Global En[illegible]

The spread of English as a global language has resulted in the emergence of a number of related fields of research within applied linguistics, including English as an International Language, English as a Lingua Franca, and World Englishes. Here, Heath Rose and Nicola Galloway consolidate this work by exploring how the global spread of English has impacted TESOL, uniting similar movements in second language acquisition, such as translanguaging and the multilingual turn. They build on a number of concrete proposals for change and innovation in English language teaching practice, whilst offering a detailed examination of how to incorporate a Global Englishes perspective into the multiple faces of TESOL, putting research-informed practice at the forefront. *Global Englishes for Language Teaching* is a groundbreaking attempt to unite discussions on the pedagogical implications of the global spread of English into a single text for researchers and practising teachers.

HEATH ROSE is an associate professor of Applied Linguistics at the University of Oxford's Department of Education. He is co-editor of *Doing Research in Applied Linguistics* (2017), author of *Japanese Writing System* (2016) and co-author of *Introducing Global Englishes* (2015). He has published in a number of the world's top journals, including *Applied Linguistics, Modern Language Journal, ELT Journal* and *Higher Education*.

NICOLA GALLOWAY is a lecturer in Education (TESOL) at the University of Edinburgh. She is author of *Global Englishes and Change in English Language Teaching: Attitudes and Impact* (2017) and co-author of *Introducing Global Englishes* (2015). She has published Global Englishes-related research in *System, ELT Journal, Journal of English as a Lingua Franca*, RELC Journal, as well as a number of book chapters.

Global Englishes for Language Teaching

Heath Rose

University of Oxford

Nicola Galloway

University of Edinburgh

CAMBRIDGE
UNIVERSITY PRESS

CAMBRIDGE
UNIVERSITY PRESS

University Printing House, Cambridge CB2 8BS, United Kingdom

One Liberty Plaza, 20th Floor, New York, NY 10006, USA

477 Williamstown Road, Port Melbourne, VIC 3207, Australia

314–321, 3rd Floor, Plot 3, Splendor Forum, Jasola District Centre, New Delhi – 110025, India

79 Anson Road, #06–04/06, Singapore 079906

Cambridge University Press is part of the University of Cambridge.

It furthers the University's mission by disseminating knowledge in the pursuit of education, learning, and research at the highest international levels of excellence.

www.cambridge.org
Information on this title: www.cambridge.org/9781107162730
DOI: 10.1017/9781316678343

First published 2019

Printed and bound in Great Britain by Clays Ltd, Elcograf S.p.A.

A catalogue record for this publication is available from the British Library.

Library of Congress Cataloging-in-Publication Data.
Names: Rose, Heath, author. | Galloway, Nicola (Linguist), author.
Title: Global Englishes for language teaching / Heath Rose, Nicola Galloway.
Description: Cambridge, United Kingdom ; New York, NY : Cambridge University Press, 2019. | Includes bibliographical references.
Identifiers: LCCN 2018040991| ISBN 9781107162730 (hardback) | ISBN 9781316614952 (paperback)
Subjects: LCSH: English language – Study and teaching – Foreign speakers. | Second language acquisition.
Classification: LCC PE1128.A2 R6378 2019 | DDC 428.0071–dc23
LC record available at https://lccn.loc.gov/2018040991

ISBN 978-1-107-16273-0 Hardback
ISBN 978-1-316-61495-2 Paperback

Contents

Figures

Tables

Preface

About the Book

With the ever-increasing global demand for English proficiency, English language teaching (ELT) has become a global industry. English proficiency, as part of the modernisation agenda in many countries, is a major part of government initiatives. English is a prestige language in many contexts. It is often a compulsory subject in school; it is a requirement to enter higher education and to graduate. It is becoming, or has already become, a prerequisite to career success in many companies that use English proficiency as a benchmark in their promotion ladders. The age for English instruction has been lowered in many primary schools, and the English language is associated with a number of perceived benefits at the individual, the institutional and the national level. As Kachru wrote in *The Alchemy of English* (1986), 'knowing English is like possessing the fabled Aladdin's lamp, which permits one to open, as it were, the linguistic gates to international business, technology, science and travel. In short, English provides linguistic power' (p. 1).

Background to Global Englishes and Its Implications

The spread of English as a global language has resulted in the emergence of a number of related fields of research, including English as an International Language (EIL), English as a Lingua Franca (ELF) and World Englishes (WE). This book groups these fields under the one umbrella term of Global Englishes in its exploration of the impact of the global spread of English on English users and learners. Our use of the term Global Englishes is not a rebranding exercise, but, rather, a consolidation exercise. As independent research fields have been exploring the diverse use of English associated with its global spread, as well as its implications, a term is needed to unite the shared agendas, ideologies and calls for change to pedagogy. We discuss these fields and other related fields, such as translanguaging and native speakerism, in our opening chapter. Chapter 1 also outlines how Global Englishes – an inclusive paradigm – resonates with similar movements in second language acquisition (SLA), such as the multilingual turn (e.g. May, 2014c), and key ideas emerging from critical applied linguistics, which are explored in greater depth in Chapter 3.

The growth of English as an international lingua franca has been coupled with a tremendous shift in usage of the language. The majority of speakers are now so-called second- or foreign-language users of English, a misnomer considering that, for many people, English has become an important language in their multilingual repertoires. These multicompetent speakers (see V. Cook, 1999, 2012, 2016a, 2016b) use the language alongside other languages for the purpose of communication in diverse and flexible speech communities. This shift in English language use has been accompanied by shifts in the needs of English-language learners for those learning the language to use as a global lingua franca.

In terms of teaching English, in just 100 years we have seen the primary purpose of English-language education move from teaching it primarily as an academic subject to teaching it for communication with first language (L1) speakers, and to teaching it for use predominantly with other users of English. As English language teaching approaches are linked with the needs of learners (Rose, 2018), this global shift indicates that a major change in the English-language curriculum is required, which is a topic covered further in Chapter 2.

The growing demand for English proficiency has further been accompanied by an increasing number of practitioner training courses, from short-term online certificate courses to full degree and postgraduate programmes. Today, there exist numerous options to obtain accreditation and further one's skills in Teaching English to Speakers of Other Languages (TESOL), accommodating those seeking credentials for a short-term working holiday to those seeking a professional career. Many leading universities also offer undergraduate and postgraduate degree programmes in TESOL. Teacher training is discussed further in Chapter 7.

This demand, for English proficiency and practitioner training, has also been furthered with the global movement towards English medium instruction, referred to as EMI. The *internationalisation* of higher education has become synonymous with *English* and, as universities seek to internationalise their curricula, the number of courses and programmes being offered in English has experienced exponential growth (Galloway et al., 2017). Europe has witnessed a tenfold increase in the number of EMI Master's programmes over a period of just ten years, led mainly by the disciplines of business, economics, engineering and technology (Brenn-White & Faethe, 2013). A widely cited report on EMI in Europe shows a similar increase in English-taught programmes in European universities, from 725 in 2001 to 2,389 in 2007, and 8,089 programmes in 2014 (Wächter & Maiworm, 2014). The EMI movement is happening worldwide (Doiz et al., 2013). In many contexts, one of the key driving forces behind this policy is to improve the English proficiency of a country's future workforce, and English skills are also a key motivating factor behind student enrolment (Galloway et al., 2017).

The rapid spread of EMI has necessitated a need for English-language support programmes. The increased use of ELF in academic settings also offers new opportunities to use English with international peers and tutors. It would seem appropriate, then, for these programmes to include a Global Englishes focus, particularly since many students will have been exposed to a monolingual native model in their high school English class. Thus, the global EMI phenomenon, discussed further in Chapter 8, clearly has implications for the field of TESOL, as well as national school curricula. However, students on EMI programmes do not always value the use of their mother tongue in EMI programmes (Galloway et al., 2017), which may stem from their attachment to 'standard' or 'native' English norms, discussed further in Chapter 4.

A Call for Change

Certainly, the rise of English as a global language has changed the foundations of how the language is taught and learned. The pedagogical implications of the change in the usage of English by global speakers have led many scholars to call for a paradigm shift in English language teaching – the likes of which last occurred in the 1970s, when communicativeness was brought to the forefront of language education with the emergence of communicative language teaching. Scholars have argued that such a shift is necessary to reframe language teaching in order to match the new sociolinguistic landscape of the twenty-first century. Underpinning this paradigm shift is a change in views of the ownership of English, the emancipation of non-native speakers from native speaker norms, a repositioning of culture within the English language, a shift in models of language and a repositioning of the target interlocutor.

Curriculum theory has been discussed in relation to the globalisation of English previously (cf. Alsagoff et al., 2012). Sembiante (2016) also discussed the implications of new perspectives on multilingualism and translanguaging in the field of curriculum studies, particularly regarding the role of language. Such contributions aim to guide practitioners to critically reflect on their teaching practice in their specific contexts, but this book further helps practitioners to consider the barriers to change in order to achieve successful curriculum innovation. This book also outlines how curricular change is part of a larger movement in applied linguistics that extends beyond TESOL to studies of SLA, identity and global mobility.

While there has been a growing debate on the need for a critical examination of English language teaching in relation to the globalisation of English, the industry continues to focus on native English norms. Teacher training manuals continue to focus on static representations of English and constrained representations of future use of the language with native speakers in Inner Circle cultures. As a result, many ELT practitioners in training continue to receive traditional views of language and language teaching characterised by adherence to 'standard' norms. This is unfortunate, given that ELF is now the most common use of the language today. This book aims at filling this gap by providing an alternative view of English language teaching, underpinned by a global use perspective.

In most books aimed at practitioner–researchers and teacher trainees, the norms of 'standard' English prevail, rather than the diversity and plurality of ELF interaction. Both Dewey (2012) and Widdowson (2012) note the need for teachers to reconceptualise the notion of language, the very subject they teach. Recent years have witnessed research flourish within the field of Global Englishes, and a number of researchers have begun to investigate more deeply what the implications are for teaching the language in the twenty-first century. Although some authored books that explicitly link EIL with TESOL have preceded this one (e.g. McKay, 2002), no definitive authored monograph on Global Englishes and language teaching currently exists.

Global Englishes for Language Teaching

This book aims to build on the growing literature on the pedagogical implications of Global Englishes research, which includes a number of book sections and chapters on the topic of ELT in Global Englishes texts (e.g. Galloway, 2017a; Galloway & Rose, 2015; Jenkins, 2015; Kachru & Nelson, 2006; Kirkpatrick, 2007, 2010a, 2010b; Melchers & Shaw, 2011; Murata, 2016; Seidlhofer, 2011), entire books (Alsagoff et al., 2012; Bowles & Cogo, 2015; Brown & McKay, 2016; Dogancay-Aktuna & Hardman, 2008; Galloway, 2017b; Matsuda, 2012, 2017; McKay, 2002; Rose & Galloway, 2019; Sharifian, 2009; Walker, 2010), articles in language teaching journals (Baker, 2012; Cogo, 2012; Cogo & Pitzl, 2016; Galloway & Rose, 2014, 2017; Jenkins, 2012; Jenkins et al., 2011; Kirkpatrick, 2011; Rose & Galloway, 2017a; Sowden, 2012; Sung, 2014; Suzuki, 2011; Syrbe & Rose, 2018; Thorn, 2013) and growing mention of Global Englishes in ELT practitioner texts (Hall, 2016; Harmer, 2007; McDonough et al., 2013; McGrath, 2013; Savova, 2008) – albeit in a superficial fashion (Galloway, 2017a). It builds on a number of concrete proposals for change being put forward, which can be grouped together into a Global Englishes Language Teaching (GELT) framework (Galloway, 2011; Galloway & Rose, 2015). This book aims to widen the debate on the need for change in ELT practice in light of such research, by offering a detailed examination of what incorporating a Global Englishes perspective into the ELT classroom (i.e. GELT) would look like. GELT is not a prescriptive model for ELT and this book intends to emphasise the diversity of global teaching practices and the diversity of students' needs around the globe. It is a student-centred framework for curricular change that aims to empower TESOL practitioners to critically evaluate their curricula in relation to Global Englishes.

Based on the proposals for change in the literature, a Global Englishes perspective of ELT emphasises the need to raise awareness of the issues associated with the spread of English and to prepare learners to use English in various global and local communities. GELT is a groundbreaking attempt to unite discussions on the pedagogical implications of the global spread of English into a single text for researchers and practising teachers. This book aims to draw on trends in educational and applied linguistics theory to better inform future English language teaching practice.

The movement towards GELT, however, requires a conceptual transition, in terms of both how the language itself is viewed and how it is taught. Such a shift in usage, as well as the evolution of the language, 'have forced a re-examination of the goals of English-language learning and teaching, as well as a reconceptualisation of the English language itself, along with sacredly held paradigms in ELT' (Nero, 2012, p. 153). As Widdowson (2012) notes, 'The first step is to raise the awareness of teachers that there is an alternative way of thinking about the subject they teach, based on an understanding of English as a lingua franca' (p. 24). Thus, this book is structured in a way that enables readers to fully understand where these proposed changes come from and to offer a critical alternative to current mainstream teacher training books. It also introduces original research that melds a Global Englishes perspective with research on materials evaluation, teacher training programmes and English medium instruction in higher education.

Book Structure

A Book in Two Parts: A Text and a Research Monograph

The book is divided into two parts. It is a key text for researchers and teachers, as well as a research monograph. The first part of the book explores the key concepts and theories underpinning a global approach to English language teaching. It explores the theoretical underpinnings of GELT, analyses GELT through a curriculum perspective, explores SLA theory through a Global Englishes lens and investigates what GELT innovation should look like. The second part of the book outlines avenues for research at the nexus of ELT and Global Englishes. It further showcases original GELT-related research in three separate studies, via an exploration of teaching materials, teacher education and language use in EMI contexts.

Part I: An Overview of Global Englishes for Language Teaching

Part I focuses on the theory behind a Global Englishes approach to language teaching and includes four chapters. Chapter 1 begins with an overview of the field of Global Englishes, introducing its connections to World Englishes, ELF, EIL, translanguaging and a number of other interrelated research paradigms. In this initial chapter, we introduce the key concepts and theories, which underpin the book, before moving on to their pedagogical implications. This chapter introduces the GELT framework and outlines the proposals that have been put forward for change to ELT practice.

Chapter 2 re-examines key concepts and theories underlying English language teaching, by exploring them through a Global Englishes lens. It takes a curriculum perspective, by exploring the implications of Global Englishes on such elements as course aims/objectives, needs analysis, syllabus design, teaching approaches, learner assessment and course evaluation. This chapter provides a structured critical overview of the field of TESOL and challenges the dominance of English-language norms, whilst providing real-life examples of GELT innovations in English-language classrooms.

Chapter 3 widens our investigation by applying a critical Global Englishes lens to the field of SLA. SLA theory holds significant influence over English-language learning and teaching practices. This chapter links trends in TESOL with parallel developments in SLA, in order to provide GELT with a theoretical anchor. Here, we provide an overview of key theories in SLA before focusing on recent developments surrounding multilingualism and movements away from monolingual reference points. Increasing awareness of the fact that multilingualism, not monolingualism, is the norm in language acquisition has led to a re-examination of key concepts in SLA. Many of the arguments within the recent 'multilingual turn' in SLA resonate with GELT; hence, this chapter highlights the synergies between the two.

In Chapter 4, we acknowledge that implementing change is challenging, and we introduce readers to the GELT curriculum innovation process. We also discuss a number of possible barriers to achieving Kumaravadivelu's (2012) 'epistemic break' (p. 14) from 'native' English-speaking norms in ELT. We also acknowledge that such a change may be rather daunting for TESOL practitioners, so offer advice on how best to introduce innovation to increase the possibility of successful institutional adoption of GELT. It is hoped that consideration of the various factors involved in the curriculum innovation process will help practitioners to maximise the opportunity to implement sustainable GELT-related curricular innovation.

This chapter concludes Part I and argues that, in order to achieve macro-level change in ELT, it is crucial not to alienate experienced teachers by telling them that their current teaching practices are irrelevant and outdated. It is also important that calls for change are grounded in classroom-based research, and not on ideological or theoretical arguments. In order to bridge the theory–practice divide, we call for more research carried out by practitioners, which leads us to the next part of the book that outlines research studies in GELT.

Part II: Research on Global Englishes for Language Teaching

Part II of the book focuses on researching GELT. Chapter 5 examines research into GELT, starting with an outline of areas in need of investigation. We especially emphasise the need for classroom-based research to evaluate the impact of Global Englishes approaches in language classrooms, in order to bridge the theory–practice divide. This chapter also explores suitable methodologies that can be employed to investigate GELT. It particularly emphasises the importance of action research, reflective inquiry and narrative inquiry as tools to examine and report on change in actual ELT classrooms, as well as introducing a number of alternative methodologies. Just as practices change, new methods of inquiry are necessary, in order to research them effectively.

Chapter 6 presents a study that investigates the global orientation of popular English textbooks, which are widely used within ELT contexts around the world. The study illustrates how the GELT framework can be operationalised as a research framework to investigate Global Englishes in teaching materials. Despite textbooks providing only one perspective into classroom practices, they remain one of the most prevalent sources of teaching and, as such, assert a major influence on the way language is taught and on the way students view the language (Matsuda, 2002). The aim of the study is to explore the extent to which a sample of textbooks position key GELT constructs, in order to ascertain whether or not these texts reflect the lingua franca language needs of modern-day English learners.

Chapter 7 examines a research project into TESOL teacher education in the UK, where a Global Englishes course is offered as an optional module within a Masters-level TESOL programme. The study uses pre-course and post-course questionnaires and interviews and post-course focus groups to examine pre- and in-service teachers' attitudes towards GELT and to examine the effects of the course on these attitudes. The mixed methods study aims to reveal the attitudinal undercurrents of the participants and to gain insight into the contexts in which they are operating. The study also aims to inform GELT course evaluation and design. We use this study as a springboard to emphasise the importance of both teacher education and conducting research with key stakeholders, thus the results will be of interest to those teaching in different contexts who are interested in ensuring that their TESOL practitioner programmes reflect the growth in ELF usage worldwide.

Chapter 8 presents reanalysed data from a recent British Council ELT Research Award project (Galloway et al., 2017), in order to more thoroughly explore the monolingual orientation within EMI programmes in China and Japan. Questionnaires were conducted with 579 students at 12 participating universities in Japan and China and with 28 members of staff at 8 of the universities. The chapter also draws on an additional 123 international students who were studying in Japan. The study builds on the results of the main project, by offering a more detailed examination into student and teacher perspectives of English-only policies within EMI, as well as their underlying attitudes pertaining to the use of other languages. The qualitative data provides insight into *why* the participants hold monolingual or multilingual perspectives of language use within these EMI contexts.

A Personal Rationale

Although we have outlined an academic rationale of this book, it also has a deeply personal rationale. Our motivations to write this book emanate from both authors' lifelong commitment to the profession of teaching, which is anchored in our combined thirty-five years of working in English language teaching and TESOL teacher education. We feel our identities are as teachers first and as scholars second, and we drew on both of these identities when researching and writing this book.

From our early years as language teachers in schools in rural Japanese towns, we both became acutely aware of the privileges afforded to us as so-called native English-language teachers working in an educational context that prized speakers of 'American English' or 'Queen's English'. As both of us came from non-standard English-speaking communities (Nicola from Scotland and Heath from rural Australia), we were highly aware from the outset of our careers that this privileged status was undeserving and misguided, but we lacked the academic knowledge to articulate why.

In these early years, we worked with many talented L1 Japanese background English-language teachers, who were not only more experienced at teaching than we were at the time, but also more knowledgeable of the standard English used in the curriculum. Our co-teachers, however, were often undervalued, especially in the commercial English language teaching industry. Such early experiences caused one of us (Nicola) to challenge such inequalities in her Master's research, and the other (Heath) to distance himself for a couple of years from the profession of English language teaching to focus his Masters research on the pedagogies of languages other than English.

After completing our Master's degrees, we both independently returned to Japan to take up lectureships at Kanda University of International Studies, which was where we first became colleagues. We worked with students who mainly aimed to use English for future careers in the tourism industry. We both were acutely aware that our learners were likely to use English with other second-language (L2) users of the language, rather than 'American English speakers', who were over-represented in the curriculum. Our university gave us a great deal of autonomy within the curriculum. The curriculum promoted learning through use, rather than a focus on form, which was quite compatible with innovations.

Lecturers were also free to propose and create content-based courses on a topic of their own interest. One of us (Heath) created and taught a course showcasing cultural and historical content related to East and South-East Asia, within the context of tourism. The decision to introduce this course was to help balance the extant curricula focus on 'British Studies' and 'American Studies'. It was also due to the perceived importance of this region for students who aimed to work in the tourist industry. As an example, in January 2018 there were 2.3 million visitors from East and South-East Asia to Japan compared to just 92,000 visitors from the USA (source: JTB, www.tourism.jp/). The other of us (Nicola) explicitly taught Global Englishes content to students, which formed data for her doctoral research. This foray into explicit Global Englishes teaching can be read in Galloway (2011, 2013, 2017a). As far as we can tell from the extensive literature we cover in this book, this course is one of the first recorded instances of teaching Global Englishes content to learners of English within a traditional language programme.

In later years, we were colleagues once more within Rikkyo University College of Business, where we worked together to integrate Global Englishes content within the existing English for Academic Purposes (EAP) curriculum. Changes included: an introductory module on the global spread and use of English; the hiring of L2 English-speaking teaching assistants for increased ELF exposure in the classroom; inviting of guest speakers who were strong role models of business ELF users; and shifting focus on communication over accuracy in assessment. Our drive to innovate the curriculum was grounded in the perceived importance of English as a business lingua franca for our students' future careers. Some of this later experience is reported in Galloway and Rose (2013) and Rose and Montakantiwong (2018). After teaching at Rikkyo University, we took up academic positions in UK and Irish universities, where we integrated our professional and academic knowledge in shaping teacher training programmes – experiences we discuss in Galloway (2017b) and Rose (2017).

We introduce this personal rationale to highlight the fact that we do not write this book sitting atop an 'ivory tower' dictating change from an ideological point of view. Sadly, this is sometimes the case when calls for change are made by applied linguistics researchers who have had limited experiences in actual language classrooms. While the perspectives we present in this book have a strong theoretical foundation, they are also entrenched in our own previous pedagogical experiences and practices in TESOL. They are reflective of our own journey and experiences as teachers of English and are bound inextricably with practice. Many of the ideas we present here have a strong professional rationale and offer our own professionally grounded answers to calls from practitioners who teach English in global contexts.

Scholars often talk about a theory–practice divide when introducing innovative pedagogical practice. However, our personal rationale highlights the fact that our research-informed practices have predominantly occurred within the very space between theory and practice. Much of the research we have reported over the years (Galloway, 2011, 2013, 2017a; Galloway & Rose, 2014, 2018; Rose & Galloway, 2017; Rose & Montakantiwong, 2018) has occurred when we have embodied a practitioner–researcher identity (for an overview of the complexities of such research, see Galloway, 2017c). Thus, this book is one way for us to consolidate this work by linking our own extant practices of Global Englishes for language teaching with current TESOL and SLA theory in order to stimulate innovation within both fields.

Acknowledgements

We would like to acknowledge the support of friends and family in writing this book, which is, perhaps, our biggest joint writing project to date. We would also like to thank the various participants in our studies, and also our research assistants, namely Takuya Numajiri and Jarek Kriukow, whose contributions to the data analysis in Chapters 7 and 8 greatly improved the volume. We would like to thank our amazing publishing team at Cambridge University Press.

Part I

Introducing Global Englishes for Language Teaching

1 Global Englishes Language Teaching

The rise of English as a global language has been well documented in research literature. In just 500 years, the world has seen English grow from a national language spoken by fewer than 3 million people to a global language learned by an estimated 2 billion speakers. The spread of English as a global language has resulted in the emergence of a number of related fields of research within applied linguistics. Paradigms for examining the spread of English include English as an international language, English as a lingua franca and World Englishes. This book groups these fields under the one umbrella term of Global Englishes in its exploration of the impact of the global spread of English on the field of English language teaching.

English has spread around the world via four channels (Galloway & Rose, 2015), which has produced markedly different Englishes as well as linguacultural contexts of language use. As part of Channel One, English spread through settler colonisation, where English-speaking emigrants created new L1 English-speaking communities in regions as far-flung as Australia, Canada, the United States and New Zealand. This gave rise to new varieties of English via the process of *koineisation* (formed by different dialects coming into contact). Channel Two saw English spread to new regions and communities via the slavery, where displaced slaves of mutually unintelligible African languages had English imposed on them, quickly becoming the first language of subsequent generations. This gave rise to new varieties of Englishes via the process of *creolisation* (formed by different languages coming into contact) in such regions as the West Indies. Channel Three (exploitation colonies) also saw new Englishes emerge via the process of creolisation (usually via pidgins), but this time to L2 English-using communities. Forts, trading ports and colonies saw English spread via this channel to regions such as Nigeria, Singapore, India and Hong Kong. In these contexts, English is still often used alongside local languages in an official or quasi-official capacity.

The final channel of English dispersion has occurred through globalisation, which has seen English emerge as a global prestige language, due to the economic and political power of English-speaking economies such as the United States. English was seen as a means to facilitate individual and national upward economic and social mobility, although we have warned previously of the dangers of such views (see Galloway & Rose, 2015). Globalisation brought an emergence of educational policies worldwide that sought to teach English in regions with no historic ties to English-speaking nations. Due to globalisation, we are witnessing a boom in numbers of English speakers in such regions as China, Japan and mainland Europe.

The rise of English as a global language has changed the foundations of how the language is taught and learned. The pedagogical implications of the change in the use of English by second language learners have led many scholars to call for a paradigm shift in the field of English language teaching. Scholars have argued that such a shift is necessary to reframe language teaching in order to match the new sociolinguistic landscape of the twenty-first century. Underpinning this paradigm shift is a change in views of the ownership of English, the emancipation of non-native speakers from native speaker norms, a repositioning of culture within the English language, a shift in models of language and a repositioning of the target interlocutor. In this book, we group these proposals within a framework of Global Englishes Language Teaching (GELT).

The term Global Englishes Language Teaching was coined by Galloway (2011, 2013) and then developed further in Galloway and Rose (2015), with further adaptations in Galloway and Rose (2018). GELT was first established as a new approach to teaching English, founded on theoretical notions from Global Englishes research. GELT is an answer to calls for an epistemic break (Kumaravadivelu, 2012) in English language teaching, which views current practices as ill-fitting for teaching English as a global lingua franca.

This chapter explores the theoretical underpinnings of GELT and rationalises a need for a new approach to teaching English in the twenty-first century. It first examines the concept of Global Englishes and establishes the boundaries of the term as used in this book. It then outlines the six proposals for change in English language teaching practices that emerged from research in the field in the early 2000s, upon which GELT was established. Finally, it outlines the GELT framework developed by Galloway and Rose in 2015 and explores adaptations to it since then. We also outline alternative models that have been proposed by researchers in the related fields of English as a lingua franca and English as an international language, in order to compare and contrast these approaches to the framework used in this book.

What Is Global Englishes?

In this book, we define Global Englishes as an inclusive paradigm looking at the linguistic, sociolinguistic and sociocultural diversity and fluidity of English use and English users in a globalised world. Global Englishes has been used by a number of authors in applied linguistics before us, whom we would like to acknowledge as informing our own understanding.

Pennycook (2007) has used Global Englishes to refer to the spread and use of diverse forms of English within processes of globalisation. Pennycook sees Global Englishes as a more inclusive paradigm compared to World Englishes, which is based on national lines and discounts 'other Englishes' in its exclusionary definitions. His work on hip-hop illustrates how users of English can take ownership of the English language, where performers reconstitute the language for their own creative purposes to 'perform and (re)fashion identities across borders' (2003, p. 529). Canagarajah (2013) has also used Global Englishes to refer to the diversity of English used around the world. He uses the term to distinguish the paradigm from the constructs of World Englishes and English as a lingua franca, which he views as too entrenched in the nativeness of speakers. Canagarajah states that 'Linguae francae should be studied in terms of contact practices, not native speaker status' (2013, p. 67). Thus, similar to Pennycook, Canagarajah views Global Englishes as a more broadly encompassing term, which dispenses with the shackles of exclusionary terms of nativeness and ownership. Whilst we would see much ELF research as being focused on contact practices, the point that Canagarajah makes is, nonetheless, reflected in much of the ELF research of the 2000s.

Scholars such as Pennycook have been observed to embrace critical applied linguistic (CAL) perspectives, which others argue is a position that some teachers have difficulty embracing:

> But the CAL position risks alienating practicing teachers, concerned as they are with the realities of classrooms, examination requirements, parents' expectations, education department policies, etc. This is in large part due to the often uncompromising ideological stance of much CAL work and the highly abstruse nature of much of its discourse.
>
> (Hall et al., 2013, p. 5)

While we see the truth in this observation, we, nevertheless, see the work of critical applied linguists as crucial in driving new ideas (and ideologies) forward. In its critique of existing constructs, as well as in its quest for more accurate and appropriate conceptualisations of language, the field is able to explore new avenues for imagining English-language use and English-language education. As teachers themselves may find such ideas difficult to grasp, it is up to educational applied linguists to apply these ideas more explicitly to English-language teacher education, as we plan to do in this book.

The term Global Englishes has also been used previously in resources aimed at language teachers and teacher educators. The term was adopted for the third edition of Jenkins's (2015) book *Global Englishes: A Resource Book for Students*, which was originally entitled *World Englishes* in its first two editions (2003, 2009). Jenkins (2015) states that the decision to change the title was in response to 'the recent massive growth in the use of English as an international lingua franca among people from different nations and first languages' (p. viii), thus the focus of the field has been adjusted to be more inclusive of newer non-nation bound uses of the English language.

Whilst we see an importance in adopting an inclusionary stance to Global Englishes, we do feel that some criticisms of Pennycook towards World Englishes, and some criticisms of Canagarajah towards English as a lingua franca, create an exclusionary environment when defining Global Englishes – a term that was created to escape exclusionary research practices. In fact, both English as a lingua franca and World Englishes have witnessed a substantial semantic widening in recent years. Indeed, much of what is called Global Englishes can be seen in the study of fluid language practices in recent ELF research, as well as from scholars of World Englishes, who have moved beyond the study of region-specified varieties. In this book, we posit Global Englishes as an umbrella term to unite the shared endeavours of these interrelated fields of study in sociolinguistics and applied linguistics. We use it to consolidate research in World Englishes, English as a lingua franca and English as an international language, while drawing on scholarship from translanguaging and multilingualism in second language acquisition. Thus, we define Global Englishes as an inclusive paradigm that embraces a broad spectrum of interrelated research that has come before it and emerged alongside it. Thus, to fully understand Global Englishes, one needs to examine more closely the interrelated fields of World Englishes, English as a lingua franca, English as an international language and translanguaging.

World Englishes

World Englishes as a discipline began as both a linguistic and a sociolinguistic school of study in the 1970s and 1980s, largely informed by the theoretical work of Braj J. Kachru and Larry Smith. It was primarily concerned with recording and codifying linguistic variation in English, with special interest in the Englishes of former British colonies. The oft-cited model of World Englishes is Kachru's (1992) groundbreaking Three Circle model, consisting of the Inner Circle, Outer Circle and Expanding Circle. The Inner Circle includes countries where English serves as a first language and spread to the country as a direct result of English-speaking colonisation and migration. Illustrative Inner Circle countries include the United Kingdom, Ireland, Australia, New Zealand, Canada and the United States. Although it is an additional language for many speakers in these countries from other linguistic backgrounds, the predominant official language is English. The Outer Circle includes countries of the former British Empire where English operates predominantly as a second language alongside other national languages (although many speakers are first language English speakers). Examples of Outer Circle countries include Nigeria, India, Singapore and Hong Kong. The Expanding Circle includes countries where English had no historical intra-national function and is taught within the education systems. In these countries, English has often been given the status of a foreign language, although, due to globalisation, it is increasing in intra-national usage and international (lingua franca) usage. Examples of Expanding Circle countries include Spain, China, Brazil and Russia.

Since its inception, the Three Circle model has been subject to much criticism for being drawn along national lines, rather than linguistic ones (e.g. Bruthiaux, 2003; Galloway & Rose, 2015; Jenkins, 2015; Pennycook, 2010), resulting in its inability to capture the diverse way English is used within and across geographic boundaries. Nevertheless, research from World Englishes has made a substantial contribution to knowledge, where it has challenged notions of standard language ideology and has sought to raise the profile and legitimacy of the Englishes of the Outer Circle. Under the umbrella of World Englishes research, scholars also sought to challenge some of the assumptions and practices of ELT, which we will draw upon later in this chapter.

English as a Lingua Franca

The limitations of World Englishes scholarship to describe English used across regional and linguistic boundaries led to growing interest in the more fluid ways English was being used as a lingua franca by speakers of different L1s. Seminal work by Jennifer Jenkins (1998, 2000), Barbara Seidlhofer (2001) and Anna Mauranen (2003) lay firm foundations for ELF research, being a field that has since flourished in its own right. Lingua franca contexts, like those seen throughout Europe, were very different to Outer Circle contexts like India and Singapore. In the Outer Circle, the emergence of English was gradual, and often involved processes of creolisation and nativisation of language. The Expanding Circle, however, is much more fluid and unstable, with the type of language contact and immediate language needs greatly influencing the way English is used from context to context. Nevertheless, early work in English as a lingua franca mirrored that of World Englishes and saw scholars focus on the linguistic features of the language used in lingua franca contexts.

However, the codifying of the 'norms' of language in flux was soon viewed as being an inappropriate task for ELF. As Canagarajah (2016) notes, 'These norms are highly variable and hybrid, changing for different communicative contexts and interlocutors' (p. 19). The field thus moved in its focus to explore the fluidity of ELF use, especially in diverse and dynamic contexts. Jenkins (2015) states that the field has since witnessed the emergence of a third phase of research, which she refers to as ELF3, where researchers further their interest in multilingualism in exploring how lingua franca English is used with other languages. Hence, like Global Englishes, ELF research has become more integrated with notions of translanguaging and plurilingualism, as:

> There is now a growing realization that English cannot be separated from other languages. This is true not only of the contemporary global contact zones where languages intermingle, but of all communication, because languages are always in contact. (Canagarajah, 2016, p. 19)

While much ELF research continues to explore English-language use, there is an ongoing body of ELF research that explicitly examines the implications of ELF on language teaching. ELF scholars have argued for a need to teach learners to adapt to a variety of communities of practice, develop communication strategies for ELF usage and to speak intelligibly, without necessarily adhering to traditional standards. Some of these concepts, and others, will be returned to later in this chapter.

English as an International Language

English as an international language, as a field of study, is often viewed as the North American counterpart to English as a lingua franca, which emerged out of a need to examine linguistic practices in Europe. This being said, ELF scholars, such as Jenkins (1998), once worked within the EIL label. However, the two fields are slightly different in the focus of their scholarship. With the growing interest in the use of English on a global scale, some researchers from such diverse fields as World Englishes, Language Policy and TESOL began to more closely examine the phenomenon of English as an international language. Unlike early ELF research, early EIL research was less focused on a linguistic study of language use, focusing more on the implications for society, and language education in particular.

The field saw important work emerge from TESOL scholars, such as Sandra McKay, who sought to examine the implications of such research on classroom practices. Just as ELF research has flourished, so, too, has EIL research; the past ten years have seen a number of important edited volumes on teaching EIL (Alsagoff et al., 2012; Matsuda, 2012, 2016; Sharifian, 2009), as well as an encyclopaedia volume (*TESOL Encyclopedia of English Language Teaching, Vol. I: Teaching English as an International Language*, 2018). In some contexts, EIL has been used as a catch-all term for the use of English in general, and as a strategy to eliminate traditional distinctions between English as a native, second, foreign and additional language (ENL/ESL/EFL/EAL), as these distinctions are viewed as being increasingly irrelevant in today's globally integrated world.

Translanguaging and Translingual Practice

It is also important to acknowledge the overlap with Global Englishes ideology and the ideology of translanguaging, and translingual practice (Canagarajah, 2011b; Garcia, 2009). Indeed, key publications in the field on translingual practice (Canagarajah, 2013; Pennycook, 2007) have also used the term Global Englishes. In our previous work within Global Englishes (Galloway & Rose, 2015), we use the term 'translingual practice', as our interpretations of Global Englishes were heavily influenced by Canagarajah (2007, 2013). Since this time, the term 'translanguaging' has flourished in the field of applied linguistics and has been used as an umbrella term to unite similarly focused research. As Global Englishes is itself an umbrella term, we too adopt translanguaging for this purpose, unless we are specifically referring to Canagarajah's work.

Translanguaging examines the processes of speakers drawing upon their entire linguistic repertoire when communicating, thus breaking down conceptual linguistic boundaries when describing communication, and challenging concepts built upon these notions, such as code switching. In terms of the implications for TESOL, this orientation goes beyond plurilingualism in TESOL (Taylor & Snoddon, 2013), which is also seen to challenge traditional notions of linguistic boundaries within the learner. Translanguaging challenges the underlying assumption that languages are separate entities, whether it is within a social, cognitive or psychological realm.

Translanguaging showcases linguistic hybridity and helps to inform our understanding of how speakers of English as a global lingua franca utilise their multilingual, or translingual, repertoires to communicate. Speakers of a global language use translanguaging – a concept that has its roots in bilingual education (see Baker, 2001; Williams, 1996) – as a strategy for communication, drawing on all of their linguistic resources. Thus, whilst World Englishes scholars were more focused on the use of English within distinct boundaries or geographical settings, we now have evidence of how global users of language negotiate communication with speakers of these so-called diverse varieties of English, developing conversational strategies that are flexible enough to adapt to their surroundings, depending on both the context and the situation.

It is also important to note that the centrality of flexible norms in GELT also resonates with recent work on transnational mobility and the growing body of research looking at the needs of migrants (Guo & Maitra, 2017). Just as ELF users are not necessarily tied to one form of English, migrants may not be tied to one place. As Guo and Maitra (2017) note:

> "Rather, they [migrants] are becoming embedded within a shifting field of increasingly transcultural identities," given the fact that migrants are becoming more "transnational and adopting fluid, transcultural identities." (p. 80)

Guo and Maitra (2017) criticise the lack of focus on, and engagement with, transnationalism and transculturalism in the Canadian public school curricula, proposing a revised version that would integrate transnational and transcultural perspectives. Similar to GELT, they propose a more ethical and inclusive curriculum, due to the fact that postmodernity and globalisation necessitate a narrative of mobility and fluidity.

Migration is now viewed as moving beyond the framework of methodological nationalism, and transnationalism challenges the rigid boundaries of nation states. GELT also calls for a more postmodern perspective, due to the fact that the use of English in multilingual contexts challenges the rigid boundaries of languages. With globalisation, the boundaries of nation states are shifting and being contested. In a similar vein, the boundaries of languages are also shifting and being contested. Migrants do not just make one single journey from one location to another, but engage in multiple and circular and return migration (Lie, 1995). Similarly, ELF users do not solely travel to a native English-speaking country, and may never do – their contexts and interlocutors are often constantly changing.

The Multilingual Turn

The term multilingual turn is used to describe the increasing importance placed on multilingualism within second language acquisition theory. The multilingual turn, which is discussed further in Chapter 3, strongly overlaps with Global Englishes. For example, while Global Englishes researchers have been calling for a change in English language teaching, similar calls have been emerging in parallel within SLA (see May, 2014b; Ortega, 2013). Thus, it seems imperative that we connect these related movements in order to provide a stronger foundation for change.

The multilingual turn describes a growing movement in the field to reject a monolingual bias that has underpinned both applied linguistics and SLA theory and research for decades and has impacted on TESOL practices. In a broader sense, therefore, translanguaging and Global Englishes can both be seen as contributing to the multilingual turn. Whilst Global Englishes has 'English' at its core, it is highly attuned to the languages that surround it. It is a paradigm informed by its multilingual users, which challenges monolingual ideologies seeks to dismantle linguistic barriers between 'varieties' and the languages of its speakers.

Ortega (2013) has predicted that the multilingual turn will impact on the field with a similar magnitude as the social turn in the 1990s, which saw the field of SLA move away from its cognitive and positivist origins and incorporate more social, individualistic and non-traditional perspectives of SLA (see Block, 2003, for details). We see Global Englishes as part of this larger trend, and we see GELT as playing a leading role in this movement relating to ELT.

Uniting the Paradigms

In sum, the field of applied linguistics has witnessed three main pillars of research into variation in the English language around the world since the 1980s – all of which focus on the plurality of English and legitimacy of such variation:

- World Englishes, which focuses on the linguistic features of English varieties and their sociolinguistic implications.
- English as an international language, which examines the implications of the spread of English as a global language, with its predominant focus on pedagogical implications.
- English as a lingua franca, which explores both the linguistic use of language across speakers of different first languages and the sociolinguistic implications of the use of English as a contact language.

There are two further related concepts, which are not confined to implications for the English language but the use of language in global, mobile communities. These concepts are highly relevant, as similar calls for innovation are emerging from their scholarship:

- Translanguaging, which challenges the monolingual orientation and looks at languages not as separate entities, but as part of an interwoven system.
- The multilingual turn, which also challenges the monolingual orientation and emphasises the importance of other languages in addition to dominant lingua francae.

All five fields have implications for research surrounding the growth of English, the world's foremost lingua franca. World Englishes, English as an international language and English as a lingua franca have shared endeavours to change the perceptions of the users of English regarding what English is, who owns it and how it should be used. Translanguaging further pushes the boundaries of conceptualising the fluidity of language, and challenges the notion of English, or Englishes, as being separate from other languages in use. We unite the shared endeavours of these five fields under the umbrella term of Global Englishes, as shown in Figure 1.1. This figure is a further adaptation of the Global Englishes figure provided in Galloway (2017a).

Importantly, all fields have implications for language teaching – the focus of this book. As Galloway (2017a) notes:

> Researchers in all of these fields have questioned the relevance of such norms for ELT in light of their research findings. Notwithstanding their different stances, such work has a similar underlying ideology, united in the desire to showcase the diversity of English

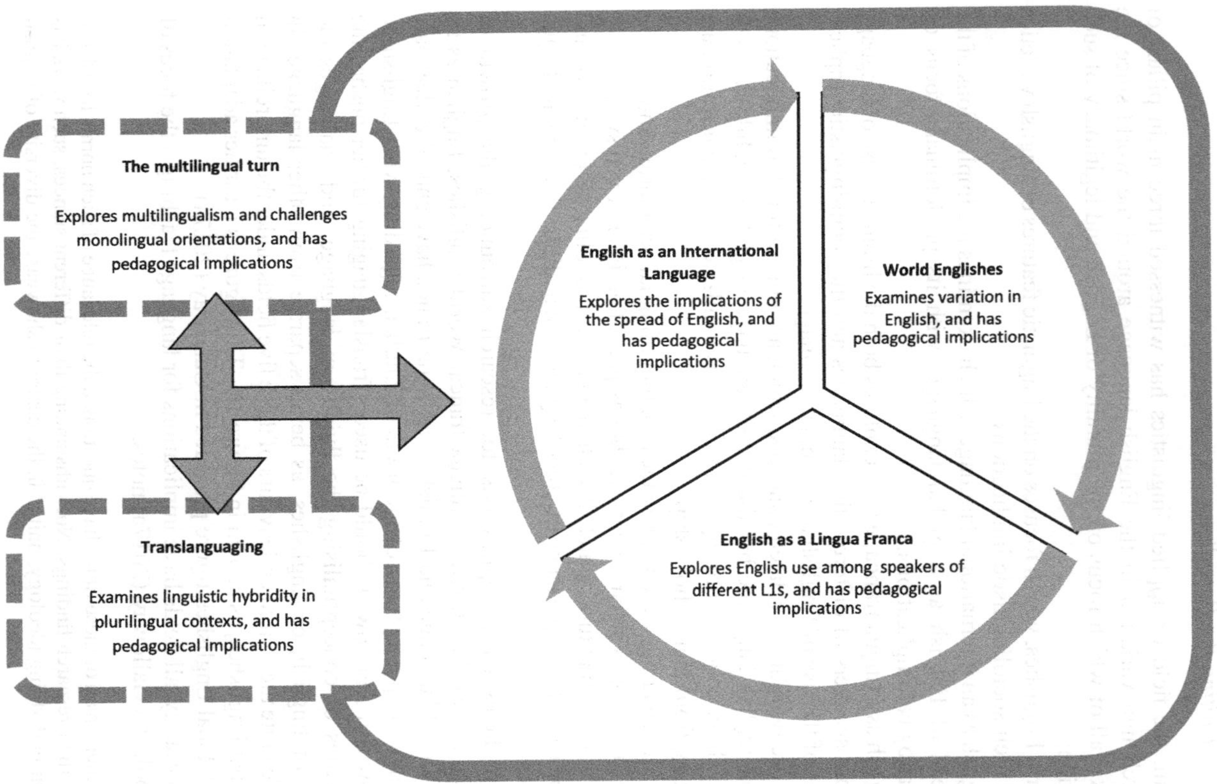

Figure 1.1 Global Englishes: an inclusive paradigm.

and to instigate a paradigm shift in ELT. As such, they form part of the broader paradigm of Global Englishes. (p. 2)

In World Englishes, it has been noted that 'pedagogy has continued to be one of the main preoccupations of the field' (Saraceni, 2015, p. 171), and this is also true for ELF research (Seidlhofer, 2011). Likewise, EIL scholarship has lobbied for a complete overhaul of English language teaching practices, as well as an epistemic break from the ideology that underpins current pedagogical practice (Kumaravadivelu, 2012). Translanguaging, having emerged from bilingual educational contexts, continues to maintain central importance in pedagogical practice. Finally, much of the theory within the multilingual turn is directly related to pedagogy, with Meier (2017) describing it as 'a critical movement in education' (p. 131), and other scholars drawing applications to not only SLA theory, but also TESOL (e.g. May, 2014c).

In defining Global Englishes, we should note that scholars use different umbrella terms to unite shared ideologies of these fields. For example, as the field of World Englishes has expanded from its linguistic origins into social realms, it, too, has been used to encompass much EIL and ELF literature. Matsuda (2017), for example, uses World Englishes to refer to research into all related fields. Thus, her definition of World Englishes would be very similar to our definition of Global Englishes. Translingual practice – Canagarajah's preferred term to describe the practice of translanguaging – has been defined as being an umbrella term itself, aiming to 'capture the common underlying processes and orientations' (Canagarajah, 2013, p. 6) that motivate 'communicative modes' in plurilingual encounters.

We choose Global Englishes, rather than these other terms, in order to highlight it as an inclusive paradigm of all shared ideologies, and in order to not limit the scope of our research interest to certain segments, regions or populations affected by the spread of English. Nevertheless, we acknowledge that other scholars of English-language pedagogy, such as McKay and Brown (2016) under the umbrella of EIL, or Matsuda (2017) under the umbrella of World Englishes, are broadly exploring similar issues as outlined in this book, while not explicitly labelling such work as Global Englishes. Thus, Global Englishes aims to bring such work together and also highlight the fact that researchers in all of the aforementioned paradigms have discussed their work in relation to pedagogy and have called for change.

Native Speakerism and Native Speaker Terminology

Global Englishes is also presented in this publication as a political ideology, where native speaker hegemony is challenged and the term native speaker is problematised. As such, it also shares an ideology with research in applied linguistics that centres on these notions. The term native speaker has been problematised and criticised for decades (see Cook, 1999; Davies, 1999, 2003, 2013; Holliday, 2005, 2015; Paikeday, 1985; Rampton, 1990), yet there has been little consensus on alternative terms to replace it (Selvi, 2011).

In our earlier work on Global Englishes (Galloway & Rose, 2015) we draw into question the accuracy of the term 'native speaker', arguing – like others before us – that the term is notoriously difficult to define, and only exists as a concept in people's minds, rather than being an identifiable reality. Because of the illusiveness of this concept, it has been described as a 'fallacy' (Phillipson, 1992b), a 'myth' (Davies, 2003) and a linguistic 'figment' of one's imagination (Paikeday, 1985). Rajagopalan (2018) notes that,

> With globalization and the resultant mass migration of people across the world on an unprecedented scale and growing contact among people from different regions at an exponential rate, the distinction is becoming more and more difficult to maintain. (p. 1)

He suggests that one should be considered a native speaker of whichever language one feels competent in.

Nevertheless, the term has been used to drive a wedge in English language-using communities – a phenomenon sometimes referred to as native speakerism. Native speakerism is a term used to describe a disparity of treatment of English users due to their perceived native speaker status, with native speakers often receiving favourable treatment over non-native speakers:

> Native-speakerism is a pervasive ideology within ELT, characterized by the belief that 'native-speaker' teachers represent a 'Western culture' from which spring the ideals both of the English language and of English language teaching methodology.
> (Holliday, 2006, p. 385)

Despite efforts from within ELT to challenge native speakerism, at least in terms of teacher-hiring practices, it prevails today, with current language teaching advertisements still illustrating a preference for native speakers over non-native speakers for certain teaching positions (Selvi, 2010). Holliday (2015, p. 13) notes 'discrimination is evident in employment practices and customer preference far beyond the English-speaking West, where "native speaker" has become a sales icon for all types of language teaching institutions and their customers'.

Native speakerism extends beyond language teaching to other English-using communities. At the essence of native speakerism is the idea of 'Othering', which creates an 'us and them' dichotomy in society where native speakers are assigned certain cultural, intellectual and linguistic attributes, and non-native speakers are assigned other qualities. However, even if these assigned attributes were justifiable (which they are clearly not), 'being a "native speaker" has nothing to do with the abilities to be a teacher of a particular language' (Holliday, 2015, p. 16).

As use of the 'native' term is problematic, many scholars have lobbied for the use of alternative terms that dissipate this dichotomy, such as 'proficient user' (Paikeday, 1985), 'native user' (Davies, 2013), 'language expert' (Rampton, 1990), 'English-using speech fellowship' (Kachru, 1992) and 'multicompetence' (Cook, 1999, 2016a). Such practices have called into question whether we should also seek to use alternative terms in this book, in order to challenge the current hegemony. However, although we acknowledge that the terms 'native' and 'non-native' are not *identifiable* realities, it is our position that they are constructed categories and *perceived* realities for the majority of people in English-using communities. That is, while the labels are not definable, they still exist in the social fabric of most English users' speech communities. By using alternative terms in this book, we feel we would be skating around the issues, rather than explicitly challenging them head-on.

Cook (2016b, p. 187) states 'that second language acquisition researchers' reliance on the native speaker is now more covert. Yet by and large, research still falls back on the L2 user meeting the standard of native speakers'. In this book, we do not want to be seen as covert, by choosing alternative terms when challenging ideologies surrounding the concept of nativeness. Therefore, it is our position that as the labels of 'native' and 'non-native' are widely used in society, and by many readers of this book, we need to use them in order to politically challenge their existence. Hence, we have decided to only use these labels in this book when the ideas surrounding them are challenged. We also choose to use these problematic labels when we are referring to a perceived, rather than defined, distinction. When the labels do not bring this dichotomy into question, we seek to adopt alternative and more accurate terms.

Implications of Global Englishes for Language Teaching

There has been a recent call within applied linguistics for a paradigm shift in English language teaching (see Galloway, 2011, 2017a; Galloway & Rose, 2015; Kumaravadivelu, 2012; May, 2014c). The last paradigm shift to occur in teaching approaches was the large-scale adoption of the communicative approach over other competing methodologies that had come before it, such as audio-lingualism in the United States, structural situation language teaching in the United Kingdom and numerous other alternative methods that emerged in the 1960s and 1970s. This historical overview will be discussed further in Chapter 2. The communicative language teaching (CLT) paradigm shift, which began in the 1970s, saw teaching approaches shift to communicative views of language learning, and was largely due to sociopolitical changes in the world that witnessed an increase in the need for learners to be able to communicate languages due to increasingly mobile communities of speakers. Since this time, the world has witnessed further globalisation and the entrenchment of English as the global language, which has caused some scholars to call for another paradigm shift to reframe language teaching in order to match the new socio-linguistic landscape of the twenty-first century. Underpinning this paradigm shift is a change in views of the ownership of English, the emancipation of non-native speakers from native speaker norms, a repositioning of culture within the English language and a shift in models of language including the target interlocutor.

Both Dewey (2012) and Widdowson (2012) note the need for teachers to reconceptualise the notion of language, the very subject they teach. 'The first step is to raise the awareness of teachers that there is an alternative way of thinking about the subject they teach, based on an understanding of English as a lingua franca' (Widdowson, 2012, p. 24). There has been headway in this field and the flourishing research within the field of Global Englishes has begun to focus on what this means for teaching the language (see Galloway, 2017a for a comprehensive overview of recent work).

Previously, we have categorised calls for change under six broad proposals referred to as the GELT proposals (Galloway & Rose, 2015), which were built upon those outlined previously by Galloway (2011). These are:

1. Increasing World Englishes and ELF exposure in language curricula
2. Emphasising respect for multilingualism in ELT
3. Raising awareness of Global Englishes in ELT
4. Raising awareness of ELF strategies in language curricula
5. Emphasising respect for diverse culture and identity in ELT
6. Changing English teacher-hiring practices in the ELT industry

In terms of the first proposal, scholars in the field of applied linguistics have long lobbied for more accurate representation of the variation in English in language-learning contexts (Gass & Varonis, 1984). This view has also extended to language educationalists, such as McKay (2012), who has argued that learners need to comprehend different varieties 'so that they are better prepared to deal with English interactions in international contexts' (McKay, 2012, p. 73). Nevertheless, there remains a lack of materials to expose students to variation in English, even in contexts where the importance of ELF usage is acknowledged. Syrbe and Rose (2018), for example, examined materials created for use in curricula in Germany. Despite a stated purpose of the curriculum being to train students to use English as a European lingua franca, their study found little representation of ELF usage in the texts, and few examples of accents outside standard Inner Circle varieties in the audio materials, with a strong received pronunciation (RP) representation.

In terms of developing respect for multilingualism, research is showing that knowledge of only English is not enough to fully function in global contexts.

Applied linguistics researchers have long been strong advocates of multilingualism, which extends into the English-language classroom. Movements in translanguaging research and the multilingual turn in SLA have further highlighted the importance of multilingualism, and have challenged the monolingual orientations that underpin much research and practice. GELT is sensitive to the fact that the ability to use other languages alongside English creates authentic contexts similar to possible future communities of practice, in which they are likely to use English alongside other languages.

The third GELT proposal emphasises the importance of raising learners' awareness of how English is used as a global language, in order for them to develop an accurate understanding of how they will use the language in the future. This proposal aims to add further authenticity to the sanitised uses of English evident in many ELT materials. Preliminary research has already shown that the direct teaching of Global Englishes can help students move beyond preconceived notions of standard language and challenge deeply ingrained native speaker norms. A study by Galloway (2011, 2013, 2017a) raised awareness of Global Englishes in traditional EFL classrooms in Japan, which resulted in learners reporting an increase in self-confidence as English users, challenging their perceptions of how they would likely use English in the future.

In order to function in these emerging global contexts, it has also become increasingly clear that learners must develop the strategies needed to adapt to different communities of language users, which forms the fourth GELT proposal. Calls in this domain have particularly emerged from the study of language in more fluid contexts – notably ELF and translanguaging. Canagarajah (2013), for example, has argued that proficiency includes an ability to be multidialectal to adjust to local, regional and global communities across and within traditionally defined World Englishes boundaries. Likewise, ELF research has highlighted the importance of strategies in ELF communication, to not only accommodate a wide range of speakers from different linguistic backgrounds but also pre-empt differences in English-language norms and bridge cultural and pragmatic differences (Jenkins et al., 2011). These strategies extend beyond the use of norms in the English language if the translingual orientation is considered (Canagarajah, 2014, 2016). The pedagogical implications 'range from facilitating language awareness among learners to developing communicative strategies that will enable them to negotiate resources from diverse languages and construct meaning situationally' (Canagarajah, 2016, p. 19)

The fourth proposal centres on the need to respect cultural differences in ELT classrooms and to widen the lens of what an English-using culture is. Will Baker's work has been highly influential within this domain (Baker, 2009, 2012a, 2015). Language curricula often posit English-using cultures as Inner

Circle, and the goal for learners is also proposed as taking part in this culture. Even when textbooks aim to widen the lens of Global Englishes, such as in the texts explored in the Syrbe and Rose (2018) study, where chapters on 'South Africa' and 'multicultural London' were included, the depictions were often of static cultures the learner must learn about in order to successfully adapt. These depictions, whilst being a step in the right direction, are somewhat out of sync with current research on culture, which shows that culture is a fluid, negotiable concept. Rather, this GELT proposal sees a need for teachers and textbooks to break away from practices of presenting static regional cultures as the contexts for language use and to, instead, emphasise the dynamic and fluid cultures that English is used in today – many of which are emerging in contexts traditionally labelled as 'EFL'. For example, English in Japan was traditionally learned to use in foreign contexts, such as travel or work abroad, or when these contexts came to Japan, such as English speakers visiting Japan. However, nowadays, it is increasingly being used in domestic settings – in universities, in laboratories, in companies and in social settings.

The final GELT proposal calls for a need in teacher recruitment and training to move away from concepts of native speakers as being experts to professional English teachers (see McKay, 2012). In considering that so-called non-native English-speaking teachers make up the majority of the profession, it has been noted that 'on a global level, the ELT profession is perhaps the world's only occupation in which the majority faces discrimination' (Ali, 2009, p. 37). While there is seemingly no shortage of jobs for non-native English-speaking teachers in the contexts of their own L1 communities, discrimination often occurs when these qualified teachers wish to take their skills to another context, and they soon find that native speaker competence is desired in addition to (and at times in lieu of) teaching qualifications and experience. While there is evidence that these practices are slowly changing, it appears that the job of the international language teacher still rests in the hands of a native speaker, who is viewed as a more 'authentic' source of linguistic knowledge, even if they have no experience of teaching, or even learning language. In this vein, World Englishes scholars, such as Kirkpatrick (2012), state that a multicomponent English teacher is a far more suitable role model for learners than a monolingual native speaker. However, we also concur with Holliday (2015) in that we need to stop this discrimination, including current research that compares the two types of teachers, as this merely reinforces the terms and suggests that there is a difference.

These proposals point to a need to innovate English language teaching in the twenty-first century to meet the changing needs of students learning a global lingua franca. As such, we concur with Kirkpatrick, who has in the past advocated that the changing sociolinguistic use of English 'has implications for language learning goals, for language teachers and for the curriculum' (Kirkpatrick, 2012, p. 131). Matsuda and Friedrich (2012) have also lobbied for innovation, arguing that the 'linguistic, cultural and functional diversity associated with English today challenges some of the fundamental assumptions of English language teaching (ELT) and requires that we revisit our pedagogical practices' (p. 17). However, even though applied linguists and language educationalists seem to agree that change is necessary, until recently a concrete plan of innovation that can be implemented into practice has been lacking. This has led to widespread observations of a theory–practice divide, which this book aims to remedy with its lobbying of a new conceptualisation of language teaching, referred to as Global Englishes Language Teaching.

The Global Englishes Language Teaching Framework

The Global Englishes Language Teaching framework (Table 1.1) was originally created by Galloway (2011) to provide a usable framework for research purposes, and to inform curriculum innovation. The original framework was informed by similar comparisons, such as Jenkins's (2006) EFL vs ELF conceptualisation, as well as earlier work by Canagarajah (2005) and Seidlhofer (2004). Galloway's (2011) framework was seen as a means to answer calls for change in ELT by consolidating interconnected themes in a reader-friendly format (see Table 1.1). Since this time, the framework has undergone adaptation as new ideas have emerged, and proposals have been put into practice.

Table 1.1 *Galloway's (2011) original GELT framework (adapted)*

	ELT	GELT
Target interlocutor	The NES	The NES and the NNES/The ELF speaker
Owners	NESs	ELF users
Cultural content	NE culture	Students' C1 and ELF cultures
Teachers	NNESTs (same L1) and NESTs	Teachers – NNESTs (same L1), NNESTs (diff L1) and NESTs/ multilingual ELF users
Norm	NE and concept of SE	Diversity, flexibility, ELF strategies and multiple forms of competence
Model	The NES	The successful ELF user
Materials	NE and NESs	NE, NNE, ELF and ELF communities and contexts
L1 and C1	A hindrance and an interference	A resource
Paradigm	Belongs to the foreign-language paradigm	Belongs to the Global Englishes paradigm

In its second incarnation, the framework appeared in our book entitled *Introducing Global Englishes* (Galloway & Rose, 2015), which was intended as an introductory text to the field. Adaptations to the framework at this time were heavily influenced by the 'pedagogical priorities' outlined by Canagarajah (2013). Categories were added and terms amended to reflect current thinking in the field. This version of the framework has appeared in a number of subsequent publications and has informed some subsequent research (e.g. Galloway, 2017a; Galloway & Rose, 2014, 2018; McKinley, 2018; Rose & Galloway, 2017; Syrbe & Rose, 2018), which applies the dimensions of the framework to critically analyse data. Meier's (2017, p. 155) 'framework for critical reflection' also uses dichotomous labels to represent shifts in thinking when she explores dimensions within the multilingual turn, thus the GELT framework sits well with other related frameworks.

Since 2015, we have made slight adjustments to the framework in order to more accurately represent research and current positions. Firstly, we have aimed to de-emphasise the divide between so-called native and non-native English speakers in light of movements to abandon these terms. While in our 2015 book we problematised the terms before using them, we want to further emphasise that GELT does not view users of English with such divisive labels. Thus, in terms of the categories of target interlocutors, ownership, norms and materials, we have dropped previous labels that aimed to include both native and non-native speakers of English to embrace more inclusive terms, such as 'all users', 'global' ownership and 'competent' teachers, who use fluid, diverse and multiple forms of the language. We have maintained use of the 'native speaker' and 'native English' labels when referring to traditional ELT, as we still feel that these provide an accurate means to describe problematic positions that have underpinned (and continue to underpin) most teaching practices. We have also replaced labels in the ownership category from speakers to contexts, highlighting that ownership of English is seen to rest within certain English-using contexts, rather than speakers. Our current thinking of GELT is illustrated in Table 1.2 and, thus, underpins the discussion of GELT that follows.

In terms of *target interlocutor*, we see a need to move away from depictions of the native speaker as being the preferred target for learners' future use of English. Research on English use has shown that twenty-first-century learners of English will need the language to engage with a global community of users, and we see that teaching practices will need to fully prepare students for this. While in some contexts a shift is apparent, research has shown that, even in somewhat ELF-aware contexts such as Germany, the target interlocutor is still widely presented to students as the native speaker. A small-scale study of German textbooks, for example, found that only one pedagogical task across four textbooks at the advanced level could broadly be defined as positioning the

Table 1.2 *The 2018 Global Englishes Language Teaching framework*

	Traditional ELT	GELT
Target interlocutors	Native English speakers	All English users
Ownership	Inner Circle	Global
Target culture	Static NE cultures	Fluid cultures
Norms	Standard English	Diverse, flexible and multiple forms
Teachers	Non-NE-speaking teachers (same L1) and NE-speaking teachers	Qualified, competent teachers (same and different L1s)
Role model	NE speakers	Expert users
Source of materials	NE and NE speakers	Salient English-speaking communities and contexts
Other languages and cultures	Seen as a hindrance and source of interference	Seen as a resource as with other languages in their linguistic repertoire
Needs	Inner Circle defined	Globally defined
Assessment criterion	Accuracy according to prescriptive standards	Communicative competence
Goals of learning	Native-like proficiency	Multicompetent user
Ideology	Underpinned by an exclusive and ethnocentric view of English	Underpinned by an inclusive Global Englishes perspective
Orientation	Monolingual	Multilingual/translingual

target interlocutor as an ELF speaker (Syrbe & Rose, 2018). We further develop such research in a later chapter of this book (Chapter 6).

Much of the emphasis on the native speaker stems from an underlying ideology that *ownership* of the English language rests within the Inner Circle. This is despite the fact that English speakers outside the Inner Circle have long outnumbered those within it – a fact that is only going to become more prevalent in the future. At the current growth rates, the number of English speakers may surpass 4 billion by the year 2050, of which little more than 0.5 billion will be defined as L1 English speakers of the Inner Circle. This will further increase the ratio of L1 to L2 speakers to a 1:8 ratio, compared to David Crystal's (2003) oft-cited 1:3 ratio. This further emphasises the need to encourage a perception in the classroom that English belongs to a global community, rather than the traditional origins of it as being the language of the Inner Circle, or more broadly of those living in nations descendent from the former British Empire. Within a GELT perspective, the owners of English are seen as being as fluid as the language they speak, moving beyond outdated notions that geographic borders and nation-based states 'contain' language and speakers. GELT's transnational view of language sits alongside similar perspectives of transnationalism (discussed further in Chapter 2). While transnationalism is challenging the rigid boundaries of nation states, Global Englishes, like ELF, challenges the rigid boundaries of languages.

Connected to changes in the representation of ownership and target interlocutors is the *target culture* in which the language is to be used. Earlier, we described a call for changes in cultural depictions in curricula to more representative illustrations of the fluid and diverse cultures where English is used today. Byram's (1997) work is important here and critical cultural awareness is central, focusing on the competence needed for communication between those from different linguacultural backgrounds. Thus, GELT aims to help learners develop this, providing them with a foundation to evaluate their own and others' 'perspectives, practices and products' (Byram, 1997, p. 63). However, in GELT, Baker's notion of intercultural awareness is more relevant, since in ELF there is no target culture, so speakers cannot be familiar with the perspectives, practices and products of all of their potential interlocutors. Thus, a more appropriate goal may be to demonstrate intercultural awareness, the role culturally based communicative forms, practices and frames of reference have in intercultural communication, and an ability to use these in a flexible and context-specific manner (Baker, 2011, 2012a). Will Baker's (e.g. 2009, 2012b, 2015) work has played a key role in leading the movement to innovate culture in language classrooms that have traditionally been underpinned by static models. GELT calls for more innovations of this type, in order for learners to be aware that new cultures emerge and develop in each instance of language use, especially in lingua franca contexts, where speakers are bringing different expectations and experiences to the speech community. Intercultural awareness recognises the need to move away from essentialist conceptualisations and highlights this fluid, dynamic and complex relationship between language and culture in ELF encounters.

The *norms* which underpin language teaching are perhaps the most resistant to change, as they are grounded in standard language ideology that a standard, or correct, version of the language exists. GELT concurs with opinions that static views of language are problematic (Widdowson, 2012). Thus, students will benefit from more fluid, diverse and multiple forms of the language during their education. Some of this fluidity can be achieved through the exposure of varieties of English, such as in Galloway and Rose (2014, 2018), while diversity can also be achieved through awareness raising, such as in Galloway (2013) and Rose and Galloway (2017). In the latter of these studies, an explicit pedagogical task involving an informed debate over Singlish and the Speak Good English Movement in Singapore helped to challenge students' standard language ideology. We will return to this study in Chapter 4.

In order to reflect global ownership of the language, GELT encourages the positioning of qualified, expert users as good *role models* for learners. While this may prove difficult, due to the prevalence of standard language ideology as discussed above, initial research shows a raised awareness of the value of expert users as role models and teachers. A study by Galloway and Rose (2013) aimed to explore the effects of hiring teaching assistants for an English-medium business course in Japan, based on their perceived value as both role models of expert ELF users (e.g. having used English in diverse contexts) and having knowledge of business concepts. Questionnaire data from students suggested that they valued qualities in the assistant, which were not connected to linguistic knowledge but the ability to engage with students, to explain key concepts and to be approachable peers. The study also saw no statistically significant differences between the reported value of the assistant and perceived nativeness. This is also supported by our own anecdotal evidence in the same teaching context, which showed that students valued having expert ELF users as guest speakers on the programme, as they represented achievable role models and inspired the learners to reach the same standards.

The positioning of authentic role models ties in with the need to position competent teachers as *ideal* English teachers, regardless of their perceived native status. After all, while native speaking teachers are often positioned as authoritative users of the language, they often make poor role models for learners, representative of a largely unachievable yardstick to which to measure their own language-learning aspirations. Non-native speaking teachers, on the other hand, were once learners of the language themselves, and have often built up a repertoire of learning practices, knowledge and experiences that have seen them become actual authoritative figures of English language teaching. Nevertheless, while making an argument for non-native speakers as authentic role models, we are not advocating that the non-native speakers necessarily make better teachers. What we would argue is that nativeness is inherently a poor criterion on which to judge a teacher's ability to teach. The issue of native speakers as ideal teachers has been challenged by teaching organisations for decades. The organisation, TESOL in 1991, for example, took to publishing an article criticising such hiring practices – a position they re-emphasised in 2006 (TESOL, 1991, 2006).

Nevertheless, the native speaker hegemony remains. One of the biggest casualties of this hegemony is that the field of English language teaching is not taking advantage of its human resources, as non-Anglophone countries are still perceived as places where native speakers of English can travel to teach, but non-native English-speaking teachers cannot find work (unless they are speakers of the local language, where this skill is valued in order to teach low-level classes through the L1 within some education systems). GELT sees the value of not only hiring qualified teachers regardless of native status but also what teachers of different L1s can bring to learners. With such expert teachers heading language classes, learners have a threefold benefit in having a teacher who is a qualified expert, has a multilingual repertoire and provides an authentic ELF setting for each class. Moreover, if hiring practices change, we can leverage the benefits of an 80% share of non-native language teachers, who can be suddenly mobile in their profession, instead of being prisoners to the current prevailing native speaker hegemony.

In terms of movements in the *sources of materials* used, GELT sees a need to draw upon a wider range of sources from global uses of English language today than is currently occurring. The ELT industry is still currently propped up by Anglocentric publications, due to a pervasive view that they are the source of authoritative experts and publications in the field (Jenkins, 2007). While there is evidence that some positive movement in more recent textbooks has occurred (see, e.g., Chapter 6, this volume) with notable additions to speaker varieties in the recorded materials of newer textbooks compared to those a decade ago, the consensus is that much more movement is needed. This particular aspect will be returned to in Chapter 6, where popular language-learning materials are investigated. For now, we argue that textbooks need to include a more representative depiction of students' future English-language use. Needs analysis is, therefore, essential in ensuring that the materials used in classrooms suit the future language needs of the students with whom they are used.

The field of English language teaching has already witnessed a significant conceptual change in our understanding of the role of the first language and culture, but some traditional ideologies remain. Despite a large body of research denouncing English-only policies in the language classroom (see Tollefson, 2007, for an overview), the ideology remains in English-language classrooms throughout the world with further gravitation towards English-only pedagogy in some national school contexts, such as in Korea. The notion that students' L1 is a crutch, or hindrance, to learning, although debased by research, remains prevalent in teachers' understanding of pedagogical practice. GELT challenges such ideologies and, drawing from similar movements within the multilingual turn, views learners' linguistic repertoire as an important resource for learning, rather than a source of interference. Similarly, GELT embraces the importance of a learner's own culture.

An uncontroversial element of needed change to move away from traditional approaches to ELT to a Global Englishes approach is a change in how we conceptualise students' *needs*. While most good teachers already see needs analysis as being central to curriculum development, the Inner Circle is often assumed to be part of this need and, as a result, is rarely problematised. Many programmes establish their curriculum around a supposition that students need to use English in Inner Circle contexts, or with speakers from such contexts. GELT challenges this notion and argues that most students' needs today – and especially those who are learning English for global use – are markedly different from the past. Therefore, teachers must make informed decisions based on the careful needs analysis of their students. While the Inner Circle may still be relevant for some students, it may not be for all.

Central to a paradigm shift in English language teaching is a shift in perspectives of the *assessment criteria* against which language outcomes are measured. Here, we concur with the observation that 'Debates about the assessment of international English have revolved around two important questions: Whose norms should we apply? And how do we define proficiency in the English language?' (Canagarajah, 2013, p. 3). Canagarajah further states that, due to a new geopolitical order, which he terms postmodern globalisation, there is a need for

> a more complex orientation that moves the discourse of proficiency to a totally different label ... This orientation also means that we have to move away from the previous paradigms of teaching to creatively devise new practices that would address our emerging communicative needs. (pp. 2–3)

Without a change in the assessment the washback effect (discussed further in Chapter 4) would continue to stifle innovation in the curriculum and, thus, both assessment and teaching must adapt in order to meet our postmodern globalisation language needs.

Language testing seeks to measure a simulation of 'relevant communicative behavior' required by the learners, which is referred to as the criterion (McNamara, 2000), and assessment is also designed with regard to such criterion. Considering the growth of English as a global language, it is clear that the target setting for using English has changed significantly and, thus, so has the criterion. The future language use behaviours of learners and test takers will increasingly involve speakers with diverse linguistic backgrounds, in addition to the first language users. A Global Englishes perspective would argue that, because the target language use context has changed for learners of a global language, so, too, should assessment criterion, if assessment aims to make an accurate inference about a learner's future performance. Language testing has been identified as being one of the areas in which the native speaker is most visible and is, in that effect, also one of the areas in which changes are most necessary. Making a change, however, is difficult, as McNamara (2012, p. 199) notes:

> Traditionally [achievement] is defined in reference to the educated native speaker of Standard English. But the majority of users of English in the contemporary world are non-native speakers using the language as a lingua franca. So the question is how far the constructs articulated in standards for English language proficiency reflect, or can reflect, the insights into the nature of communication represented by research on English as a lingua franca.

A GELT perspective, however, does not seek to replace one standard with another. Indeed, ELF research has indicated that the very idea of a standard is incompatible with the fluid nature of ELF usage. Instead, GELT argues for assessment criterion to be based on communicative competence, rather than accuracy according to such a standard. Thus, the central criterion to any piece of assessment that aims to make inference about a learner's ability to use English in a global context should make its evaluations of the speaker's ability to communicate effectively and concisely in that type of environment.

In terms of the *ideology* underpinning GELT, we see that the approach is underpinned by the inclusive paradigm of Global Englishes, which embraces the diversity of English used today. We posit Global Englishes as the means through which an epistemic break can be achieved in English language teaching, which Kumaravadivelu (2012) has defined as a thorough reconceptualisation and reorganisation of knowledge systems. He argues that

> The native-speaker episteme has not loosened its grip over theoretical principles, classroom practices, the publication industry, or the job market. What is surely and sorely needed is a meaningful break from this epistemic dependency if we are serious about sanitizing our discipline from its corrosive effect and sensitizing the field to the demands of globalism and its impact on identity formation. (p. 15)

In our exploration of GELT, we hope to provide a roadmap for change in current practices so that this break can be better facilitated.

Global Englishes *for* Language Teaching

Finally, we want to emphasise that our vision for change in English language teaching does not suggest that we need to abandon previous practices entirely. Just as Larsen-Freeman and Anderson (2011), who provide an overview of techniques and principles in language teaching, note that they 'do not seek to convince readers that one method is superior to another, or that there is or ever will be a perfect method' (p. ix), GELT is not proposed as a superior teaching approach. Instead, it challenges the assumptions about English that pervade into teaching practices, saturate teaching materials and permeate into the ideologies of learners. GELT calls for a re-evaluation of current practices in light of the changing sociolinguistic uses of the language. GELT answers calls by scholars such as Matsuda and Friedrich (2012), who have previously argued for a complete revision of teaching programmes 'using one's understanding of the use of English in international contexts as a foundation that influences every single aspect of the curriculum' (p. 25).

Similar to other scholars who examine teaching approaches (e.g. Richards & Rogers, 2014), we want to emphasise that teachers will have to adapt the ideas and concepts presented in this book to their own contexts, depending on their student needs and their curriculum constraints. GELT is an ideology that can be used to inform, rather than direct, teaching in the twenty-first century. In order to emphasise GELT as a framework for action, which can also be used to evaluate progress, we have inserted a seemingly trivial (but actually very important) *for* in the title of this book. The reason for this insertion is to emphasise that GELT should be viewed as a tool *for* language teaching, rather than an approach that is used *to* teach. In this way, GELT should not be seen as an alternative to current approaches used to teach but a way to inform these approaches. Indeed, methods of teaching need not change, but, rather, it is the ideology that underpins curricula that is to change.

GELT offers a new perspective on how we view language, encouraging practitioners and curriculum planners alike to question norms and monolingual ideology. It acknowledges the importance of bi/multilingual speakers' whole language repertoire and semiotic system and aims to emancipate them from adhering to strict native norms. Thus, it offers an opportunity for learner agency, enabling learners to draw on their languages to suit the purposes of communication, recognising the hybrid use of languages and how it changes. The work on translanguaging (Garcia, 2009; García & Wei, 2014) aims to move the field past dividing these languages, and emphasises the valuable use of the entire repertoire. As opposed to learning how to communicate in one set way, it acknowledges learners' ability to adapt according to their interlocutors and the situation.

GELT can also be used for research purposes for investigations of language teaching practices. In the latter half of the book, we will illustrate the use of GELT as a research framework used to measure innovation in course curriculum and materials, where innovation is occurring within a variety of teaching contexts. In this way, we show how Global Englishes *for* language teaching is being used to innovate and to highlight areas where further innovation can occur.

2 The TESOL Curriculum and GELT

As outlined in the previous chapter, GELT requires a conceptual transition in the field of TESOL. In order to facilitate this, we examine some of the fundamental key concepts and theories underpinning English language teaching through a Global Englishes lens. Global Englishes research, and the expansion in the use of ELF, raises numerous questions about how English should be taught and learned. Good teaching and successful curricula meet the needs of learners, yet in today's globalised world, learners' needs have changed and, as such, it is questionable how far 'traditional' approaches that focus on 'native' English-speaker norms are meeting these needs. This has implications for English language teaching, especially: programme goals and objectives; the content to be taught and learned (the syllabus); how it should be taught (the methodology); and how learners should be evaluated (assessment).

In this chapter we take a curriculum perspective, exploring GELT by focusing on needs analysis, syllabus, methodology, assessment and curriculum evaluation. In doing so, we aim to problematise the centrality of 'native' English speaker norms and the role of Western-centric notions of teaching and learning. A number of the concepts and theories introduced have their roots in second language acquisition theory, discussed in the next chapter. In our examination of the main trajectories in the field, we also aim to help map future directions in curriculum innovation.

TESOL: A Changing Context

In the introduction to a special issue of *Modern Language Journal*, Kramsch (2014) notes a changing context of language teaching, which is entirely applicable to the field of TESOL:

> There has never been a time when language teaching and learning has been more interactive and more imaginative than today ... Communicative pedagogies have made the classroom more participatory, electronic chatrooms have loosened the tongues and the writing of even the shyest students, video and the Internet have made authentic materials available as never before, telecollaboration and social networks have increased students' access to real speakers in real cultural environments—and yet

> there has never been a greater tension between what is taught in the classroom and what the students will need in the real world once they have left the classroom. In the last decades, that world has changed to such an extent that language teachers are no longer sure of what they are supposed to teach nor what real world situations they are supposed to prepare their students for. (p. 296)

It is this tension and preparation for real-world situations that GELT aims to address. This certainly poses a dilemma for teachers in deciding what they are supposed to teach, particularly if their textbooks, tests and institutional or governmental ELT policies continue to promote 'native' English speaking and monolingual norms. As discussed in Chapter 1, debates over the dominance of 'native' English-speaker norms are not new, nor are they unique to the field of Global Englishes. Nevertheless, research within the Global Englishes paradigm throws a new perspective on these debates, illuminating the need to reconceptualise the 'E' in ELT and TESOL – and in EMI for that matter (discussed in Chapter 8). Growing research in the field of Global Englishes has prompted a shift in the perspective of language, corresponding with other movements such as the multilingual turn. It is this new perspective that the GELT framework (Figure 2.1) attempts to address, encouraging a movement away from the monolingual orientation.

In order to understand where TESOL is heading, we must first understand where the field has come from, although it is beyond the scope of this chapter to provide a detailed overview of each major development. As with Canagarajah (2016), who examined the history of the field via a content analysis of *TESOL Quarterly*'s issues over the past fifty years, we also adopt Widdowson's (2004) approach to the history of ELT, focusing on 'the underlying trends and tendencies' of the profession (p. 353). However, in doing so, we do this within the context of the curriculum. Good teaching is, after all, 'Dependent on understanding the context for teaching, the needs of teachers and learners, the careful planning of courses and materials, as well as the monitoring of teaching and learning' (Richards, 2001, p. xi). It is dependent on a number of interrelated factors and processes referred to by Richards (2001) as *curriculum development*. By anchoring our discussions within familiar concepts such as the curriculum, we hope to avoid alienating teachers with our critical perspectives, which has been previously observed as being an issue in connecting theory with pedagogical practice (Hall et al., 2013).

Curriculum theory has previously been discussed in relation to the globalisation of English (cf. Alsagoff et al., 2012). Such contributions also aim to help guide practitioners to critically reflect on their teaching practice in their specific contexts. Sembiante (2016) also discussed the implications that the shift in the perspective of language prompted by researchers discussing multilingualism and translanguaging have for the field of curriculum studies, particularly the role of language. In a similar vein, the GELT framework helps practitioners to consider not only innovations but also barriers. Thus, in the following sections, we examine the field within the context of the curriculum through a Global Englishes lens to showcase how GELT embraces and informs shifting perspectives in the field.

Curriculum

The curriculum is often conflated with teaching methods, which are often viewed as being the most important factor in ensuring the success of an education programme. As such, the field of TESOL has been preoccupied with a quest for the best method. However, as Richards (2001) notes, '[a] perspective often missing from the method-based view of teaching is that of how methods interact with other factors in the teaching-learning process?' (p. ix). A curriculum can be defined as 'an inventory of what is to be taught, and how it will be taught and assessed for the realisation of particular goals or specific needs. It is primarily a selection of content, resources and activities organised and sequenced for consistency and continuity of instruction, and for the assessment of change or development' (Mickan, 2013, pp. 24–5).

A curriculum, therefore, includes:

1. Needs Analysis: Who are the learners/the target group? Why are they learning English? What is the context like? How is English used in their country/domain?
2. Goals and Objectives: What is to be achieved? What is their purpose?
3. Syllabus: What is to be taught?
4. Methodology: How should it be taught?
5. Assessment: How can we measure whether learners are learning the content and the goals have been met?
6. Evaluation: How can we ensure that it is effective?

Needs analysis often acts as the anchor for curriculum development and evaluation. If learners' needs change, the whole curriculum may need to be re-examined. Postmodern globalisation has clearly changed learners' use of the English language, and thus impacts on all other curriculum elements. Taking a curriculum perspective to GELT enables us to consider how the various elements relate to one another, allowing us to ask key questions to help ensure successful and sustained curriculum innovation (see Figure 2.1).

The GELT framework is designed to guide practitioners to evaluate and design curricula. It illuminates the *why, what, when, where, how* and *with whom* to learn. An effective curriculum or course design makes the educational principles that underlie the curriculum explicit (Graves, 2016) and, therefore, we began this book with an overview of the field of Global Englishes and GELT. The beliefs and values of curriculum planners are also important. As Guo & Maitra (2017) note:

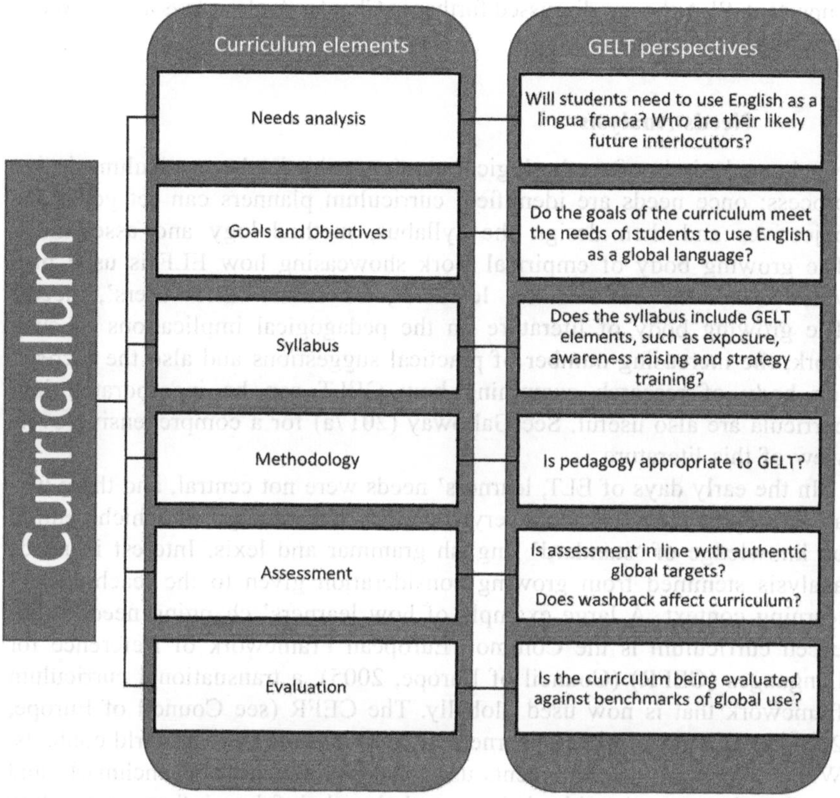

Figure 2.1 The interrelated elements of the curriculum in relation to GELT.

It is important to pay attention to the ideology and politics behind curriculum planning, for people in positions of power, provincial governments, school authorities, and other stakeholders are often primary agents when decisions are made on the content of the curriculum, as well as instructional materials and texts chosen, thereby legitimating and enforcing what students should learn and teachers ought to teach (Bickmore, 2005; Skerrett, 2015). (p. 82)

Beliefs about the purpose of English-language education are often evident in national education policy statements, and these can have a powerful impact on curriculum change. The Council of Europe's adoption of communicative competence as a curricular goal, for example, impacted national curricula across Europe, and indeed around the world. We recognise that curriculum planners are not always the government, nor education ministry officials, and the beliefs of practitioners, students, parents and other stakeholders are also important. SLA theory, discussed further in Chapter 3, also plays a large role in informing curriculum change.

Needs Analysis

Needs analysis is often the logical starting point in the curriculum design process; once needs are identified, curriculum planners can set goals and objectives and then design the syllabus, methodology and assessment. The growing body of empirical work showcasing how ELF is used provides a wealth of data on learners', or future ELF users', needs. The growing body of literature on the pedagogical implications of such work, the increasing number of practical suggestions and also the increasing body of research examining how GELT can be incorporated into curricula are also useful. See Galloway (2017a) for a comprehensive overview of this literature.

In the early days of ELT, learners' needs were not central, and there was an assumption that learners everywhere had the same goals, which centred on knowledge of 'standard' English grammar and lexis. Interest in needs analysis stemmed from growing consideration given to the teaching and learning context. A large example of how learners' changing needs influenced curriculum is the Common European Framework of Reference for Languages (CEFR) (Council of Europe, 2005), a transnational curriculum framework that is now used globally. The CEFR (see Council of Europe, 2001, p. 9) aims to prepare learners to communicate in real-world contexts. While some 'can-do' statements use 'native' English as a benchmark, and are therefore questionable, it is nevertheless helpful to inform curriculum developers of the students' can-do needs to use the language in the 'real' world. However, as Galloway (2018) notes: 'The "real world", then, appears to be a world where learners will use the target language with native English speakers' (p. 469), which seems somewhat incompatible with GELT.

Needs analysis also grew in importance as language courses started having to justify or secure funding (Richards, 2001). Education is certainly a competitive industry and in many contexts, courses have to provide evidence that they are serving a need. This is certainly not problematic for GELT, given the flourishing Global Englishes research providing empirical evidence on learners' needs today. Indeed, the 'establishment of World Englishes and ELF research has provided powerful arguments for the need to reconceptualise models of English in ELT' (Llurda, 2016, p. 56). While 'the lack of descriptive work on ELF initially made it difficult for teaching professionals to incorporate an ELF approach into their teaching practice' (Llurda, 2016, p. 56), this is not the case today. One of the very aims of this book is to encourage curriculum planners to draw on such work and recognise the significance it has for the English-language curriculum.

Necessities

Nation & Macalister (2010) refer to three types of target needs: ***necessities, lacks*** and ***wants***. There is plentiful evidence of learners' necessities, in terms of the required knowledge needed by those learning English to use as a global lingua franca. Global Englishes research highlights a mismatch between what is currently taught in the 'traditional' ELT curricula and how the language is used as a lingua franca. It showcases, for example, that 'errors' and 'mistakes', often highlighted in mainstream ELT materials and assessments, do not necessarily result in a communication breakdown.

Corpus linguistics as a field of study grew out of a focus on 'authenticity' and 'real' English, alongside developments in technology, and, today, many course books are based on corpora – electronic databases of 'real' contextualised examples of 'authentic' language. Examples include the *Touchstone* series (Cambridge English) and the *Empower* series (Cambridge English). However, the native English corpora upon which such textbooks are based do not reflect the needs of all learners, particularly those who will use English as a lingua franca. Emerging ELF corpora, such as VOICE 2.0 (2013), ACE (2014) and ELFA (2008), provide alternatives and they showcase how ELF users utilise their multilingual repertoires and negotiate communication in multilingual encounters.

There is also a wealth of data available for those working in different domains, such as business English as a lingua franca (Ehrenreich, 2009, 2015; Kankaanranta & Louhiala-Salminen, 2018; Kankaanranta & Planken, 2010), ELF in social contexts (Pietikäinen, 2014, 2018), electronically mediated intercultural communication (Sangiamchit, 2018), translation/interpreting (Albl-Mikasa, 2013, 2015, 2018; G.Cook, 2012; House, 2014), academia (Jenkins, 2014; Murata & Iino, 2018; Smit, 2018) and migration (Grazia Guido, 2008, 2018), all of which can provide insights for curriculum planning. We recognise that ELF users may not all have the same needs and 'native' English norms may still be appropriate for some learners. Indeed, GELT is based on the context-sensitive nature of such communication and aims to increase learners' choices, recognising the diverse needs of learners today, thus drawing on the notion of 'communities of practice' (Wenger, 1998).

Wants

With regard to the subjective needs, the 'wants' (Nation & Macalister, 2010), or attitudes, of various stakeholders, some studies have concluded that positive attitudes towards native norms can be used to justify the use of this model, given that it meets learners' self-professed needs (Kuo, 2006; Timmis, 2002). However, such studies have been criticised for failing to investigate the underlying factors behind such attitudes, including the very dominance of native norms and standard language ideology (Galloway, 2013, 2017a; Galloway & Rose, 2015). Just because learners 'want to be native speakers . . . does not mean these attitudes are right' (Cook, 1999, p. 196), and such 'attitudes are the product of the many pressures on them to regard L2 users as failed natives' (p. 199). Recent studies have also revealed the important influence of ELF awareness and experience (Galloway, 2011, 2013, 2017a; Wang, 2013, 2015; Wang & Jenkins, 2016) and the positive influence of Global Englishes instruction on attitudes (Baker, 2012b; Derwing et al., 2002; Galloway, 2011, 2013, 2017a; Galloway & Rose, 2013; Shim, 2002; Sung, 2015). Indeed, the field is dominated by monolingual ideology, and therefore, we have included this in Table 2.1, where we present the ideological perspectives influencing ELT curricula.

Students' desire to learn native English should not be dismissed, but as we argue in Chapter 5, we urge researchers, and practitioners, to explore these attitudes, and students' needs, in more depth. As McKay (2003) notes:

> many language learners today are studying English not because they are being coerced to do so by speakers of Inner Circle countries, but rather because of the benefits knowledge of English brings. An effective EIL pedagogy, then, must consider the specific goals that lead learners to study English and not assume that these goals necessarily involve attaining full proficiency in the language. (p. 5)

An effective GELT curriculum should not only be based on an understanding of learners' goals and motivation for learning the language, but also on their needs. However, it must also refrain from assuming that all students have the same needs. Needs will always differ; for some, it may well be native English-speaker proficiency, but we also have to cater for those who may wish to strive to become a more successful ELF user.

Lacks

Some of the studies investigating students' attitudes in relation to Global Englishes reveal that ELF familiarity and experience influence attitudes (e.g. Galloway, 2011, 2017a; Wang, 2015). This is not always a straightforward task, however, and language awareness and the need for reflection will be discussed further in relation to syllabus and methodology. Galloway and Rose (2014), for example, found in their listening journal study that learners lacked the metacognitive skills to reflect on their ELF experiences.

Table 2.1 *Richard's (2001) curriculum perspectives from a GELT perspective*

Curriculum Perspective	Richard's (2001) Perspective	Further GELT Perspective
Academic rationalism	Emphasises the intrinsic value of the subject matter, mastery of content and developing the learners' overall intellect and rationality.	GELT embraces new ideas in academia, and thus further enhances intellectual knowledge surrounding English language.
Social and economic efficiency	Emphasises the practical needs of learners and society and the need to produce learners who are economically productive.	Emphasising the practical and functional skills in English can be easier in GELT since it is more needs based. By preparing students to develop intercultural communicative competence and sensitivity to using English in multilingual contexts, they are more likely to meet social and economic needs.
Learner-centredness	Emphasises learner-centredness, the individual needs of the learners and the importance of self-reflection, self-expression and critical thinking and learning strategies.	GELT offers opportunities for critical thinking and promotes learner autonomy, focusing more on the process than the product, and thus emphasising learner agency.
Social reconstructionism	Emphasises the role of education in addressing social injustices and inequality.	GELT doesn't see curriculum development as a neutral process and encourages students to examine the possible biases or social divisions that English has created. GELT is in line with critical pedagogy, seeing teachers and learners as being involved in a joint process of exploring and constructing knowledge.
Cultural pluralism	Emphasises the need to prepare learners to participate in several different cultures, not merely the culture of the dominant social and economic group.	GELT aims to develop intercultural competence to work in fluid ELF cultures. GELT highlights the importance of L2 users and challenges L1 cultural, linguistic and social hegemony.

Situational Needs and Specific Purposes

Context is central to GELT and information on the 'Situation needs' (Brown, 1995), or information to help with the 'Environment analysis' (Nation &

Macalister, 2010) or 'situation analysis' (Richards, 2001) is abundant in the field of Global Englishes. In addition to research in different domains, Global Englishes research is also increasing in varied geographical settings, including Europe (Sherman, 2018), ASEAN (Kirkpatrick, 2018), China (Wang, 2018), Japan (D'Angelo, 2018; Galloway, 2011, 2013, 2017a), Brazil (Gimenez et al., 2018) and South Africa (van der Walt & Evans, 2018). Business students studying English at a university in Korea, for example, may have different situation needs for learning English than comparable business students at a university in Mexico.

The centrality of learners' needs in GELT resembles an English for Specific Purposes (ESP) approach, where the goal of an ESP course is to prepare learners to use English in a specific context or within a specific set of tasks. Starfield (2016, p. 150) notes that:

> The ESP learner is not learning the language for general educative purposes or for the study of literature in which the language is the subject matter of the course, but rather as a means to the "acquisition of some quite different body of knowledge or set of skills".
> (Robinson, 1980, p. 6)

In GELT, the specific purpose can be said to be to use English in lingua franca or global contexts and acquire a specific set of skills to use English in such contexts. This is different to the knowledge and skills taught in a curriculum based on monolingual native norms. GELT, or EIL in McKay's (2003) words,

> must recognize the various ways in which English is used within multilingual communities. Typically these bilingual users of English have specific purposes for using English, employing their other languages to serve their many additional language needs ... One purpose they all share, however, is to use English as a language of wider communication. (p. 18)

Context and content are also central to ESP (Starfield, 2013) and to GELT, where awareness should be raised of how ELF functions in dynamic, flexible situations with speakers from diverse linguacultural backgrounds. As in ESP, needs analysis in GELT is an ongoing iterative process that continues throughout the course as practitioners learn more about their learners, their goals and their target situations.

A further similarity is that the emergence of ESP was related to post-Second World War needs with globalisation, ideologies of progress and the desire to facilitate international communication (Starfield, 2016), which is also true of GELT's links to globalisation. ESP was also perceived as a 'radical' break from previous approaches (Starfield, 2016). There are various subfields of ESP, such as English for law, EAP, English for business and English for science. As new needs emerge, a new subfield emerges. Many of these have their own course books and some, such as EAP, have become established fields in their own right with their own journals. In a similar vein, Global Englishes has become an established field, with associated journals (*World Englishes, Journal of English as a Lingua Franca*), conferences and publications. As such, it could be seen as a new subfield of ESP.

However, in drawing comparisons with ESP, we have to be careful so that we do not promote the use of a fixed set of lexical items or phrases deemed appropriate for ELF communication. As mentioned in Chapter 1, while this type of work formed part of the first phase of ELF research, it is not central to current research (ELF3) and is incongruent with the ideology of Global Englishes. Nevertheless, there are similarities, and it is also worth noting that the globalisation of English and the associated pedagogical implications have been acknowledged within the field of ESP. Nickerson (2005), for example, refers to the use of ELF alongside other languages, and Nickerson (2013, p. 451) notes the need to move away from native speaker models to think about 'functional nativeness' in lingua franca contexts. Starfield (2016) highlights the large number of articles written by L2 English speakers in the ESP journal and the fact that the majority of ESP practitioners around the world are not L1 speakers. Further, in discussions of how to adopt a critical approach to ESP, Nickerson (2005) discusses the need to focus on strategies for communication in business 'regardless of whether the speaker/writer is a native or non-native speaker' (p. 369), indicating a shift in the field from language skills to language strategies, which resonates well with GELT. Nickerson (2013) also discusses a shift to ELF perspectives and Starfield (2016) refers to the VOICE corpus that 'will provide instances of spoken interaction that may help drive these changes' (p. 159). There have also been discussions on how to encourage multilingual learners to reflect on their self-perceptions of their cultural identities and positioning (Belcher & Lukkarila, 2011). This movement towards seeing learners as multilingual subjects in the field of ESP is promising for GELT and Starfield (2016) recognises that this has implications for ESP curricula and has the potential to move the field away from deficit views.

Goals and Objectives

Many policy-level curriculum developers perceive instrumental benefits in English proficiency, both for the learner and for the wider society, and thus measurable development in learner proficiency is the main objective of most language curricula. As Wedell (2003) notes, these perceived benefits 'have for several decades provided an impetus and rationale for numerous English language curriculum change (sometimes called "reform" or "development") projects' (p. 439). While goals and objectives 'are near-synonyms and thus are often used interchangeably' (Graves, 2016, p. 87), subtle differences exist. Goals (sometimes referred to as aims) are often broader, outlining what learners should achieve by the end of a course/programme.

They are often the foundation for the objectives, shorter term statements of what learners need to know or be able to do to reach these goals – they are designed to be measurable and observable; 'thus objectives "unpack" the goals' (Graves, 2016, p. 87). Setting goals and objectives is a critical step in curriculum development. In some contexts, practitioners are afforded a degree of autonomy to create their own; in others, they are published and enforced by higher authorities.

It was often 'taken for granted in the past that the aim of an English course is to make the learners communicate like native speakers. This is for most learners an inaccessible goal; and these days it is not even an appropriate one' (Ur, 2012, p. 6). As noted, the CEFR continues to be used to develop goals; yet can-do statements are somewhat out of sync with modern ideas regarding the benchmarks of learners, as is indicated in the following statements that appear in the CEFR (Council of Europe, 2001):

- learners are able to make 'assimilations and deletions comparable to native-like speech';
- learners are able to appreciate 'fully the sociolinguistic and sociocultural implications of language used by native speakers and can react accordingly';
- learners 'can sustain relationships with native speakers without unintentionally amusing or irritating them or requiring them to behave other than they would with a native speaker'.

In a GELT curriculum, the native speaker is not the assumed benchmark. A proficient learner may be able to 'interact with a degree of fluency and spontaneity that makes regular interaction with native speakers quite possible without strain for either party' (Council of Europe, 2001, p. 24), but this may not indicate that the learner can achieve mutual intelligibility in an ELF encounter. As Llurda (2016) notes:

> We need to question the common assumption in ELT that native speaker English should be the target for learners. What is the point in teaching specific aspects of a particular variety spoken by a restricted number of people if the goal is to communicate with a much wider and more global population? (p. 56)

In contexts where the CEFR has to be used, we urge practitioners to adapt it, making even the slightest changes to the benchmarks used in order to situate goals within global contexts, rather than native speaker ones.

In the Bilingual Business Program (Bilingual Business Program, 2010) at Rikkyo University (where both authors once worked), programme members devised and published learning outcomes for the overall language programme, as well as each language course within the programme. Although these outcomes were benchmarked against the CEFR, the can-do statement did not reference L1 using norms. Examples of language-related outcomes include an outcome that students will be able to 'follow and contribute to complex interactions during group discussions' (p. 11). The document also includes globally orientated non-language-related outcomes that link to critical pedagogy, such as goals to 'Exercise increased sensitivity to identify my own cultural biases and distinguish stereotypes from general cultural patterns by seeking evidence behind the given claims' (p. 8).

Clear goals and objectives are essential, and also ensure that a programme is open to evaluation, particularly given the focus on programme accountability in recent years and the increased demand for programme evaluation reports to justify funding. In Table 2.2, we outline some possible additional goals and objectives for a GELT curriculum. Also, see the lesson plans in the appendix of Galloway (2017a) and activities on the accompanying website to Galloway and Rose (2015).

One of the overall goals is to prepare students to use ELF. A GELT curriculum focuses on being intelligible, not acquiring native-like proficiency; being able to successfully deliver a message, not deliver it in a way that a small group of native speakers would; convey a message and negotiate forms, not communicate in constrained forms. When formulating goals and objectives, it is important that the goal is not to help learners produce 'accurate' English that adheres to a fixed set of 'standard' norms but to use the language flexibly. The inability to produce the language in a predetermined 'fixed' way does not equate to being an unsuccessful language user. As Dewey (2014) notes, 'in second language pedagogy, grammar is predominantly seen as a precondition for communication. In short, grammatical accuracy is regarded as an important factor in determining communicative success, and so intelligibility is conceptualized as being norm dependent' (p. 15). The role of grammar will be discussed further with regard to syllabus, but it is important to note here that the goal of GELT is not accuracy. It embraces linguistic diversity – as such, it aims to raise learners' awareness of the sociolinguistic use of English as a global lingua franca and their awareness of multilingualism. This clearly has implications for the syllabus, which should expose them to how meaning is negotiated, how ELF users exploit their linguistic resources to negotiate communication and how they adapt it to suit their purposes.

The goal is to expose them to the agency of ELF speakers, something that exposing students to one or two select native varieties of the language will not achieve. The aims of GELT are to help learners develop both their receptive and their productive skills for ELF contexts. However, its main foundation lies on the need to move away from native English norms and expose them to the inherent variability in the language when it is used as a global lingua franca. As discussed in Chapter 1, a further goal is successful intercultural communication. In relation to culture, Baker (2011, 2012a) critiqued Byram's (1997) notion of intercultural communicative competence, given that, in ELF encounters, there are not necessarily clearly

Table 2.2 *A multilayered content-based and skills-based syllabus integrated with GELT (adapted from Galloway & Rose, 2018)*

Module	Week	EAP Skills Focus	Global Englishes Topic Focus
The spread of English	1	Introduction Reading: reading for meaning	History of English; English speakers
	2	Listening: taking notes skills Debate: introducing opinions	Advantages and disadvantages of the spread of English
	3	Writing: brainstorming Presenting: structure	Issues related to the spread of English
World Englishes	4	Reading: issues and opinions Listening: summarising	English in Kachru's Three Circles; English and power
	5	Debating: agreeing/disagreeing Writing: paragraphs	Variety and ownership
	6	Presenting: voice Presenting: non-verbal communication	'Standard' English
ELF	7	Reading: skimming and scanning Listening skills: listening for gist	English use in Europe
	8	Introduction to presentation task Debating: boosting and hedging	English use in Japan
	9	Writing: citing sources Writing: essay structure	English use in higher education
Main tasks	10	Student presentations Student presentations	Varieties of English
	11	Presentation reflections and feedback Listening: organising notes	Varieties of English; English in Singapore
	12	Student debate preparation Student debate	'Standard' English in Singapore
	13	Review of main topics End-of-term assessment	Review

established relationships between a language and a particular culture. Flexibility is key and ELF scholarly work has explored how intercultural competence can be translated into classroom practice (Baker, 2012b). When using ELF, there is no clear language–culture nation correlation, so goals and objectives that encourage students to show awareness of cultural differences are inappropriate. GELT aims to move away from simplistic representations of culture, something that can still often be found in textbooks (highlighted in Chapter 6) and move more towards goals and objectives that aim to develop intercultural communicators.

For GELT, both performance objectives and process objectives are important. Objectives should not only focus on language development, but also on developing critical thinking, autonomous learners. It is also important to note that due to the centrality of learners' needs, and learner agency, learners should be involved in formulating goals and objectives, where possible. A GELT curriculum focuses on the whole process of learning, on real-world knowledge and participative learning, autonomy and reflective/active learning. It is not viewed as a top-down 'product', where knowledge/language is fixed and learners are passive.

Syllabus

A GELT curriculum calls for the replacement of goals that aim to produce learners who can accurately reproduce standard versions of native English with goals focusing on intelligibility and the global ownership of English. This shift then has implications for what is to be taught in the classroom – whether in the form of a formal written syllabus, a plan, or a list of items for a lesson. A syllabus may or may not be a published document and can be sequenced in different ways (e.g. from easy to difficult; by theme; or by skill). A syllabus also often recommends preferred methodology or materials (Ur, 2012).

The issue of what to include in the ideal English-language syllabus has been discussed at length and several scholars have discussed the various developments in syllabus design over the years (Graves, 1999; Richards, 2001). Different syllabi types emerged from a variety of factors, which correspond to three main developments in language teaching:

1. the product-orientated focus phase (structural formal syllabi);
2. the communicative phase (syllabi based on the use of language but also sociocultural approaches to teaching focusing on intercultural competence);
3. the learning how to learn/postmodern phase (learners given more responsibility and focus on learning content).

These can also be broadly divided into product and process syllabi (Figure 2.2). While GELT ideology could be positioned within any syllabus type, it may be more attuned to syllabi that do not focus on forms of the language, as much Global Englishes ideology lobbies for flexible language norms. That being said, we have had moderate success in integrating GELT into product-based syllabi such as the skills-based syllabus reported in Galloway and Rose (2018) and the content-based and EAP syllabus reported in Galloway (2011, 2013, 2017a). Thus, it is worth reviewing all types via a Global Englishes lens before outlining what a GELT-orientated syllabus might look like.

The Synthetic Syllabus

Synthetic syllabi, still common in many contexts, focus on form and are based on assumptions that language is best taught in discrete units of studies.

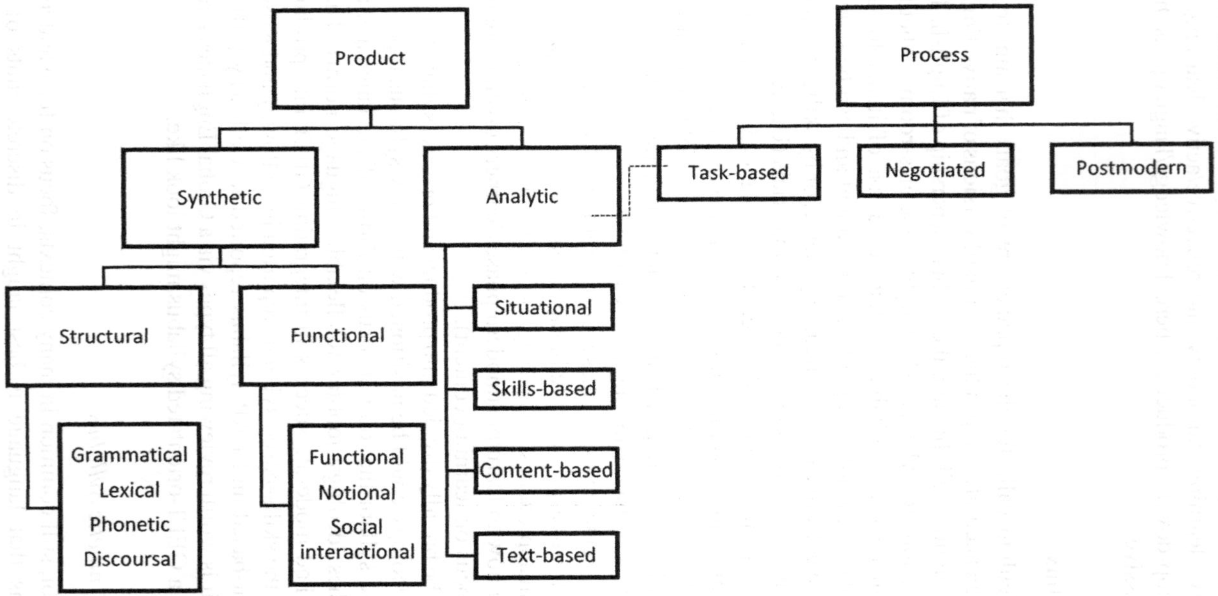

Figure 2.2 Syllabus types.

Structural (or formal) syllabi were one of the first types of synthetic syllabi. Linguistic knowledge is introduced by separate bits of grammatical or lexical features that can be built up to form patterns and sentences. Synthetic syllabi first flourished alongside structural linguistics. At this time, linguists believed that humans all developed language in the same way and that an L2 was acquired in the same way as an L1, with grammar being central. Even when Chomskian notions were introduced in the 1960s, ideas regarding the importance of building blocks of language remained. Thus synthetic syllabi remained, even if teaching approaches changed. The 'native' English speaker was posited as the authority, the ideal speaker in a homogeneous speech community (Chomsky, 1965, p. 3).

Some may argue that synthetic syllabi are simpler to design: simple sentences can be introduced before embedded clauses and present tense verbs before irregular and conditional verb forms (Mickan, 2013, p. 25). This may seem easier than basing one on learners' needs, or indeed one that presents language as a fluid and dynamic construct. Grammar is not central to GELT and the overall goal is certainly not mastery of native English. When working with structural syllabi, it is important to encourage learners to see such examples as merely one way of communicating an idea.

In the 1970s and 1980s, there was a major shift in how language was viewed in the field. The emphasis on 'communicative competence' (Hymes, 1966, 1972) saw increased emphasis placed on language in use. Communicative competence, which was defined as knowing 'when to speak, when not, and . . . what to talk about with whom, when, where and in what manner' (Hymes, 1972, p. 277), aimed to be more inclusive of not only grammar and sentence structures, but also feasibility and performance. It challenged the notion that language resided in the mind of the native speaker as the ideal speaker–listener. Communicative competence significantly widened the scope of language teaching and therefore extended the goals of teaching (Thornbury, 2016). Previous product-based structural syllabi were criticised for failing to prepare students to use the language communicatively.

A second major phase of syllabus development language emerged where language was not viewed as a set of components, but as socially situated communication, a tool for communication. Types of functional syllabi emerged, informed somewhat by linguistic developments in systemic functional linguistics, which also viewed language as performative of functions.

The functional–notional syllabi emerged out of the Council of Europe Modern Languages Project – the threshold syllabus in the early 1970s that aimed to reform and standardise modern-language teaching in Europe and devise a framework for adult learners based on their needs (Thornbury, 2016), as discussed in relation to needs analysis. This was a reaction against the structural syllabi and there was an emphasis on needs analysis. When designing the components of this needs-and-purposes-driven curriculum, Wilkins's (1976) work on notional syllabi was adopted by the Council of Europe in their development of a communicative language syllabus. Wilkins (1976) proposed that a curriculum that aimed to enable learners 'to function effectively' should be 'organized in terms of the purposes for which people are learning language and the kinds of language performance that are necessary to meet these purposes' (p. 13). Such aims were clearly the precursors to the later creation of the CEFR. The functional–notional syllabus contained semantic–grammatical meaning (e.g. time, duration, frequency), modal meaning (modality, scale of certainty) and communicative function speech acts, such as requests, complaints, apologies, compliments and suggestions. In these syllabi, the units of grammar featuring in previous types of syllabi were restructured and organised in this way.

Thus, despite major changes in approaches to teaching and ways to view language, the synthetic syllabus was preserved through major developments in linguistic theory. Even though functional–notional syllabi were sequenced around language used to carry out topics and language functions, the core idea of structuring the syllabus around sequenced discrete objects of study remained. From a GELT perspective, of the two main types of synthetic syllabi, functional syllabi are easier to work within, as the core of the syllabus presents learners with numerous language choices that can be used to carry out a function in the target language. This concept is relevant for GELT, which also places emphasis on what people want to do through the language, rather than just mastering the language structures. Nevertheless, the synthetic syllabus still focuses on controlled norm-driven structured patterns. While GELT constructs can be integrated into a functional syllabus type, flexible rather than synthetic syllabus designs are needed for GELT ideologies to reach their full potential.

The Analytic Syllabus

Analytic syllabi are a third type of product-based syllabi, organised around formulaic communicative abilities or functions as opposed to seeing the linguistic items (e.g. grammatical structures or function-based language structures) as the starting point. The functional movement in syllabus design was challenged in the early 1980s, with criticisms that teaching a set of functions or special purpose language was limiting. Many felt that communicative language teaching was being weakened by an attachment to syllabi that still had grammar-based or function-based linguistic structures at their core.

Situational and *topic-based* syllabi were seen as a more flexible alternative, where lessons focused on 'Getting around a city' or 'At the airport' or such topics as 'The family', 'School' and 'Hobbies'. Within these situations and topics, teachers and learners were free to explore a range of language choices. While the flexibility of this syllabus type worked well in small-sized communicative language classes, in reality it was often layered with other synthetic syllabus types. The result was a weak version of communicative language teaching, which combined a situational–structural language teaching approach, where language structures were embedded in situations, and grammatical accuracy was once again promoted. A good example of this hybrid is the *Streamline* (Hartley & Viney, 1978) and *New American Streamline* (Viney et al., 1994) textbook series, which repackages a structural syllabus in a situational structure and is promoted as communicative. While such situations and topics are certainly relevant for GELT, the return to structural approaches is irrelevant for a learner today.

Moves towards communicative language teaching also led to syllabi being designed around language as a resource for meaning-making in context, exploring the languages used for various genres, texts and content. *Genre* syllabi and *text-based* syllabi are organised around the context of use and the texts rather than language structures. *Skills-based* syllabi involve lessons being organised around language-related skills, such as giving a presentation, writing a cover letter or listening for effective note-taking. Similarly, *content-based* syllabi involve lessons being organised around the content, taken a step further with CLIL (content and language integrated learning), which focuses on the use of English for the teaching of other school subjects or specific content.

Genre, text-based, content-based and skills-based syllabi offer good opportunities for GELT integration. In Galloway and Rose (2018), we describe a skills-based syllabus, where Global Englishes content had been layered within the materials and tasks. An overview of the syllabus is shown in Table 2.3. In a skills-based syllabus, GELT content can easily replace the existing content used to introduce and practise the taught skills, and does not necessarily need to disrupt the structure of the units (skills) being used for sequencing purposes.

A similar success story is described in Rose and Montakantiwong (2018), where elements of an existing skills-based syllabus were replaced with Global Englishes content. The authors explain:

> Students still learned the required EAP reading skills, note-taking skills, essay-writing skills, and presentation skills that underpinned the curriculum. What had changed was that instead of reading a generic EAP passage for reading comprehension, we gave them adapted articles based on World Englishes and English as a Lingua Franca literature. Instead of practising note-taking to generic lectures, they listened to TED-talk presentations.
> (Rose & Montakantiwong, 2018, p. 8)

Table 2.3 *Example additional goals and objectives in a GELT curriculum*

Example Goal	Example Objectives	Example Outcomes
To raise learners' awareness of Global Englishes	Students will gain awareness of how English is used globally	The students will be able to: *-demonstrate an awareness that English is fluid;* *-demonstrate knowledge of basic features of salient varieties of English, including their own;* *-comprehend (listening) salient examples of ELF communication.*
To teach ELF strategies	Students will learn strategies for use in ELF contexts	The students will be able to: *-demonstrate an awareness of ELF strategies;* *-apply appropriate repair strategies when they are not understood;* *-accommodate their use of language to their interlocutor's needs.*
To understand attitudes towards English	Students will explore attitudes towards English, including their own	The students will be able to: *-demonstrate an understanding of their own, and their peers', attitudes towards English;* *-demonstrate an awareness of factors that influence attitudes;* *-reflect on their own attitudes and the factors that may influence them.*

Similar adaptations could be made to genre, text and content-based syllabus types, where Global Englishes ideology is integrated into the genres, texts and content being studied by learners. Indeed, the syllabus reported in Galloway's extensive research into a Global Englishes course in Japan (Galloway, 2011, 2013, 2017a) embodied a content-based structure, while still delivering language-related goals.

Process-Based Syllabi

A further major category of syllabi includes process syllabi, which allow for classroom decision-making (Breen, 1984). '[N]egotiation about the purposes, content and ways of working' are seen as a 'meaningful part of the content of lessons' (Breen, 2001, p. 154). Of course, this may not be possible, or relevant in certain contexts, but process syllabi, which focus on how learning is undertaken and actively involve learners in the selection of content for the syllabus, are useful to explore here, as these ideals are clearly compatible with GELT.

As noted above, GELT embodies process objectives, aiming to promote self-efficacy and self-direction and learner agency. Encouraging learners to go beyond the native speaker code and be creative with the language may lead to greater agency in future language use. As noted with regard to product-based syllabi, simply introducing formulaic expressions does not allow for learner agency, and certainly does not present an accurate reflection of how English is used today.

The most well-known process-based syllabi are *task-based* syllabi, which grew out of calls for stronger versions of a communicative approach. It is worth noting here that weaker versions of task-based syllabi can also be categorised as analytical syllabi, especially when tasks involve a focus on form (the product). However, a strong focus on tasks that mirror what learners will do in the real world is clearly in sync with a GELT approach. Tasks are designed to develop communicative competence and are based on an understanding of language as context-dependent. While there is a debate over whether this is product-orientated or process-orientated (depending on what type of tasks are used), it is important to point out that the main focus is on the task itself and on interaction and negotiating meaning. Thus, of all the product-based syllabi, a task-based syllabus seems to be a good fit for GELT, where practitioners are welcome to organise their lessons around communicative tasks rather than around various discrete items that learners are expected to master through practice.

Focusing on using the target language 'for a communicative purpose (goal) in order to achieve an outcome' (Willis, 1996, p. 23) in GELT could be used to offer opportunities to use ELF. Task-based syllabi can pave the way to introduce real ELF-interaction tasks, where students from different L1s work together to complete lesson activities. In monolingual classrooms, ELF interaction tasks could be facilitated through Skype exchanges or out-of-class activities, as has been illustrated in Vettorel (2013) and Sung (2018), respectively. We are not proposing that a GELT curriculum should include a task-based syllabus, but we want to point out this compatibility. We should also note that the debate continues regarding whether analytic syllabi enable learners to notice language forms implicitly, or whether they need to be accompanied with some degree of explicit instruction.

GELT is also in line with postmodern syllabi that embrace new ideologies of language. GELT requires us to see grammar in a different light and views language as a complex adaptive system. As discussed in the next chapter, language learners have come to be viewed in a different light in the field of SLA over the past fifty years or so with a trend towards empowering the learner (see Larsen-Freeman, 2012). However, in order to achieve this fully, Larsen-Freeman (2012) argues that we need an alternative view of language, one inspired by complexity theory and one that respects learner agency. This fits well with GELT which does not promote a fixed, static view of language, where creativity is seen as an error, rather than an innovation. Such a 'goal of language instruction, although never explicitly stated, was conformity to uniformity. But, such a goal, even if it is desirable, is not achievable' (Larsen-Freeman & Cameron, 2008, pp. 300–1). As noted above, the objectives of GELT are to enable learners to exploit the meaning potential of language, 'not just to internalize a ready-made system' (Larsen-Freeman & Cameron, 2008, p. 301).

However, this certainly raises questions as to how to present a language that is recognised as emergent and being in a constant state of flux. A GELT syllabus should enable learners to utilise different parts of their language resources, teach them how to adapt their speech and to negotiate and co-adapt with their interlocutors. It requires a reconceptualisation of the English language to take a broader view. The form, meaning and use are important, but we need to present this in a flexible way and present grammar in more dynamic terms, raising learners' awareness that when grammar is used in communication in ELF encounters, it is not always determined by rule-governed structures. This, then, clearly has implications for methodology, which should encourage learners to seek reasons as to why it is used in different ways. A GELT syllabus, then, does not merely include rules but focuses more on encouraging learners to seek reasons for such rules and also exploit their potential and take advantage of their agency and creativity. In doing so, this will help GELT achieve the aim of empowering ELF users to go beyond conforming to form-based rules.

Larsen-Freeman (2006) calls for grammar teaching to help develop capacity within students, not formal grammatical competence. Capacity is 'an active force for continuing creativity' (Widdowson, 1983, p. 27), and involves learners using lexicogrammatical resources for the creation of meaning. It is that which enables language learners to move beyond the memorised formulas and static rules they employ and acquire 'a way to create and understand meaning' (Larsen-Freeman, 2009, p. 530).

GELT-Informed Syllabus Design

In this discussion of syllabus types, we have aimed to show how GELT does not necessarily have to follow one syllabus type and also that a Global Englishes perspective can be incorporated into any type of syllabus. However, needs analysis, which should be an iterative process, is central and therefore a flexible approach to syllabus design is clearly a better fit. Whatever syllabus type is chosen, it should be in accordance with other elements in the curriculum to ensure alignment. A multidimensional, or mixed/layered, syllabus is another option, particularly for those who have to work with enforced syllabi. When selecting content, it is important to understand that GELT questions the separation of languages and recognises the bi/multilingual practices of individuals.

The content should be sequenced or graded according to the specific context and the needs of the learners.

There is a growing body of studies showing how GELT can be incorporated into different kinds of courses (Baker, 2012b; Derwing et al., 2002; Galloway, 2011, 2013, 2017a; Galloway & Rose, 2013, 2014; Kubota, 2001; Shim, 2002; Sung, 2018) and, as discussed in Chapter 1, there has been much discussion in the World Englishes paradigm on the need to expose students to different varieties of English, given the link between intelligibility and familiarity. However, a GELT syllabus is more than merely replacing one 'norm' with another. We recognise that exposing learners to speakers of English from different contexts may help to raise awareness of the diversity of English, but it will not help them to be productive, or to learn how to use the language as a lingua franca. Global learners will have different needs and, therefore, this makes choosing what 'varieties' of English, or ELF encounters, to introduce problematic. It is also more complex than merely providing examples of the use of English in different contexts and domains. If the goal is to produce global English-using citizens, then the syllabus should allow for a degree of reflection. This highlights the need for language awareness or explicit knowledge about the language itself. Llurda (2016) notes that much mainstream ELT pedagogy did not pay much attention to language awareness throughout the twentieth century. He also notes that it was thought to be irrelevant for those aiming to achieve general language competence.

We encourage syllabus designers to move teachers away from giving problematic advice based on English language teaching of the twentieth century, such as the belief that, in EFL settings, English is 'neither widely used for communication, nor used as the medium of instruction' and that EFL learners have 'limited exposure to the language outside of the classroom, and often limited opportunity to use it' (Carter & Nunan, 2001, p. 2). In this book, Carter and Nunan (2001) further inform practitioners that this may be problematic for teachers who are 'non-native speakers of English who may lack opportunities to use the language, or lack confidence in using it' (p. 2). These extracts from teacher education resources less than twenty years ago show how much the field has developed in terms of timely advice for syllabus design. The division between ESL and EFL settings, and between native and non-native English speakers, is no longer relevant and should not be used as a basis to organise the content of a GELT syllabus.

Methodology

There is often confusion over what constitutes a *method*, and an *approach* and a *technique*. Here, an approach is defined as a model of teaching based on theories of SLA (e.g. the communicative approach), a method is a collection of teaching procedures that correspond to a certain approach (e.g. the audiolingual method) and a technique is a teaching practice (e.g. Presentation–Practice–Production).

The quest for the 'best' teaching method has dominated the field over the years and a variety of approaches, methods and techniques have been tried and tested, soon to be replaced by a more fashionable method (Figure 2.3). Changes in methodology were usually the result of changing ideas within SLA, or changes in students' language-related needs, which often grew from sociopolitical trends. Figure 2.3 is a general timeline of major methods, and other versions of this timeline exist. Larsen-Freeman and Anderson (2011) list eleven methods, and Richards and Rodgers (2014) list sixteen approaches and methods. Hall (2016) notes that the differences in these accounts show there is no definitive list. We would add that our indicated start and end years in the timeline are also not definitive – we still find grammar–translation methods around the world today, and 'new' methods almost always grew out of existing practices.

Methods and Geopolitical Circumstances

As Cook (2003) notes, 'Different approaches to teaching English did not occur by chance, but in response to changing geopolitical circumstances and social attitudes and values, as well as to shifts in fashions in linguistics' (p. 30). In the 1800s and early 1900s, the *grammar–translation method* prevailed, where learners practice grammatical structures and lexical patterns and focus on accuracy and writing. At a time before mass travel, few people were learning languages and the goal was often to develop intellectual abilities and enable literature to be read in the original language, not necessarily to communicate (Richards & Rodgers, 2014; Hall, 2016). This met the needs of those learning English as an academic subject, but not for the purposes of communication. As communication is central to GELT, the grammar–translation method is clearly incompatible.

Rose (2018) states that '[s]ince the early years of mass language education, approaches have adapted according to the needs of the learner' (p. 6). The *direct method* emerged around the 1920s in response to the needs of a more mobile population, which required spoken communication skills in foreign languages. Linked to an increased interest in 'natural learning' and the belief that language is learned by direct association with the target language, it places emphasis on using the target language. Question and answer techniques and demonstrations to communicate the meaning of words are used, thus moving away from isolated sentences and lists of words to oral classroom methodology. The direct method has had a major influence on the field of TESOL, particularly by promoting the use of the target language and avoidance of the mother tongue. As Hall (2018) points out 'logically, this principle has

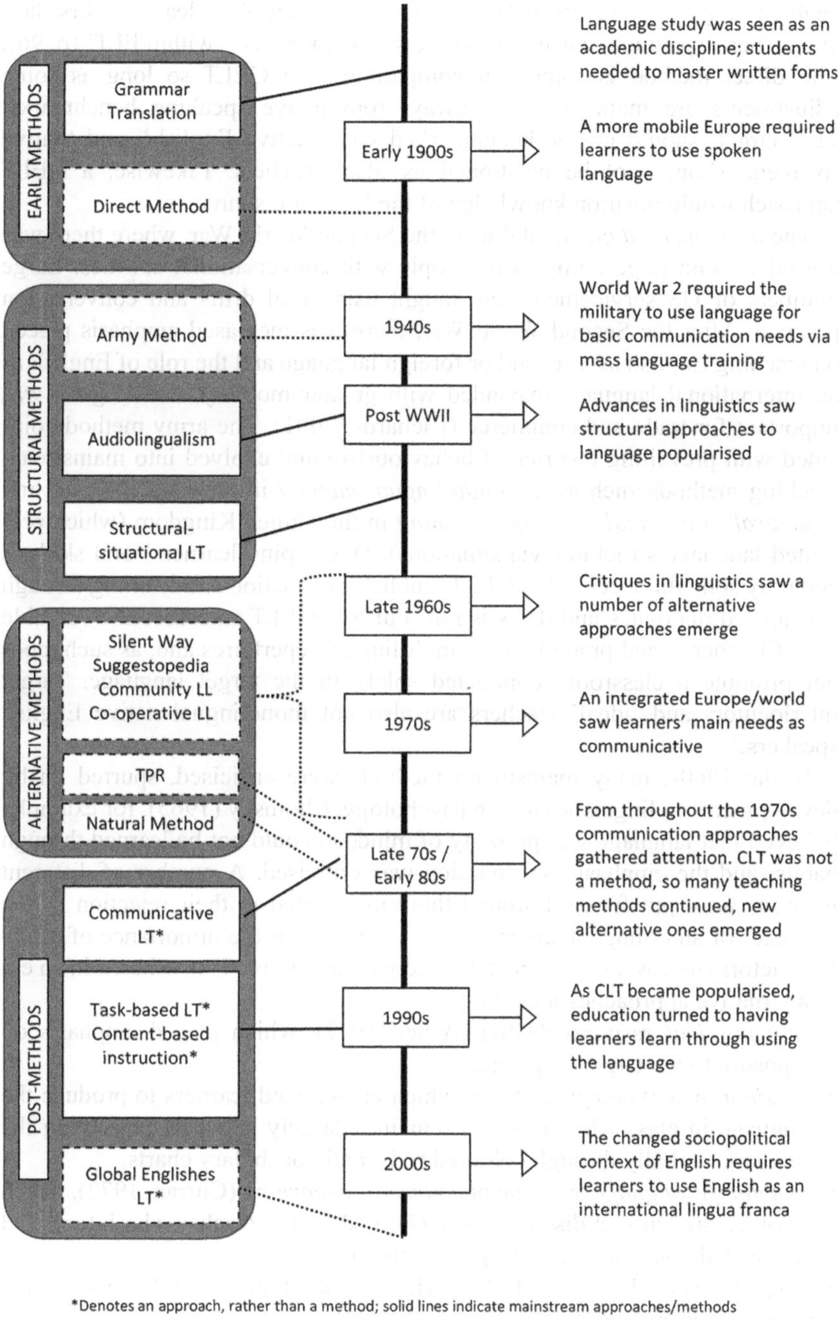

Figure 2.3 Major methodology trends from early to mid-20th century in the quest for the 'best' method.

enabled language teachers to teach without knowing their learners' first language, hence paving the way for 'native speaker teachers' within ELT' (p. 96). The direct method is somewhat compatible with GELT so long as some adjustments are made to move away from native speaking benchmarks. The 'target' should not be benchmarked with 'native English', and 'native speakers' should not be positioned as ideal teachers. Likewise, a GELT approach would position knowledge of the L1 as a resource.

The *army method* emerged during the Second World War, where there was a need to train large numbers of people with conversational abilities. Large numbers of US servicemen were taught using oral drills and conversation practice. After the Second World War, there was increased emphasis placed on teaching English as a second or foreign language and the role of English as an international language expanded with greater mobility, and English was important for trade and commerce (Richards, 2001). The army method coincided with prevailing theories of behaviourism and evolved into mainstream teaching methods such as the *audiolingual method* in the United States and *structural–situational language teaching* in the United Kingdom (which presented language structures via situations). Developing learners' oral skills is certainly something central to GELT, but habit formation and learning through teacher-led dialogues and drills is not. Further, GELT embraces the valuable use of learners', and practitioners', multilingual repertoires and, as such, does not promote a classroom conducted solely in the target language. Target interlocutors and 'ideal' teachers are also not monolingual native English speakers.

In the 1960s, many mainstream methods were criticised, spurred on by developments in linguistics and in psychology. Chomsky (1965), for example, believed that language was property of mind, so could not be learned through habits, and the emphasis on imitation was criticised. A number of different methods were put forward around this time, united in their rejection of the 'science' of audiolingualism and their acceptance of the importance of affective factors such as motivation and anxiety (Hall, 2016). This ushered in an era of alternative approaches including:

- *total physical response* (TPR) (Asher, 1977), which placed emphasis on exposure to the target language;
- *the silent way* (Gattegno, 1972), which encouraged learners to produce the language in class while teachers remained largely silent by presenting the language verbally through coloured rods, and vocabulary charts;
- *community language learning* or *counselling learning* (Curran, 1972), which involved student-led discussions, facilitated by the teacher who interpreted the needed vocabulary and language structures;
- *suggestopedia* (Lozanov, 1978), which centred on the influence of the unconscious on learning.

Richards & Rodgers (2014) note the 'unusual demands' (p. 313) that these methods placed on both learners and teachers were one of the reasons they did not become popular.

The emergence of communicative language teaching has been documented 'as the most significant development within ELT over the last fifty years. It is generally regarded as a clear paradigmatic break with the past' (Hall, 2016, p. 214). The communicative approach instigated a shift from a focus on form to meaning, positing English as a tool for communication. It reflected a change in thinking about language, 'a reaction against the view of language as a set of structures; [and] a reaction towards a view of language as communication' (Brumfit & Johnson, 1979, p. 3). It saw a shift away from form and mastery of the written language to language in use, and from an emphasis on reading and writing to an emphasis on speaking and interaction.

While communicative language teaching appears on the surface to complement GELT, we have still to witness a shift away from native English-speaking norms, thus GELT requires a further paradigmatic break. Communicative competence is still based on native competence. As McKay (2003) notes, some of the assumptions

> are not appropriate for the teaching of EIL, particularly its reliance on native speaker models to inform a definition of authentic materials and cultural appropriateness. On the other hand, CLT's emphasis on actual language use, meaningful tasks, and learners' personal experiences could well be productively applied to the teaching of EIL. (p. 15)

GELT, too, which we see as including the teaching of EIL, shares a lot of the same fundamental principles as CLT; the goal is to be able to communicate in the target language and develop communicative competence. Activities involved in 'real' communication use meaningful tasks; the classroom is learner-centred and promotes learner autonomy. As discussed with regard to syllabus, strong forms of CLT, such as task-based language teaching, can be a useful way to encourage students to engage in real-life tasks using ELF, although the focus on form is not necessarily on a native speaker form. For Samuda and Bygate (2008), a task is defined as

> a holistic activity which engages language use in order to achieve some non-linguistic outcome while meeting a linguistic challenge, with the overall aim of promoting language learning, through process or product or both. (p. 69)

Such definitions fit GELT, especially considering that task-based language teaching allows learners to complete tasks via non-prescribed language forms to achieve the outcome (Willis & Willis, 2001).

In GELT, the learners' L1 is seen as a valuable resource and learners are encouraged to utilise their multilingual repertoires. In GELT, tasks should aim to reinforce learners' positive self-image as a legitimate speaker of the language and, therefore, teachers should refrain from correcting 'errors' that ELF researchers class more as innovations. As Willis & Willis (2001) note:

> The challenge for TBL, therefore, is to devise a methodology which affords learners the freedom to engage natural learning processes in the creation of a meaning system, but which also provides them with incentives to 'restructure' their system in the light of language input. (p. 174)

With developments in online language learning, there are increasing opportunities to engage in real-life ELF communication to negotiate tasks, and task reflection could include looking at the strategies used.

However, CLT has come under severe criticism as a 'centre'-based methodology often incompatible with certain contexts. Discussed further in Chapter 4, several studies have documented such incompatibility and the need for locally sensitive methods. A critical strand emerged looking at the relationship between method and issues of power and control within ELT (Hall, 2016). Pennycook (1989) suggests 'methods' favour the West, as most have originated in the United Kingdom or the United States, and thus represents the interests of one group at the expense of others. People have started to speak of 'The death of the method' (Allwright, 1991), the 'postmethod condition' (Kumaravadivelu, 1994) and 'beyond methods' (Kumaravadivelu, 2006).

The increased emphasis on the local challenge led to criticism of the notion of methods in the 1990s, leading to the *post-methods* era. It was argued that a 'postmethod condition' (Kumaravadivelu, 1994) was needed to encourage practitioners to develop context-specific ideas and draw on a range of methods and principles at different times depending on the needs of their students. This resonates well with GELT, which places emphasis on understanding the situation/context when thinking about pedagogy. 'The de-linking of English from the culture of Inner Circle countries also suggests that teaching methodology has to proceed in a manner that respects the local culture of learning' (McKay, 2003, p. 18). In order to move forward, we have to stay attuned to what is happening in local classrooms, and to move away from a methods-based perspective, and towards pedagogy. In this sense, GELT is more of a bottom-up approach that aims to empower the periphery.

Another trend has been critical pedagogy, a philosophy of education that applies the principles of critical theory (Giroux, 1983). Education is seen as a political act, knowledge is not seen as a neutral concept and education is seen to have the potential to improve social justice by developing active citizens (Freire, 1996). Emancipation is central and 'unlike traditional ELT which tends to strive for neutrality, critical pedagogy acknowledges positionality in terms of class, race, gender and ethnicity (Benesch, 2001), and teaches students to oppose and reorganise social forms that are exploitative and damaging (Brookfield 2003)' (Jeyaraj & Harland, 2016, p. 588). Here, language is analysed to look at how it contributes to asymmetrical power relations. Learners are given the opportunity to engage in dialogue with other learners and the teachers and they are encouraged to be reflective and critically question the material. GELT draws on such perspectives, encouraging learners to be critical of native hegemony in their material. In GELT, learners are active, not passive, in the learning process. GELT advocates a critical approach to ELT that recognises that theories may not translate well, and it aims to address power imbalances, not perpetuate them. As promoted in the lesson plans in the appendix of Galloway (2017a), GELT draws on real-world resources to encourage a dialogue with students about language and power imbalances.

Assessment

Language assessment is usually for the purpose of evaluating how well a learner has reached the stated goals of the curriculum. In a curriculum where communicative competence is at the core, the constructs of any piece of language assessment are merely a proxy for their estimated performance in real-world communicative situations, as measured by their ability to meet the curriculum standards. A construct in assessment refers to the definition of target language abilities, in such a way that they can be measured. As Rose & Syrbe (2018) note:

> Tests are a means of gathering information based on which we make an inference about someone's language ability, rather than a direct observation of the test taker's abilities in the real world. In other words, we are making an assumption about the assessee's performance in a real-life target setting. In that sense, the test is a simulation of the "relevant communicative behavior", which is referred to as the criterion (McNamara, 2000) in this target setting. (p. 3)

Thus, good pieces of assessment are devised in respect of real-world criterion, which requires a detailed understanding of the language in use. Global Englishes research challenges the validity of traditional English-language assessment practices, especially when the criterion of language assessment practices no longer represents the 'relevant communicative behaviour' in the real world. Today, global users of English use the language within local and global communities of practice, where it is used in its plurality and within fluid cultures and diverse contexts. Thus, language assessment needs to reflect learners' ability to use English with such flexibility and within such diversity. Global Englishes research argues that good assessment practice must be able to make an inference about learners' future performance according to this evolved criterion. In short, bad assessment practices occur when a test construct does not match the target criterion.

There has been considerable debate over whether the construct for Global Englishes assessment should be based on standard English or ELF (Elder & Davies, 2006). If an assessment construct is based on standard English, then some accommodation to ELF usage is necessary, such as only penalising language forms that impede communication, since successful communication is the criterion of assessment. A further option would be to define the construct in terms of ELF, which raises further complications. As Chapter 1 has shown, ELF is not a codified variety of English, and its features are fluid, and thus ill-fitting to operationalise as a test construct. Therefore, good assessment constructs, rather than being defined according to language form, are better defined according to success in communication. Llurda (2016) notes that:

> An appropriate benchmark of proficiency would be the measurement of how a message was successfully delivered and understood as opposed to whether an L2 user's production matches the production of a selected group of native speakers. (p. 57)

Thus, constructs of assessment in a GELT curriculum need to focus on measuring success in communication, using ELF settings as the benchmark for the target criterion (assuming, of course, this matches the students' language needs). Shohamy (2017) states that 'the vast amount of research on ELF should be channeled into the development of ELF tests, rating scales and rubrics' because '[t]hese findings are instrumental in developing the testing construct' (p. 591).

GELT further emphasises the importance of assessing students' strategic competence in using the language and in negotiating meaning. In short, GELT lobbies for a shift away from assessing learners' *linguistic knowledge of English* towards assessing learners' *strategic use of English*. This complements Widdowson's (2012) assertion that good language assessment should centre on *how well* learners understand the language in terms of its use, rather than on *how much* learners understand the language in terms of its form. It also supports Canagarajah's (2007) claim that assessment needs to 'focus on one's strategies of negotiation, situated performance, communicative repertoire and language awareness' (p. 936), and Hu's (2012) argument that the constructs of EIL assessment must encompass intercultural strategic competence and accommodation skills.

GELT assessment practices, therefore, could involve learners displaying their strategic ability to:

- use spoken English to take part in a successful oral task with a classmate on a given topic related to the syllabus;
- negotiate meaning in a communication breakdown;

- use written English to communicate ideas effectively on a topic and genre related to the syllabus;
- comprehend ELF interactions of speakers of both familiar and less familiar Englishes;
- complete a project with classmates using English as a lingua franca, while being able to draw on their other linguistic resources.

It is important to note that communicative assessment tasks such as role-plays, written assignments, interviews, presentations and group projects are more appropriate to the criterions central to Global Englishes, rather than traditional standardised tests that usually require standardised norms.

At a curriculum level, GELT assessment practices are, therefore, quite achievable, so long as the curriculum goals and objectives are ones that move learners towards becoming global users of the language in lingua franca settings. It is essential that curriculum elements are in alignment, for example, needs analysis will elicit appropriate assessment criterion, goals and objectives will ensure learners are moving towards this criterion and assessment practice will ensure the constructs being tested match these needs and goals. External to the curriculum, however, washback from major standardised tests can disrupt this alignment, as major proficiency tests still have standard English-language norms as their core constructs. Washback from standardised tests as a barrier to change is discussed further in Chapter 4.

Evaluation

As Richards (2001) points out, 'once a curriculum is in place, a number of important questions still need to be answered' (p. 286). Curriculum evaluation is an ongoing process and as discussed above, given the context-sensitive nature of GELT, ongoing classroom-based research is called for to ensure that GELT meets the changing needs of learners today. Thus, even if GELT is incorporated successfully, practitioners are encouraged to evaluate their innovations on a regular basis.

Curriculum evaluation has several purposes. If the purpose is to determine whether or not the goals of the curriculum have been met, evaluation may involve looking at the assessment results of the learners. However, it is clear from the preceding section that this will be pointless if assessments based on native norms continue to be used. If the purpose is related to the overall curriculum, then it will include an evaluation of teaching and materials, and analysing information about the course/programme. An example of GELT evaluation is the quasi-experimental studies located in the field (Galloway, 2011, 2013, 2017a), which had the dual focus of investigating the influence of the course on students' overall attitudes towards English and ELT and also gaining feedback on the course itself. Chapter 7 also presents a similar study with regard to teacher education. Evaluation can guide classroom teaching, showing what works and does not work, and, therefore, GELT requires action research (see Chapter 5).

Curriculum evaluation can be formative, or summative, and ideally, an institution should employ both to provide regular up-to-date information. By examining GELT from a curriculum perspective, we aim to reduce the risk of misalignment between the various elements. In an edited volume on curriculum in L2 teaching, Graves (2016) notes issues with when curriculum design processes are undertaken by different people before the curriculum is then given to teachers and learners. He notes that this can result in curriculum incoherence and thus calls for more alignment between these processes by the actors of each stage (Graves, 2016). It is clear from the literature that there is currently a misalignment between programme content and student needs throughout TESOL, especially when the curriculum is derived from actors who are external to the classroom. In order to reduce the risk of curriculum misalignment, we want those developing curriculum guidelines and principles to take account of contextual factors. Of course, we must also ensure that the programme is not 'aspirational', but realistic for the learners (Graves, 2016). Thus, the reporting and sharing of curriculum implementation and evaluation between practitioners are essential – a point discussed further in Chapter 5.

Conclusion

In a sense, GELT reflects an ecological approach to curriculum. As Van Lier (2009, p. 53) notes from an ecological perspective:

> The curriculum does not start out by specifying and sequencing materials that is to be "covered", but it starts out with the activities, needs and emergent purposes of the learner. On the basis of activities and emergent needs, the teacher makes resources available in the environment, and guides the learner's perception and action towards arrays of affordances that can further his or her goals.

We concur that '[t]he process curriculum also reflects the view of the classroom as a learning community (Wenger, 1998; Van Lier 2004, 2009)' (Richards, 2017, p. 17). This is conducive to a GELT curriculum as learning is not viewed as mastery of fixed, predetermined content. Learners are encouraged to construct new knowledge together and to explore the meaning potential of the language together.

Examining the field from a curriculum perspective helps us to understand its various elements and how they interact with one another, which is particularly important when advocating a new approach to ELT. The needs of learners have changed, necessitating different goals, content and methods. GELT aims to instigate a paradigm shift away from native English norms and also away from the cycle of colonial relations in the field of TESOL. It is no longer relevant to look to the West for the best method and it is important to point out that GELT is a bottom-up approach, which acknowledges the global dominance of English and promotes a critical approach. The need to move away from native norms is not new, but GELT throws a new perspective on this debate. The transient nature of the English-speaking population in today's globalised world requires a different approach and requires us to reconceptualise some of the fundamental concepts and theories underpinning the field. The language is likely to be further globalised, and we need a flexible approach that will respond to such changes, such as a new form of ESP, a subfield. This all requires a lot from the teacher, as it devolves responsibility to teachers and learners, which is a challenge that will be discussed in Chapter 4.

3 Second Language Learning Theory and GELT

In the previous chapter, we examined key concepts and theories that underpin the field of TESOL through a Global Englishes lens. In this chapter, we do the same for the field of second language acquisition (SLA). SLA is an important field of inquiry and it is clear from the preceding chapter that it holds significant influence over the English-language curriculum, particularly with the increased focus on the learner and the learning process. Here, we provide an overview of key developments in the field, before focusing on recent developments surrounding multilingualism and movements away from monolingual L1 English-speaker reference points. Increasing awareness of the fact that multilingualism, not monolingualism, is the norm has led to a re-examination of key concepts in SLA. Many of these arguments resonate with GELT, and this chapter highlights how GELT is in line with parallel trends in SLA.

Second Language Acquisition: An Overview

SLA refers to the processes by which someone acquires an additional language, the study of how learners learn. Established in the 1960s (Creagh, 2017), it has become a thriving field of study. It is an interdisciplinary field and has been influenced by the fields of language teaching, linguistics, sociology, anthropology, psychology and brain science among others, and more recently bilingualism and multilingualism (Creagh, 2017; Ortega, 2009; Tarone, 2015). As such, there is a lot of epistemological diversity, which is covered by several comprehensive overviews of developments in SLA (e.g. Atkinson, 2011; Mitchell et al., 2013; Ortega, 2009).

The main developmental periods in SLA can be segmented in numerous ways. SLA can be seen as both systematic (e.g. focuses on the actual language learners acquire as they pass through a series of stages) and variable (e.g. learners acquire the language at different rates), so a common divide can be made between studies that focus on the product and the process of acquisition. Lines have also been drawn between cognitive and social approaches in SLA. Meier (2017) identifies four strands of developments (cognitive, integrated, socio-critical and multimodal understandings of language). A further theoretical perspective has resulted in an increased focus on multilingualism, and is the main focus of this chapter.

It is clear from the previous chapter that these developments in SLA research have influenced the TESOL syllabus and teaching methods in many ways. For example, structural syllabi emerged during an era that focused on the linguistic aspects of acquisition and was accompanied by such approaches as audio-lingualism and structural situational language teaching. Many of the alternative teaching methods emerged during an era which focused on the cognitive-psychological aspects of SLA. Many learner-focused syllabi such as the task-based syllabus have emerged alongside sociocultural perspectives of SLA. However, SLA research is not solely conducted to inform pedagogy, of course, and we are wary of directly translating research findings into the classroom context. Nevertheless, understanding research on how learners acquire a language has clear implications for TESOL and, therefore, for GELT.

SLA has also been the focus of much attention within the field of ELF and World Englishes (for an overview, see Berns, 2015). Yamuna Kachru (1986) criticised Gass and Selinker (1983) for failing to take into account multilingual societies and the communicative needs of learners in their research. Seidlhofer (2011) refers to the 'mismatch between the purpose for which English is most learnt in the world, namely ELF use, and what is focused on in SLA, namely ESL/EFL' (pp. 11–12). Jenkins (2006) maintains that 'mainstream SLA research can no longer afford to ignore the massive growth in the use of English as a Lingua Franca (ELF)' (p. 137).

Notwithstanding the monolingual bias in the field in recent years, multilingualism has been at the centre of recent discussions in SLA. This development has been referred to as the multilingual turn and is a movement that Global Englishes situates itself within. The idea that English is a stable construct has long informed the field of SLA, but recent years have seen many reconceptualise established concepts in light of the growth of multilingualism: 'Multilingualism, it seems, is the topic du jour – at least in critical applied linguistics' (May, 2014b, p. 1). V. Cook (1999, 2012, 2016a, 2016b), for example, has reframed the concepts of 'competence' as multicompetence. Scholars are increasingly critical of the focus on the monolingual native speaker, highlighting that the use of English by non-native speakers should not be viewed as deficient and inferior. Instead, the competencies of bi/multilingual learners are seen to be the basis for successful language learning. As discussed in Chapter 1, there is an increased focus on the blurred boundaries between languages and, overall, the dominant ideology of monolingualism, native speakerism, and standard language ideology is being challenged. The multilingual turn in SLA resonates well with GELT; however, before examining this further, we need to evaluate the main developments in the field that preceded it.

In this section, we review some main concepts in SLA research in order to explore potential connections to GELT. Our review of historical theories is hardly exhaustive and is provided as a foundation for an in-depth exploration of the multilingual turn, which we see as being most clearly connected to movements in Global Englishes. Nevertheless, in order to understand the implications of SLA for GELT, it is important to examine some fundamentals of SLA through a Global Englishes lens.

SLA as a Focus on Language as a Product

As discussed with regard to the syllabus, the structural approach stressed an emphasis on the formal aspects of the language, the structure. A learner's first language was believed to influence the acquisition process, resulting in errors. Thus, early SLA research examined the similarities and differences between a learner's first and second language. This began with Lado's (1957) work on contrastive analysis, which looked at the comparison, and interaction, between the learner's first and second languages, not at the language they were producing. The belief that patterns can be predicted based on the learner's first language and that this could result in either positive transfer or negative interference led to beliefs about interference. Languages, then, were seen to be discrete entities and it was believed that separate structures could be studied (Saussure, 1966).

Saussure (1959) made a distinction between the features and rules of a language and the use of language. At this time, Chomsky (1965), who reformulated Saussure's (1959) notions of language, was influential. Chomsky (1965) believed that all people are born with the ability to learn a language: just as we are built with an ability to walk, so are we to learn a language. His universal grammar theory is built on the idea that there is a set of basic grammatical elements common to all languages, so there is no need to teach grammar explicitly. Chomsky (1965) distinguished between competence and performance, in regard to one's knowledge of a language versus one's situational use of it. This notion of linguistic competence led to the study of language by comparing native speakers, who had the ideal knowledge of a language, and non-native speakers, thus positioning the native speaker as central, and with whom to compare non-native speakers.

Cognitive understandings of language, then, see grammar as a system that can be processed by humans; therefore, language is conceptualised monolingually, as a stable system that is independent of the people that use it. These ideas influenced developments in the field, including the study of the development of learners at various stages according to their linguistic systems, and comparing language learners with native speakers (e.g. Ellis, 1994). As behaviourism was challenged in the 1960s, there was a shift towards looking at how learners communicate in the target language. Corder (1967) and Selinker (1972) rejected the contrastive viewpoint, stressing the importance of patterns in the target language. Corder (1967) stressed the importance of examining learners' errors and error analysis was seen as being an important part of the learning process. Researchers examined the systematic errors produced by learners, who seemed to move through various stages of learning as their proficiency developed. This was coined 'interlanguage' or 'interim language'. Thus, unlike the contrastive view, three language systems (not two) were seen to be important: the native, the target, and an interim language. An associated term was fossilisation (Selinker, 1972), referring to a plateau in a learner's interlanguage. Terms still used today, such as *ultimate attainment*, *native-like*, *target-like*, *near-native*, *interlanguage* and *fossilization*, stem from this era of SLA. This era also laid the foundation of an underlying assumption of monolingualism and the superiority of native speakers. Criticism of such terms and concepts is not, of course, unique to the field of Global Englishes.

Input, Output and Interaction

In the 1970s and 1980s, Chomskian ideas influenced Krashen, who was prominent at this time in theory development in his introduction of five hypotheses. Krashen (1982) argued that learners drew on subconscious knowledge to communicate meaning. To Krashen, grammar is not central, but rather meaningful language communication is important to activate existing grammar principles as part of an innate 'language acquisition device'. Krashen believes that we acquire rules in a predictable order and language can be acquired subconsciously with comprehensible input, with the grammar provided by the 'language acquisition device'. His input hypothesis stressed the importance of the linguistic environment. Speakers of the target language, and their speech, provided learners with linguistic input through listening opportunities and he believed that learning to communicate was a result of internalising this input. Learners had to comprehend linguistic items at a stage slightly beyond their current level (i+1). However, Krashen also believed in the need for a silent phase to reduce interference and help with pronunciation. While GELT is not compatible with Krashen's views of interference and silence, we do concur with Richards and Rodgers (2014) in that there are many implications of Krashen's theory that are relevant for language teaching. Comprehensible input is clearly important for successful learning and communication and is not too different from Global Englishes views on the importance of accommodating to an interlocutor's language needs.

Such researchers as Long (1983a, 1983b, 1985, 1996) and Doughty and Pica (1986) also shifted the focus from form to meaning and showcased how using the language interactively facilitates L2 development, because of conversational and linguistic modifications. Thus, the focus started to be placed on interaction. Long was a prominent interactionist in the field, and this resonates with GELT as interaction is at the core of Global Englishes work. Interactionists are interested in how speakers engage in conversations to negotiate meaning, and many relevant ideas emerged at this time, such as highlighting the importance of conversational modifications, comprehension checks, clarification requests, paraphrasing, repetition and so forth. These concepts are clearly important for ELF communication. However, Long often referred to the native speaker as the target interlocutor, which is not the case for those learning to use the language as a lingua franca. Long (1983) notes that negotiation for meaning that leads to modified interaction between the native speaker and non-native speaker helps with their acquisition as it connects input and output, and makes language comprehensible. However, discussions of native speakers simplifying language, such as foreigner talk (see Ferguson, 1971), are not compatible with GELT, even if the strategies are. ELF further views interaction as a cooperative engagement, where speakers negotiate meaning as they communicate. Hall (2017) notes that:

> Most research into interaction has taken place in Western cultural settings, with little being known about the negotiation strategies followed by L2 learners in other cultural contexts. (Mitchell, Myles and Marsden, 2013) (p. 124)

We would concur with Hall, in that much of Long's revised (1996) interaction hypothesis is based on Western ideologies, with the native speaker positioned as central to interaction. Since this time, however, we have witnessed a large amount of ELF research, which has filled gaps in knowledge of communication strategies used outside such settings.

Swain (1985, 1995, 2000, 2005) challenged Krashen's comprehensible input hypothesis with her 'comprehensible output' hypothesis, believing that learners needed opportunities to produce the language to develop their knowledge. Unlike Long's model, Swain's model contradicts Krashen, rather than complementing it. She believes that giving learners the opportunity to practice enhances their fluency. It can also help their grammatical competence and accuracy; as they struggle to produce output, they pay attention to grammar. In short, producing the target language may serve as 'the trigger that forces the learner to pay attention to the means of expression needed in order to successfully convey his or her own intended meaning' (Swain, 1985, p. 249), and output helps learners to notice the gap between their linguistic resources and the target language (Swain, 1995, 2005). Swain's (1995) 'pushed output hypothesis' noted that learners look at their linguistic system when they fail to meet their communication goals. This idea resonates with Gass's (1997) observation that task-based methodologies force learners to *notice* gaps.

The work in this era sparked much debate over consciousness in successful L2 learning and the role of implicit versus explicit instruction. Long (1983, 1988) and Ellis (1990) reviewed numerous studies concluding that conscious learning contributes to successful L2 learning. Schmidt's (1990) 'noticing hypothesis' has been influential; however, this principle rests on the belief that learners must be able to notice the gap between their own language ability and that of a native speaker to help them to develop proficiency. Van Lier (1996) observes that:

> To learn something new one must first notice it. This noticing is an awareness of its existence, obtained and enhanced by paying attention to it. Paying attention is focusing one's consciousness, or pointing one's perceptual powers in the right direction, and making mental 'energy' available for processing. (p. 11)

Sharwood Smith (1981), who was one of the first to define conscious raising, proposed that teaching formal aspects of language did not necessarily have to involve rules and drills but could involve highlighting relevant aspects.

As discussed in Chapter 2, the focus on output and meaning led to an emphasis on the process of learning and to methods such as task-based language teaching. While task-based language teaching could be seen as a stronger version of communicative language teaching, some incarnations of task-based teaching include a heavy focus on form (Norris & Ortega, 2000; Skehan, 1996; Willis, 1996), and therefore we should not assume compatibility with GELT ideology. Output-based or interaction-based approaches to language teaching do not necessarily mean a movement away from a focus on form. Indeed, Long (1991), Ellis (1993, 1997), and Ellis et al. (1999) proposed the need for a focus on form, as did Skehan (1996) who notes that learners' language will develop better if a focus on form is included in the task cycle. Willis's (1996) task cycle includes a focus on both form and meaning, in stating that 'task-based learning combines the best insights from communicative language teaching with an organised focus on language form' (p. 1).

The same challenge is applicable to GELT with regard to whether or not to explicitly focus on form, although it becomes more complex when we view 'form' or norms in more dynamic and flexible terms that encourage learner creativity and agency. As discussed in Chapter 1, there has been much discussion on language awareness, metalinguistic rules and terminology. In GELT, a more inductive, implicit way is preferred that focuses on meaning and context. It is compatible with Long (1996), who distinguishes between form within a meaningful context and a focus on forms (driven by grammar). Thus, we propose that in a GELT curriculum, input enhancement (e.g. make the input more noticeable) is important, but explicit form-focused instruction and implicit form-focused instruction (learners work out the rules for themselves), if used, should not focus on native speaker-benchmarked forms. In solving a problem in a task, for example, learners should be encouraged to utilise their entire multilingual repertoire to complete a task. Indeed, ELF researchers have stressed the importance of language awareness classes. In a sense, we advocate a consciousness-raising approach to teaching grammar. We reject the linear view of introducing grammar, seeing it as more organic, and we encourage future ELF users to form hypotheses about the language, linking it with what they know, what they need to do and how they can negotiate successful communication. Thus, although reference points have changed, noticing and awareness are clearly fundamental concepts in GELT.

SLA as a Focus of the Process of Acquisition

Throughout the 1970s and 1980s, research that looked at learning as a cognitive process began to become the predominant theory underpinning SLA research. In this 'cognitive turn' (Meier, 2017, p. 135), research looked at the path learners followed as they acquired the language, the interaction between the learners' internal 'cognitive' processes and their external environment (Creagh, 2017). Thus, the field witnessed a shift from the product to the process of acquisition. Acquisition of the target language was seen as being independent of the learners' L1 and there was a focus on their mind and the brain, looking at psychological aspects of learning and the learner-internal or cognitive processes that underpin language acquisition. Thus, this cognitivist and psychological view of SLA was based on notions that learners develop patterns and have to make sense of input provided by their surrounding environment. Research looked at how paying attention to language influenced acquisition, intake, working and long-term memory (computational model), and how the human mind processed the second language (Creagh, 2017).

This led to an increased focus on the learner, placing them central in the learning process. However, it also cemented the position of the native speaker as central, seen as the best model and also the best teacher. As discussed in Chapter 2, soon after Chomsky proposed defined competence and performance, there were criticisms and advocates for a more communicative view of second-language teaching. In contrast to the separation of language use and knowledge, Hymes (1972) introduced the notion of communicative competence, emphasising the ability to use grammatical competence in communicative situations (a sociolinguistic perspective). Success in SLA came to be seen as requiring more than merely acquiring grammatical accuracy, and this new notion of communicative competence generated an interest in the relationship between language and social context, and more emphasis on the meaning of language and how it is used. These ideas received a lot of attention in the 1970s and 1980s from applied linguists interested in SLA and language testing and the concept was developed. Nevertheless, these views still emphasised native

English-speaker norms, as competence in both Chomsky's and Hymes's terms implied conformity to such norms – to linguistic norms in Chomsky's case and to social appropriateness in Hymes's case (Larsen-Freeman, 2007, pp. 45–6).

Canale and Swain (1980) and Canale (1983) defined communicative competence as the underlying system of knowledge and skill needed for communication, defining three types of knowledge: knowledge of grammatical principles; knowledge of how to use language for communication; and knowledge of discourse principles. Canale (1983) also distinguished between one's underlying capacity and how this capacity is manifested in real communication or performance. Savignon (1972, 1983) put more emphasis on this aspect of ability, in explaining 'the ability to function in a truly communicative setting – that is, in a dynamic exchange in which linguistic competence must adapt itself to the total informational input, both linguistic and paralinguistic, of one or more interlocutors' (Savignon, 1972, p. 8). She saw ability as something dynamic, not static, and defined by context, which is a key concept that clearly resonates with GELT.

Sociocultural Aspects of SLA and the 'Social Turn'

Cognitive approaches that looked at SLA in a slightly decontextualised way came to be criticised in the field, as it was argued that focusing on cognitive and mentalist aspects led to deficit perspectives of language learners (Block, 2003; Firth & Wagner, 1997). Some researchers shifted from a monolithic understanding of language to look at how language is used by examining the language-learning process in a socially contextualised way. The 'social turn' came as an answer to increased calls for a reconceptualisation in the field, which urged SLA researchers to take into account socio-historical aspects of learning as opposed to just cognitive and mentalist perspectives. Firth and Wagner (1997) stressed the centrality of context and that SLA studies should account for and also be studied within context. As Sembiante (2016) notes, while Firth and Wagner (1997) were not the first to make this call (see Frawley & Lantolf, 1984, 1985, and also Beebe, 1980; Block, 1996; Norton, 1995; Tarone, 1983; Young, 1988), they were definitely instrumental in uniting a number of socially orientated researchers, who pioneered this new direction in the field.

Sembiante (2016) notes that the basis of many arguments made by May (2014b) and his colleagues in the multilingual turn – discussed next – 'stem from these initial propositions' (p. 51), and it is clear that this focus on interaction and the learners' context resonates with GELT. As discussed in Chapters 1 and 2, when devising goals and subsequently learning objectives in a GELT-orientated curriculum, we urge practitioners to take the learners' varying contexts into account. GELT learners do not all have the same needs: they are active agents in the learning process and play an active role in how they shape the language, and therefore the language they are learning. GELT also recognises that they are shaped by their environment (see Larsen-Freeman, 2011; Larsen-Freeman & Cameron, 2008).

The sociocultural framework, influenced by Vygotsky (1978), became more prominent in education throughout the 1980s, and also in language education. Learning was seen as a social activity, so focus moved towards interaction, which complemented communicative trends occurring around the same time. Researchers looked at how second languages were acquired through co-construction between experts and novices utilising notions such as scaffolding for learners to move towards autonomous learning (Lantolf, 2011). Core concepts within sociocultural theory complement GELT, such as notions that teachers should be able to assist individual needs with resources at hand for learners. Meier (2017) notes that 'As this perspective is open to the use of other languages, such as the first language, to support additional language learning (Moore, 2013), I argue that this pedagogy could be described as potentially but perhaps not explicitly cross lingual' (p. 137).

Others in the field of Global Englishes have also drawn on sociocultural theory. More than a decade ago, Jenkins (2006) noted that sociocultural theorists do not focus on native speaker contexts of use, but on the interactions that non-native speakers participate in, where language is learned through the mediation of interaction. Here, learners are 'socially constituted and always situated beings' who 'undeniably belong in their second self-chosen world, not as observers but as fully-fledged participants' (Pavlenko & Lantolf, 2000, p. 169). Similarly, 'In the case of TESOL, much of the meaningful classroom interaction is ELF, with learners being present and future members of an international community made up predominantly of other NNS [non-native speakers]' (Jenkins, 2006, p. 155). She also notes that sociocultural theory places emphasis on the transformative agency of L2 learners (Donato, 2000), which is clearly in line with GELT, where learners do not just conform to the rules of native English, but are creative and innovative, as they 'transform' the rules to negotiate meaning. As Jenkins (2006) points out:

> Again, this is an aspect of sociocultural theory which contradicts the fundamental conformist tenet of mainstream SLA but on the other hand has much in common with an ELF perspective, whose claim is that ELF speakers, to use Donato's turn of phrase, are transforming their (English) world by means of their lingua franca interactions. It also links with Brutt-Griffler's (2002) position, which holds that ELF speakers (although she does not actually use the term) are not merely recipients of English but, more importantly, agents in its spread and development. (p. 148)

Jenkins (2006) also notes that the notion of identity in sociocultural theory is important and, indeed, many researchers have looked at identity in ELF contexts (Jenks, 2013; Sung, 2014a, 2014b; Virkkula & Nikula, 2010). For many, the goal is no longer to integrate into a native English-speaking community and ELF provides a range of new 'identity categories' (Jenks, 2013, p. 168) for those learning English.

It is important to highlight that social constructivist perspectives of learning are very different to interactionist perspectives of SLA, even though both superficially appear to see learning as a product of language interaction (Hall, 2017). Interactionists place cognition at the core of learning, whereas social constructionists see learning occurring through the process of social activity. In sociocultural and post-structuralist views, language learning is seen as being based on co-construction of meaning, but also about interpersonal interactions, where 'participants actively and dynamically negotiate not just textual meaning, but also their social relationships' (Kumaravadivelu, 2005, p. 70).

Individual and Group Differences in SLA

Through this time, the field of SLA has continued to develop its interest in psychological aspects of language learning and has witnessed a growth in research focusing on the variation in language learning according to learners' individual differences. Individual and group differences include such variables as age, personality, motivation, anxiety, aptitude, and learning strategies.

The critical period hypothesis – the belief that in order to master a language one must learn it before a critical age – prevailed for decades. Despite scarce research evidence that supported the importance of age in instructed second language acquisition environments (as opposed to immersive environments) many countries have sought to lower the age of instruction. Even though substantial evidence now exists to contradict 'the younger, the better' ideology (Pfenninger & Singleton, 2017), many institutions still promote such educational policies. The introduction of language at earlier ages in education has implications for Global Englishes. As argued by Galloway (2011, 2017a), GELT is needed in primary school contexts, particularly since stereotypes certainly form at a young age, thus promotion of native norms in primary school is concerning.

Another large area of research on individual differences is motivation, which has implications for GELT. Motivation has consistently been proven to be a good predictor of language-learning success (Dörnyei & Ryan, 2015). Motivational research in SLA began with seminal work by Gardner and Lambert in bilingual Canada. Gardner posited two key orientations for language learning motivation: the instrumental motive and the integrative motive, of which the integrative motive was deemed more powerful (Gardner, 1985). Gardner viewed success in language learning as being highly dependent on the learner's attitudes towards the linguistic-cultural community of the target language, in addition to other factors such as: motivational intensity/effort;

the desire to learn the language; attitude towards learning the language; and attitudes towards the learning context, including the teacher. Learners were described as having integrative motivation if they had a positive attitude towards the target language and an interest and willingness to interact with members of the target language group (Gardner, 1985).

As the sociopolitical status of English has changed, we also need to reassess the importance of instrumental motives for learning, as these motives may have grown in importance. Ur (2012) notes that 'learners today need English for a variety of instrumental purposes rather than in order to join a particular English-speaking community' (p. 10). English has become an important language with high capital value and is a prerequisite to academic and career success in many contexts. For many learners, instrumental motivation, rather than integrative motivation, has become a more powerful driving force for learning English for career or academic success.

Dörnyei and Csizér (2002) re-examined the notion of integrative motivation, referring to its ill fit with English as an international language. Kormos et al. (2011) found that the most important language-learning goal was 'related to the status of English as a lingua franca' (p. 513). The influence of indirect and direct intercultural contact (Kormos & Csizér, 2008) has been found to be important and indeed, as discussed in Chapter 2, research has revealed the influence of ELF awareness and experience influences attitudes towards English (Galloway, 2011, 2013, 2017; Wang, 2013, 2015; Wang & Jenkins, 2016). Attitudes towards speakers of the target language are important; however, with the globalisation of English use, this target community has significantly widened. Gardner's integrative motive may have accounted for motivations of Anglophone Canadians to integrate with the Francophone community, and vice versa, but is seen as being more problematic when looking at motivations for learners of a global language, with a more fluid English-using community.

This mismatch has in part been addressed by Yashima's (2002) notion of international posture, which is defined as an 'interest in foreign or international affairs, willingness to go overseas to study or work, readiness to interact with intercultural partners and ... a non-ethnocentric attitude toward different cultures' (p. 57). Research in this area has focused on learners in the Expanding Circle who learn English for use with an international English-using body, rather than speakers of a fixed L1 community. Research has shown that high levels of international posture are related to positive language-learning attitudes in Chilean learners (Kormos & Csizér, 2008) and that high levels of international posture exist among young language learners in Indonesia (Lamb, 2012). GELT, however, might challenge some descriptions of international posture, by arguing that ELF use is not just an 'international' construct and that there are increasing opportunities to use English in domestic settings.

Dörnyei's (2009) *L2 Motivational Self System* was introduced as an alternative construct via which to examine motivation. This system places the learner at the centre of his or her system of language-learning motivation, where learners depict their future selves. These selves, termed possible selves, 'denote a powerful and at the same time versatile motivational self-mechanism, representing individuals' ideas of what they might become, what they would like to become, and what they are afraid of becoming' (Dörnyei & Ryan, 2015, p. 87). This self-system, therefore, consists of multiple versions of one's future self, termed as the *Ideal Self* (the type of learner one ideally wants to become), and the *Ought To Self* (the type of learner one thinks they should become to meet external expectations or to avoid negative outcomes). If a learner's current language ability is different to either of these future selves, the learner might develop a desire to learn, and therefore be motivated to develop their ability to learn a language (Dörnyei & Ryan, 2015). The opposite is also true: if the future self is not that different, then the goal cannot be said to be desirable to the student, and then an issue will occur with the learner's ability to reach that goal. Dörnyei's (2009) 'L2 Motivational Self System' is helpful for GELT, as it is a useful way to conceptualise motivation. Here, attitudes towards the target language community are related to an ideal language self-image, rather than a problematic 'other', which has traditionally been posited as a 'native' speaker.

This perspective of motivation highlights the importance of previous experiences with the target language and previous intercultural contact with members of the target language community, which may lead to, or perhaps diminish, their 'linguistic self confidence' (Dörnyei et al., 2006, p. 15). With regard to motivation, GELT aims to increase learners' motivation by raising their awareness of the use of English as a global language, by increasing their confidence as legitimate speakers and not comparing them to L1 norms or presenting them as deficient in any way. Confidence is linked to a higher self-perceived and actual language competence (Sampasivam & Clement, 2014), thus GELT aims to increase this second-language confidence or linguistic self-confidence. While Kachru (2005) may note that '[t]here is enough evidence in sociolinguistic literature to show that users of institutionalised varieties are secure in their identities and do not wish to acquire the identity of either an American or British speaker of English' (p. 160), we do have to recognise that some learners will desire to learn native English. Thus, learners' ideal L2 self may be a native English speaker or an expert ELF user. GELT acknowledges that learners' ideal L2 self is defined by the learners themselves, and not imposed by the curriculum or others.

More researchers started looking at identity, seeing it as something subjective and constructed socially and also as a post-structuralist perspective, something actively produced and reproduced, rather than something that is fixed

(Jenks, 2013; Norton, 2014; Virkkula & Nikula, 2010). Researchers were critical of those in the cognitivist tradition who viewed individual differences (e.g. motivation, age) as stable traits (Larsen-Freeman, 2011) and the field has moved towards looking at unique local particularities of learners as self-reflective agents. Thus, in this era of SLA research, individual differences began to be viewed through a sociocultural and post-structuralist lens, where language learning involved co-construction of meaning and interpersonal interactions. There was recognition that learners are different and learn in different ways (Meier, 2017).

Multilingualism and the Multilingual Turn

Ortega (2013) notes that the epistemological diversity in the field today has been fuelled by the social turn, initiated in the mid-1990s. As noted above, it emphasised social dimensions of SLA, questing cognitive understandings. This led to a division of research; those that argued that it happened in a learner's mind and those that felt it had social dimensions. This led to ontological differences in how language, language learning and language learners were conceptualised and understood (Meier, 2017). Ortega (2013) points out that, after the social turn, the field started to take on a lot of diversity and started drawing on such constructs as emergentism, connectionism, dynamic systems and complexity theories, with seminal papers in the mid-1990s (Ellis, 1996; Gasser, 1990; Larsen-Freeman, 1997; MacWhinney, 1997; O'Grady, 1996). With the social turn now complete, this opened the door to examining social dimensions of language and she predicted a move towards a bilingual orientation in SLA, noting that:

> I believe it is the ability for SLA researchers to invest in future positive reframings of the late-learned, bi/multilingual nature of L2 acquisition that will most radically impact on the field's continued and growing transdisciplinary relevance in the 21st century. Moreover, I predict it will take a bi/multilingual turn in SLA, one of similar depth and magnitude as the earlier social turn SLA experienced (Block, 2003), for these reframings to flourish. (Ortega, 2013, p. 14)

Indeed, an increasing number of researchers in the field of SLA are challenging the monolingual bias in SLA in light of the fact that multilingualism and multiculturalism are a reality around the globe. An increasing body of research acknowledges 'that SLA nowadays should be seen as the acquisition of multilingual and multicultural competencies, even if the object of instruction is one standard linguistic system' (Kramsch, 2012, p. 108).

It is important to note, however, that foundations for the multilingual turn had been laid in previous decades, from both cognitivist and social standpoints. The interdependence hypothesis (Cummins, 1979) argued that bilinguals have an underlying integrated proficiency and not separate monolingual competences. Meier (2017) notes that from around the 1980s, a new integrated (or cross-lingual) way of looking at language started. This hypothesis, which has since been accepted based on neuroscience and psychology research, confirmed, for example, that multilinguals have an integrated multilingual lexicon (Kroll et al., 2013; Lowie et al., 2014) on which they draw for all communication, placing language in the minds of users. Complexity theorists have furthered our understanding of language 'as a complex adaptive system, which emerges bottom-up from interactions of multiple agents in speech communities' (Larsen-Freeman, 2011, p. 49) that constitutes a 'system [that] is in constant flux' (ibid., p. 50).

May (2014a) notes that the increased focus on superdiverse linguistic contexts in the field foregrounded multilingualism, rather than monolingualism, as the new norm of applied linguistic and sociolinguistic analysis. Many ELF researchers have drawn on Vertovec's (2007) notion of 'superdiversity' and we have certainly seen a movement towards focusing on the blurred boundaries between languages, looking at it all from a more fluid perspective. Increased globalisation has highlighted the dynamic and hybrid nature of multilingual encounters. As part of this term, new vocabulary was required to capture new ideas and SLA saw the emergence of many neologisms to explain complex multilingual practices, including translingual writing (Horner et al., 2010), multiliteracies (Cope & Kalantzis, 2000), codemeshing (Canagarajah, 2011a), polylingual languaging (Jørgensen, 2008), translanguaging (Garcia, 2009; García & Wei, 2014), metrolingualism (Pennycook, 2010), lingua franca multilingualism (Makoni & Pennycook, 2012), contemporary urban vernaculars (Rampton, 2011), flexible bilingualism (Creese & Blackledge, 2011), plurilingualism (Canagarajah, 2011b) and mobile resources (Blommaert, 2010).

It is clear that recent years have witnessed an increasing view of languages as being dynamic, multifaceted, heteroglossic, and adaptive. They evolve through contact between people from different language backgrounds and there is recognition that, in their hybrid use of languages, speakers adapt to different situations. As noted in Chapter 1, translanguaging has its origins in bilingual education, where stigmatisation of the use of minority languages and restricting access to multilingual repertoires in schools were criticised for having detrimental effects on bilingual students' success in school. In recent decades views on bilingualism have matured from constrained labels built around language proficiency and temporal benchmarks, to how bilinguals use the languages according to context, and we have seen new understandings emerge, such as the flexible bilingual (Blackledge & Creese, 2010), dynamic bilingual (Garcia, 2009) and multicompetent users (Cook, 2012).

These critical multilingual perspectives add to debates surrounding monolingual and the native speaker bias in SLA and TESOL and such terminology has increased awareness of fuzzy boundaries surrounding language, particularly in superdiverse contexts. All of this work combined has led to a multilingual turn in SLA (May, 2014c). The multilingual turn also stems from work of Pennycook (2001) in critical applied linguistics, discussed in Chapter 1, who questioned labels used to describe the global spread of English, as well as challenging power relationships involved with language use. Pennycook's postcolonial work, like many movements in the multilingual turn, aims to emancipate L2 users of English from constrained communities, models and views of language, which were underpinned by a monolingual bias.

It was at the 2012 American Association for Applied Linguistics annual conference where Stephen May referred to a 'multilingual turn in SLA' within a colloquium that brought together these ideas. In this colloquium, Kramsch (2012) notes that Ortega explored what kind of research would be needed to support a multilingual outlook on SLA research – a notion further explored in Chapter 5. The colloquium eventually led to an edited volume on the topic by May (2014c), in which the purpose of the book is stated to 'resituate the issue of multilingualism more centrally in applied linguistics and, in so doing, to make more permeable some of its key subdisciplinary boundaries particularly, those between SLA, TESOL, and bilingual education' (May, 2014a, p. 2). With contributions from SLA, TESOL, and bilingual education scholars, the book shows how researchers address the monolingual bias and treatment of the 'acquisition of an additional language (most often English) as an ideally hermetic process uncontaminated by knowledge and use of one's other languages' (May, 2014a, p. 2).

Thus, as with GELT, the multilingual turn urges a paradigm shift in how we view language, questioning dominant norms and discourses and stereotypes. It calls for a critical approach that embraces multilingual practices and translanguaging, and, as with GELT, it respects language learners' hybrid language practices and entire linguistic repertoire, aiming to legitimise such practices. Those advocating a multilingual turn contend that there is a need to break down boundaries between languages. Blackledge et al. (2014), for example, point out that 'the traditional distinction between languages is no longer sustainable, so the distinction between monolingual, bilingual and multilingual speakers may no longer be sustainable' (p. 193). Also in the book, Block (2014) develops his earlier critique of monolingual bias in linguistic-cognitive SLA and makes a call to address the issue of multimodality. Block argues that the field of SLA needs to focus more on multilingualism, an approach that should embrace embodiment and multimodality, which includes such aspects as intonation, proxemics, posture, gesture and clothing. Block is interested in what people do when they communicate, which connects with ideas of Canagarajah (2016), who argues that semiotic resources are used in communication and are therefore part of language. 'For Block, multimodality and embodiment move beyond linguistics (the bias of SLA) to a holistic communicative act, and he argues that SLA should be concerned with all possible semiotic forms of communication' (Creagh, 2017, p. 70).

Thus, a movement within the multilingual turn has led to an evolved understanding of language as part of a multimodal repertoire, as an 'intricate web of social meaning woven from grammar, intonation, gaze, gesture, head movement, bodily orientation, and additional semiotic resources' (Atkinson, 2011b, p. 147). As discussed in Chapter 1, Cook's (2012) notion of the multicomponent learners is very much in line with GELT, and thus many notions within the multilingual turn are as well. When using ELF, learners use other semiotic resources, not just linguistic knowledge. Thus, all of this has implications for how language competence is defined and taught, thus bringing us back full circle in forcing us to readdress what is meant by competence and proficiency in TESOL of the twenty-first century.

Much of Ortega's (2013, 2014) work reverberates with GELT, such as her calls for the abandonment of concepts of nativeness and monolingual as organising principles in SLA, particularly in the field of linguistic-cognitive SLA. She calls for 'usage-based linguistics', the study of language from a functional perspective, which can be a helpful theoretical framework for an epistemic reorientation of SLA. Usage-based linguistics sees language as an emergent thing; a process, not a product, that is shaped by experience. It also recognises the multiple discursive practices of language learners. Since knowledge of a language comes from using it in the local context, and experience is important, this is in contrast to Chomskian ideology and universal grammar. She is further critical of concepts that stemmed from this ideology, such as 'native-like', target-like', 'interlanguage', 'fossilisation', and 'ultimate attainment'. Such thinking clearly echoes our own views of language use within Global Englishes.

Sembiante (2016) notes that a functional language perspective supports teachers to adopt critical language pedagogy, which is relevant to GELT:

> A functional language perspective encourages teachers and students to develop critical language awareness, or the understanding of how language varies across social contexts, how they use language in different ways and for different purposes and how language functions differentially in genres and content areas across the curriculum. (p. 56)

In Chapter 2 we outlined how GELT embodies aspects of critical pedagogy. In a thematic decomposition of two books with the phrase multilingual turn in their title (Conteh & Meier, 2014; May, 2014b), Meier (2017) notes that, while there is no explicit reference to critical pedagogy in any of the chapters, the findings presented are 'consistently concerned with concepts that are central to critical pedagogy' (p. 152); thus we are not the only ones to see the link between the two. Meier (2017) notes that:

> There is an over-arching critical, and arguably ideological, theoretical perspective associated with the multilingual turn, which questions widely held assumptions about language, learners and learning, as well as the nature and location of knowledge, social relationships and power; all concepts associated with critical pedagogy (see McLaren 2013; Norton and Toohey 2004). Teachers, learners, parents, and schools may make linguistic decisions that are shaped by widely accepted monolingual and standard language norms and prevailing ideologies. (p. 154)

As with GELT, there is an aim to move away from monolingual bias and the shift resonates well with GELT, which also places two opposing ideologies at either end of its continuum to indicate a needed 'turn' in perspective. GELT compares an approach loosely guided by traditional, monolingual assumptions, and one guided by critical, multilingual assumptions to try to force this turn.

Three chapters in May's seminal book (Canagarajah, 2014; Leung, 2014; Norton, 2014) focus on TESOL, indicative of it being central, rather than peripheral, to the multilingual turn. As noted in Chapter 1, Canagarajah's earlier descriptions of language in global contexts informed the original GELT framework, and thus we see a natural ideological thread that connects GELT to similar movements pertaining to TESOL within the multilingual turn. As Creagh (2017) notes, ideas within the multilingual turn 'point to pedagogical transformation in the field of TESOL' (p. 150).

Accomplishing the Turn

Nearly three decades ago, Sridhar and Sridhar (1986) criticised the assumption that learners want to achieve native-like proficiency, noting that '[p]aradoxical as it may seem, Second Language Acquisition researchers seem to have neglected the fact that the goal of SLA is bilingualism' (p. 13). Further, while there is criticism that the field of SLA has taken a more psycholinguistic approach and has neglected social (sociolinguistic, socio-psychological, and sociocultural) factors, Jenkins (2006) notes that '[m]any of those who have identified problems with mainstream SLA have tended not to take issue with its basic premise of NS [native speaker] normativity' (p. 144). She further criticises the field for focusing on 'ways of facilitating the acquisition of as near native-like competence as required by the learner, teacher, or "system," be this by means of tasks, scaffolding, comprehensible input/output, or whatever' (p. 139). To some extent, this is now untrue, given the work described above in the multilingual turn. However, while it is clear from this chapter that the field of SLA has witnessed several 'turns', as with the field of TESOL outlined in the previous chapter, monolingualism and associated terms (e.g. native speaker) still dominate.

'Turn is a name given to a development that has established itself, or is in the process of establishing itself' (Meier, 2017, p. 132). Meier (2017) further states that a turn is not necessarily a new occurrence, but something that develops over some time, growing in significance in terms of its importance. Global Englishes is not only an established field, but there is an increasing body of work focusing on its pedagogical implications. Moreover, many advocates of change in language teaching are not those researching in fringe fields, but rather leading scholars in applied linguistics. Thus, we must ask the same question as Ortega (2013):

> With such distinguished SLA advocates, and with such powerful and increasingly comprehensively articulated arguments, why has SLA had such difficulty breaking away from the straightjacket of the comparative fallacy, the target deviation perspective, and the monolingual native speaker bias? (p. 15)

We could argue the same for TESOL, in that with such a growing body of evidence spanning decades calling for a change in teaching practices and curriculum from key figures in TESOL (e.g. McKay, Widdowson, Larsen-Freeman), why does change appear to be so slow in gaining traction?

Sembiante (2016) observes that progress has been slow since the publication of the multilingual turn with 'some proponents of the linguistic–cognitive perspective arguing that traditional understandings and constructions of SLA will continue to trump those emerging from the new sociolinguistic movement' (p. 54). Ortega (2013) also notes that time may be necessary for changes to take full effect in SLA. For GELT, matters might be worse, as change tends to take even longer in TESOL. Many practising teachers infrequently return to teacher training. Thus, new ideas sometimes require a new generation of teachers to become fully realised in practice. Our discussion of the obstacles and environmental constraints to GELT, in Chapter 4, aims to speed up this process by problematising these barriers and discussing ways in which they can be dismantled. However, we have argued previously that attachments in the field to standard language and the monolingual ideology are barriers to GELT and, as we see it, the multilingual turn.

Nevertheless, future prospects of a turn are looking positive. Translanguaging has been well received in the field and might encourage movement in other areas, as it is highly applicable to TESOL, having grown from bilingual educational practices. There is an increasing body of studies revealing the positive influence of Global Englishes instruction on attitudes (Baker, 2012b; Derwing et al., 2002; Galloway, 2011, 2013, 2017a; Galloway & Rose, 2013; Shim, 2002; Sung, 2015). The more we can share successful practices in TESOL to a wider audience of language teachers, the more quickly we can accomplish the turn. A call for such research is discussed further in Chapter 5.

Conclusion

This chapter has highlighted that the monolingual bias is evident in the field of SLA as well as TESOL. Nevertheless, there we are clearly witnessing a paradigm shift in the field of SLA, which bodes well for parallel shifts in the related field of TESOL due to the natural links between the two. Just as shifts in teaching English in global contexts have been gathering traction in classrooms and teacher training programmes, the multilingual turn is gathering momentum in SLA. This is promising for GELT, where the yardstick of competence and reference points for learning are not the L1 monolingual English speaker. GELT positions language users as L2 users in their own right and recognises learner agency. More scholars are now critical of the monolingual bias and recognise the value of utilising learners' entire linguistic repertoire, viewing them as multicompetent users of language.

Nevertheless, in addition to theoretical issues that are at the heart of debates in SLA and TESOL with regard to global language use, there are also practical issues to consider. TESOL is, after all, a profession; and like any profession, it is bound by real-world limitations and a range of push-and-pull forces that can affect the implementation of new ideas. For example, teachers have to contend with pull factors such as the need to prepare their students for real-world English use, and with push factors such as teaching to tests, working within set curricula and juggling different stakeholder expectations, including their own. They may, after all, have their own internal battles to contend with regarding the importance of standard language education. While often described as a theory–practice divide, we believe there to be a gaping lacuna between the criteria outlined within the GELT framework and current mainstream classroom pedagogy. Even teachers who want to instigate change may not know how to do so due to a lack of knowledge. They may also lack access to necessary tools, such as the materials to do so. Even if teachers embrace SLA theory that promotes the importance of multilingualism, the fluidity of language, and sees language learning as a social practice, they may face difficulties regarding how this translates to classroom practices. Similarly, they may be at a loss in terms of how the focus on form should be approached, if this is how they were taught to teach. Even though new ideas may be circulating throughout the SLA research realm, this does not guarantee that TESOL practitioners will even be familiar with them. Many practitioners will have their own ideologies and will work in different contexts. There are numerous barriers to applying SLA theory to TESOL, to initiate change. These barriers can be both internal and external to the teachers and students, and may pose substantial obstacles for successful GELT implementation. These barriers to innovation are discussed in detail in the next chapter.

4 Curriculum Innovation and GELT

As noted in Chapter 1, GELT is not a prescriptive one-size-fits-all model for practitioners, nor is the purpose of this book to tell teachers what to do, or to suggest that they have to abandon current curricula and pedagogical practices familiar to them. The preceding three chapters have highlighted the need for change to pedagogical practice in light of Global Englishes research. In this chapter, we discuss GELT curriculum innovation in more depth, examining the process of implementing innovation and the factors that influence it, including possible 'barriers' (Galloway & Rose, 2015) or 'environmental constraints' (Nation & Macalister, 2010) present in different contexts. In doing so, we also discuss the possible barriers to accomplishing the multilingual turn in the field of SLA, although, here, our main focus is on instigating a paradigm shift in the field of TESOL. Our in-depth discussion of the curriculum innovation process, and the variables that influence it, aims to increase the potential for successful and sustained GELT curriculum innovation. We draw on innovation theory to examine the process in full and, as elsewhere, we do not make value judgements regarding the learning and teaching context in a particular culture. In this chapter, we aim to further aid practitioners to make informed decisions about GELT, its relevance for, and feasibility in, their contexts.

The Innovation Process

Despite the increasing attention given to the need for change at the theoretical level, 'the native-speaker episteme has not loosened its grip over theoretical principles, classroom practices, the publication industry, or the job market' (Kumaravadivelu, 2012, p. 15). It is also clear from the preceding chapter that, despite the increased attention given to multilingualism, monolingual ideologies still dominate and also present obstacles to fully achieving a 'turn', or paradigm shift. In order to facilitate curriculum innovation, and ultimately widespread change, we feel it is 'important to pay greater attention to what innovation theory suggests about ways of making the practice of ELT innovation more successful than hitherto' (Wedell, 2009, p. 398). Thus, this chapter draws on innovation theory to explore the complexity of incorporating a GELT perspective into ELT classrooms. By examining the curriculum innovation process in full, we aim to provide readers with ample information to consider and, ultimately, to help them 'develop a more rationalised, informed perspective on the (de) merits of selecting language norms in the classroom' (Dewey, 2012, p. 166). As Rogers (2003) notes:

> Getting a new idea adopted, even when it has obvious advantages, is difficult. Many innovations require a lengthy period of many years from the time when they become available to the time when they are widely adopted. (p. 1)

Curricular innovation can be a challenging and complex phenomenon, and GELT requires a conceptual transition in not only how English should be taught and learned, but in how the language itself should be viewed. We recognise that change may not be imminent; indeed, many of the proposals that inform GELT were made more than thirty years ago and, as we argued elsewhere, the native speaker yardstick has been questioned for decades outside calls within the field of Global Englishes. Incorporating a GELT perspective fully into a curriculum may take time and certainly requires more research, the subject of our next chapter. There are definite barriers, as we have outlined elsewhere (Galloway & Rose, 2015), but this does not make it impossible, nor should they be a deterrent to making the curriculum more relevant to the needs of learners in today's globalised world. By examining the curriculum innovation process, and giving consideration to the various factors involved, the potential 'barriers' to innovation and the various phases/stages that innovations go through, we aim to improve the success for GELT innovation institutionalisation.

Successful and sustained innovation certainly depends on having a strategic approach and it is important to understand the many factors involved, which has been given a lot of attention in the literature (Chang, 2011; Fullan, 2007; Henrichsen, 1989; Owston, 2007; Rogers, 2003; White et al., 1991). Several models have also been proposed to describe the various phases and factors that impact curriculum innovation (Fullan, 2007; Henrichsen, 1989; Rogers, 2003), which we draw on in Figure 4.1 to produce a framework to help practitioners understand curriculum innovation and the various factors involved, both in general (Figure 4.1) and in relation to GELT (Figure 4.2). We also draw on Wedell's (2003) list of questions for planning TESOL curriculum change, which help guide planners to consider change in their own contexts, and White et al.'s (1991) overview of managing curriculum development and innovation.

There are different phases to curriculum innovation and research is needed at every stage to maximise the likelihood of innovation success. We draw on Fullan's (2007, pp. 65–9) three broad phases (initiation, implementation and institutionalisation) and Roger's (2003) five steps in the innovation decision-

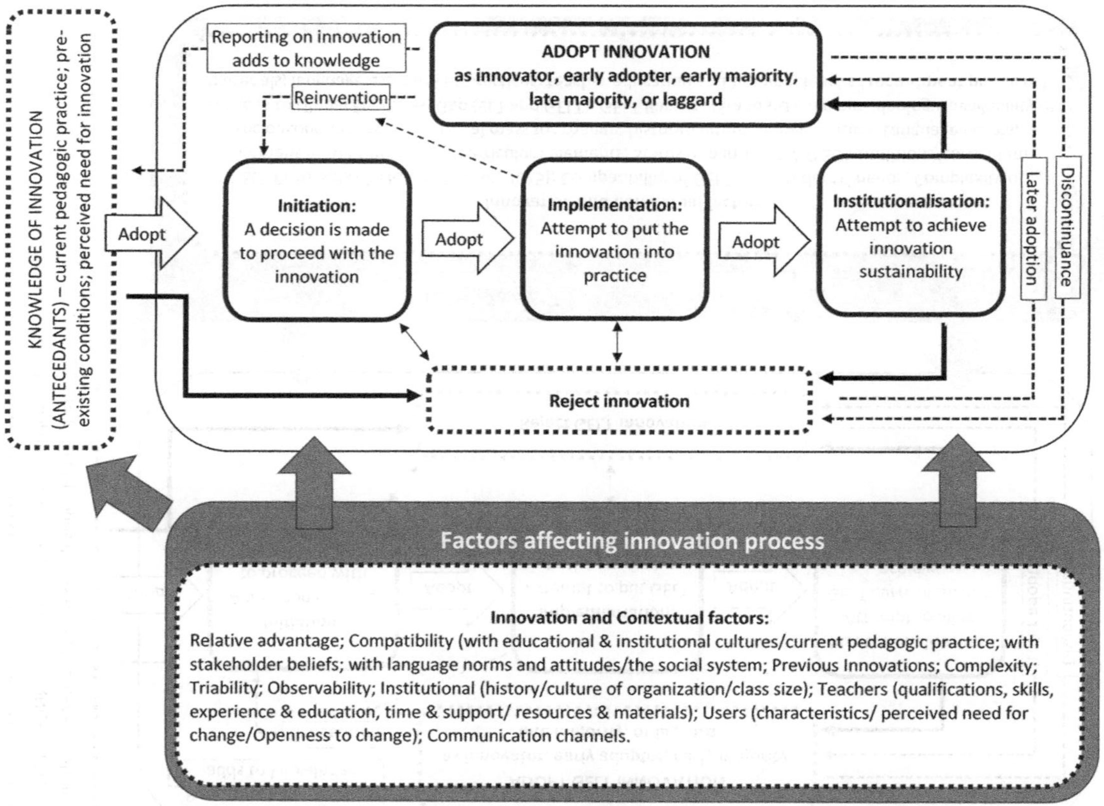

Figure 4.1 Curriculum innovation cycle.

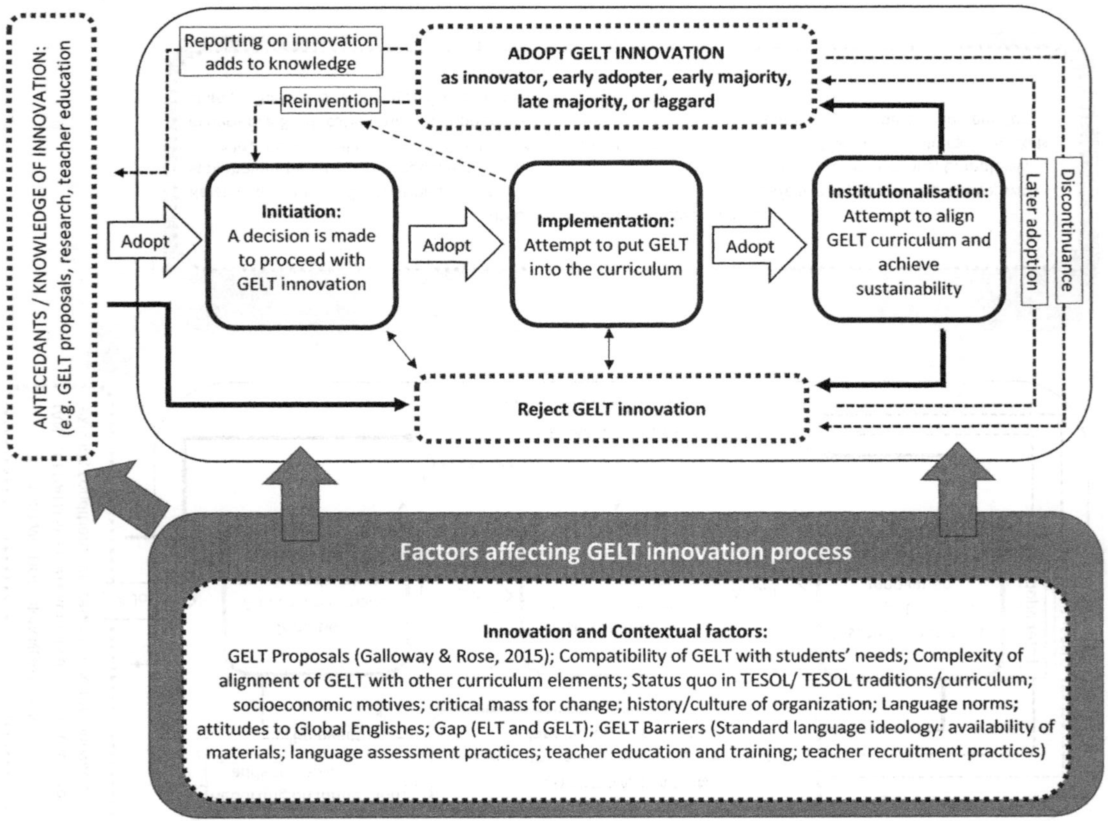

Figure 4.2 GELT curriculum innovation cycle.

making process: (1) knowledge, (2) persuasion, (3) decision, (4) implementation and (5) confirmation (p. 20). In our figure, we depict four phases:

1. The 'knowledge' phase (exposure to the innovation first with no knowledge and then more information in the persuasion stage, where the advantages and disadvantages are assessed – e.g. the perceived characteristics – relative advantage, compatibility, complexity, trialability, observability.
2. The 'initiation' phase (or Roger's decision phase – a decision is made to proceed with or reject the innovation).
3. The 'implementation' phase (attempt to put the innovation into practice, leading to the next stage, rejection, or reinvention, which starts the process again).
4. The 'institutionalisation' phase (attempt to achieve innovation sustainability, leading to rejection, adoption, and possibly reinvention, which starts the process again).

As indicated in Figure 4.1, it is not a linear, but a cyclical process and innovation rejection can happen at any stage. The model is also transformative in non-typical flows: initial rejection can lead to later adoption, just as initial adoption can later lead to discontinuance. As Waters (2014) points out, it is unfortunate that, despite its importance, research on the institutionalisation phase appears to have been somewhat neglected in the research of English-language education management. This is certainly the case with regard to GELT. There is growing research on the attitudes of students and practitioners towards English and ELT in relation to Global Englishes (see Galloway, 2017a; Galloway & Rose, 2015; Jenkins, 2007 for an overview), but only a small number have explored what a Global Englishes approach would look like in the classroom (see Galloway, 2011, 2013, 2017; Galloway & Rose, 2014, 2017; Rose & Galloway, 2017; Shim, 2002; Sung, 2014, 2018), and few studies have been conducted on the influence this has on students' attitudes (Baker, 2012b; Derwing et al., 2002; Galloway, 2011, 2013, 2017; Galloway & Rose, 2013; Shim, 2002; Sung, 2015), and, to date, there have been few longitudinal studies.

This phase of curriculum innovation may occur last in chronological terms, but a successful GELT innovation strategy requires consideration of successful institutionalisation from the outset, which includes attention to the various factors influencing the process as part of a needs analysis. As White et al. (1991) note, 'the questions to be dealt with here are concerned with clarifying the current situation *before* looking to the future' (p. 172). We highlight the importance of considering the institutionalisation phase first in Figure 4.1 and we have also aimed to make it clear that there are many factors influencing the complex process of curriculum innovation. Some of these relate to the innovation itself, and others relate to the resource system, the users and the alignment between the various factors. The figure aims to help practitioners to consider all of these factors to determine if GELT can exist as 'part of the "fabric" of the "host" system into which it has been introduced' (Waters, 2014, p. 98). We also show in Figure 4.1 that consideration of some of the innovation and contextual factors, such as current resources and degree of openness to change, which Wedell (2003) calls 'level 1' questions, can also lead to changes in the innovation introduced (reinvention). This then leads to further questions (Wedell's level 2), which involves considering the alignment of the components, e.g. the adjustments that will need to be made to restore balance between the curriculum elements.

Research on teacher beliefs and teacher education is certainly important, but GELT will be implemented in different ways in different contexts. As such, more research is needed on what happens after teacher training and teacher education. Research should focus on contextualised investigation of how the innovation is introduced, in order to examine what happens in the classroom when GELT is incorporated into the curriculum. Indeed, referring to the widespread recent English-language education innovations, including CLIL and ELF, Waters (2014) notes that:

> It would also be particularly useful if such analyses (especially those involving local innovations) were carried out both prospectively (before implementation) and retrospectively (after implementation), to increase understanding of the predictive value of this kind of study in managing innovation. (p. 96)

In their study of curriculum innovation in China, Li and Edwards (2013) found that, on arrival, teachers could be characterised as 'early adopters' at the start of the UK-based course. However, post-course evaluations revealed that they had made the transition to the 'decision phase' (p. 394). Such research on how teachers move through different stages at varying lengths of time is important to see how practitioners move towards the implementation or confirmation stages. Li and Edwards's (2013) study also highlights that facilitating factors for curriculum innovation in China include the dissatisfaction of teachers regarding the current ELT practices in China. Their conclusions indicate that a supportive policy environment may positively influence teachers to accept new teaching approaches, via promotion of the relative advantage of innovation. For GELT, we need to ensure teachers fully understand the relative advantage of this innovation, in order that change can be fully realised.

True adoption occurs when an innovation has been institutionalised to the point that it is no longer construed as a new idea or practice (Rogers, 2003). Fullan (2007) also refers to adopter commitment, which is a key variable to determine whether an innovation will survive. Thus, it is important that GELT research does not only focus on the attitudes of stakeholders prior to its incorporation and we call for more longitudinal studies in the next chapter to examine whether it produces lasting changes. Such research is likely to reveal whether GELT will undergo *mutual adaption*, which is described as 'adaptation of the innovation to fit the local setting and adaptations by local users to fit the innovation' (Waters, 2014, pp. 136–7), or *reinvention*, which is described as 'the degree to which an innovation is changed or modified by a user in the process of its adoption and implementation' (p. 180). This relates to what Richards (2017) refers to as the 'enacted curriculum', referring to how teachers individualise curricula according to their unique contexts. This is even more likely with regard to GELT, due to its context-sensitive nature and flexible approach to student needs. GELT curriculum innovation ultimately aims to be a bottom-up process that will be informed by students' needs analysis carried out by practitioners in diverse contexts around the globe. The success of innovations in various contexts can then be shared more broadly via reported action research so that teachers can learn from innovations in broadly similar contexts.

Whether the decision is to reject, adopt or reinvent (Figures 4.1 and 4.2), we need to encourage research, so that teachers and curriculum planners can share their experiences with innovative practice. We must also recognise that, even if GELT is incorporated initially, it may be discontinued. At the moment, GELT is an idea that needs to be fully implemented and evaluated and, thus, should not be treated as a full-blown teaching approach. Rogers (2003) notes that *discontinuance*, a decision to reject an innovation after it has previously been adopted, occurs for a variety of reasons. With GELT, we imagine that discontinuance may occur for any number of reasons, such as:

- a lack of teacher training and resources to fully realise the innovation
- washback from high-stakes examinations
- backlash from standard language ideology of key stakeholders, including teachers and learners, resulting in a lack of acceptance.

Thus, reporting on both successful and unsuccessful innovation is essential in the adoption process (Figures 4.1 and 4.2).

As Rose and Montakantiwong (2018) note, 'whether it is a success story or a cautionary account, recognising the pedagogical value of others' experiences is one of the most prominent takeaways' (p. 99) of sharing innovation implementation experiences. The reasons for discontinuance of GELT innovation, therefore, are as important to share as the success stories, so that educators can learn from others' experiences. Of course, the ultimate aim is to promote sustained innovation with regard to GELT and it is hoped that the growing body of research at different stages will provide insights into why this may happen. However, consideration of the factors outlined in this chapter aims to reduce the chances of discontinuance and to navigate around some of the reasons an innovation may be rejected.

Factors Influencing the Innovation Process

In the educational research literature, Carlson (1968) defines an innovation as 'a new idea or practice' (p. 10), noting that idea-based innovations are more difficult to implement than practices-based innovations. GELT is both: it is theory-driven, as new ideas are being applied to pedagogy; and it is practice-driven, as teachers seek ways to consolidate their efforts to teach English as a national language. As outlined in this book thus far, GELT may not be entirely 'new' in the sense that it is not completely different to other approaches to ELT and it is also compatible with a range of current syllabus types and methodological approaches. However, 'newness in an innovation needs not just to involve new knowledge' (Rogers, 2003, p. 12) and a person may have known about it for a while, 'but not yet developed a favourable or unfavourable attitude towards it, nor have adopted or rejected it' (p. 12). Indeed, Chapter 1, documents the growing attention given to the pedagogical implications of Global Englishes research for TESOL and it is a topic that is certainly gathering momentum. In this sense, it may not be a completely 'new' concept to all. We also examined the predecessors to GELT in Chapter 1, several of which also compared this with 'traditional' forms of English language teaching. Nonetheless, given the dominance of native norms, GELT may be 'new' to many, particularly in the sense that it involves a new way of looking at the English language.

It is clear from Figure 4.1 that many factors influence the innovation process and also the innovation itself with regard to GELT. When introducing an innovation, people often want to know what the innovation is, how it will work, how it will be an improvement on the status quo, what advantages it is intended to bring and whether there will be any drawbacks. In Chapter 1, we presented a detailed overview of the innovation itself (the theoretical underpinnings of GELT). As White et al. (1991) point out, 'explicitness is an important characteristic of an innovation. If an innovation can be clearly described, people are more prepared to take notice of it. Also, if the innovation is well developed and in tangible form, it will be more acceptable' (p. 183). Thus, the explicitness of an innovation should be considered alongside the antecedents (Henrichsen, 1989) to the innovation, as well as the background to the innovation, which includes considering factors such as current pedagogic practice, the intended users, the need for innovation and also previous innovation attempts. Much of this was covered in Chapters 2 and 3 with our overview of the current situation ('traditional' ELT and historical perspectives within the field of SLA), as well as our overview of the perceived need for innovation.

We have also highlighted the importance of understanding the context, including the users/receivers of the innovation (in our discussion of needs analysis), current pedagogic practices (in our discussion of methodology), and the experiences of previous innovation attempts (our discussion of the introduction of CLT and the social and subsequent multilingual turn in SLA). In essence, Chapters 1–3 provided an in-depth understanding of the background to GELT (the current situation), which is important to increase the potential for successful and sustained innovation. It is also hoped that this will provide practitioners and curriculum planners with a consideration of the factors beyond their immediate educational system, given that context does not merely relate to their own classroom and successful innovations in one context can have direct application to other contexts (although consideration of the immediate institution is also important, of course, as shown in Figure 4.1). Here, sharing of innovative practice becomes important. Rose and Montakantiwong (2018) emphasise the importance of sharing experiences (both good and bad) within a wider professional community, in order to learn from both successful and unsuccessful innovation.

Rogers (2003) highlights that five factors determine innovation success: relative advantage (whether it offers an improvement on the status quo); trialability (the ability to experiment with it); observability (the degree to which it is observable to others); complexity (the degree to which an innovation is perceived as difficult to understand and use); and compatibility (how it fits in with existing beliefs and practice). GELT aims to be compatible with a variety of institutions, from language schools or centres, to state schools and online courses, and the small body of research that has been conducted on GELT in the classroom has been conducted in both classroom settings and online programmes. Institutions will differ with regard to class sizes, linguistic composition, resources and ideology of education. As such, we call for research in various settings, which will also involve examining who will be involved in the innovation process. Ideally, GELT would involve a collaborative effort with teachers and institutions to ensure that people have ownership, a bottom-up perspective to curriculum innovation. On a larger scale, this would also involve materials designers, policymakers, practitioners and even parents.

In Chapter 1, we outlined the attributes of GELT in our discussion of the benefits and the rationale for this much needed paradigm shift. These attributes lay the foundations for the first step of identifying the 'relative advantages' of the innovation (Figures 4.1 and 4.2), which 'may be measured in economic terms, but social prestige factors, convenience and satisfaction are also important factors' (Rogers, 2003, p. 15). It is early days for GELT, yet the increasing body of studies examining the impact of GELT on learners' attitudes (Baker, 2012b; Derwing et al., 2002; Galloway, 2011, 2013, 2017a; Galloway & Rose, 2013; Shim, 2002; Sung, 2015) show that they have positive attitudes/show satisfaction. Further, as will be discussed in Chapter 7, there is also an increasing body of studies reporting positive responses to incorporating a GELT perspective into TESOL practitioner education programmes (Blair, 2015;

Dewey, 2012; Dilek & Özdemir, 2015; Doan, 2014; Hall et al., 2013; Lopriore, 2016; Sifakis, 2017; Sifakis & Bayyurt, 2015, 2018; Suzuki, 2011; Vettorel, 2016; the study reported in Chapter 7). Potential adopters can learn a lot from these studies, helping them to decide whether it is worthwhile and whether it offers benefits over the status quo, and also how GELT can be incorporated into diverse contexts and curriculums in varied ways.

Practitioners and curriculum planners will always want to know why an innovation is better than what they have at present. They will need to be convinced as to why the existing pedagogical practices that uphold the status quo need to change. Thus, the growing body of research on the positive effects of GELT is important to communicate to curriculum planners. We also hope that, by offering research directions in the next chapter, future research will add to the knowledge base and help make the relative advantage more 'observable'. Rogers (2003) defines observability as 'the degree to which the results of an innovation are visible to others. The easier it is for individuals to see the results of an innovation, the more likely they are to adopt it' (p. 16). This book, alongside others that serve a similar purpose, should help with raising observability, but we also need more research to offer hard empirical evidence that GELT innovation can succeed in a wide range of practices.

Of course, economic profitability may be an issue, and, as Galloway (2018a) argues with regard to materials, given that publishers want to make money it is uncertain whether they will 'dare to be different' (McGrath, 2013, p. 198) and move away from native English norms. The testing industry is also a moneymaking industry, and something we return to later in the chapter. Social prestige is also a problem, and is discussed further in relation to attachments to standard language ideology later in this chapter.

For successful and sustained GELT innovation, it is, therefore, important to understand how GELT is viewed by the receivers of the innovation: the students, the practitioners and other key stakeholders. We have to be careful not to assume that they will see innovation in a positive light and, therefore, this relates to the importance of communicating the relative advantage, the benefits of GELT, to them. Standard language norms prevail and we have to recognise that many potential adopters may have been socialised into thinking that native English is not only right, but that native norms are best. GELT may be daunting and the status quo may be seen as safer. Indeed, as Meier (2017) notes:

> In the current climate of uncertainties, such as climate change, economic downturns, political changes, refugee crises and terror threats, multilingualism may be seen by some as a further destabilising force, and be one of the reasons for the perpetuation of monolingual and standard language norms by stakeholders in schools and society. (pp. 153–4)

GELT, with its promotion of multilingualism, may, then, be viewed suspiciously by some people.

Standard language ideology is promoted through language and education policies and 'gatekeeping academies', such as international standardised testing. Indeed, Johnson (2016), drawing on Jenkins (2006), makes a similar point to us in relation to Global Englishes research that, despite an observable increase in the legitimacy of ideas in the field of World Englishes, there has been very little pedagogical implementation within TESOL. Johnson (2016) notes that this may be related to the prevalence, in certain contexts, of 'high-stakes exams, language policies and/or public discourses that view varieties of English as linguistic deficiencies' (p. 129). Attachments to standard English clearly present a possible barrier to GELT and also influence other barriers, including teacher recruitment practices and testing – both of which are included as part of Galloway and Rose's (2015) barriers to GELT, which we turn to next in our discussion of compatibility.

Compatibility

Compatibility with Educational and Institutional Cultures and Pedagogic Practice

When considering implementing innovation, it is important to consider such factors as compatibility (Figures 4.1 and 4.2). Thornbury (2006), for example, notes that the grammar–translation method may have survived because of its ease of implementation, particularly in places with large class sizes. A simple and easier to implement innovation will be more attractive, but it is also important that it fits with existing beliefs and practice. It is also important to look at the factors within the resource system and institution, and the inter-elemental factors (Henrichsen, 1989) that operate 'between' elements, for example, the degree of proximity of the resource and user system. If there is a good degree of fit between the elements, then change will be implemented more easily. Consideration of such factors also involves thinking about what kind of support they will need to make the transition and what kinds of adjustments will have to be made. Understanding such factors regarding the context of the innovation could, of course, be considered part of phase one (antecedent/knowledge), but here we focus more on the specific teaching context in which practitioners are operating, as opposed to the field of TESOL/SLA as a whole. They are also part of the institutionalisation phase, as they are unlikely to be fully adopted and institutionalised if the innovation does not fit within the institutional context.

It is clearly important to consider whether GELT may be compatible or incompatible with the sociocultural values and beliefs, current pedagogical practices and also the stakeholders' needs. Indeed, the GELT framework emerged in response to the changing needs of English learners in today's globalised world. 'One indication of the compatibility of an innovation is the degree to which it meets a felt need' (Rogers, 2003, p. 246) and it is clear from Chapter 2 that GELT meets a specific need – the need to prepare students to use English as a global language. However, '[T]he classroom is a socially defined reality and is, therefore, influenced by the belief systems and behavioural norms of the society of which it is part' (Tudor, 2001, p. 35). GELT may well meet the needs of learners in today's globalised world preparing to use ELF, but there is also a need to examine the sociocultural context, including prevailing norms and beliefs about English and ELT.

Culture is the 'defining aspect that needs to be understood for innovation to be successful' (Wedell, 2003) and it is important to point out that the 'context' does not only relate to the classroom itself, but also to the sociocultural processes and norms of education that influence learners and teachers and, therefore, the curriculum. In his chapter 'Achieving Cultural Continuity on Curriculum Innovation', Holliday (2001, p. 169) restates Jacob's theory (1996) on curriculum innovation, noting that 'cultural continuity' emphasises the need for sensitivity to the cultural needs of different stakeholders (the recipients of innovation), whether they be students or teachers encountering new teaching methodologies, or stakeholders in curriculum projects. In order to achieve cultural continuity, more research is needed that focuses on building bridges between the culture of GELT-related innovations and the traditional expectations of the key stakeholders in diverse classrooms to ensure we have an in-depth understanding of different contexts, and also an in-depth understanding of how GELT is viewed by those from diverse contexts. Cultural continuity necessitates that innovations are adjusted to, and informed by, institutional environments to ensure successful integration (Holliday, 2001).

Compatibility with Stakeholder Beliefs

Thus, when examining the context, it is also important to examine the belief systems of the curriculum planners, institutional and national education and language policies, and other stakeholders, as discussed in Chapter 2. As Breen et al. (2001) point out:

> any innovation in classroom practice from the adoption of a new technique or textbook to the implementation of a new curriculum has to be accommodated within the teacher's own framework of teaching principles. (p. 472)

Practitioners' attitudes, discussed further in Chapter 7, may not only influence the curriculum but also help explain any possible reluctance or resistance to change. White et al. (1991) point out:

> It has to be realized that the view of an innovation differs according to where you stand in the system. There are two quite different viewpoints: that of the *change* agent – the person advocating the innovation – and that of the *receiver* or *changer* – the person who is being asked to put the innovation into effect . . . Failure to take the receivers' viewpoint into consideration will almost invariably lead to difficulties, because, in the process of dissemination and implementation, an innovation will tend to be 'reinvented' by the adopters. (pp. 179–80)

Thus, it is imperative that stakeholders' views are considered when making curriculum innovation, and GELT is no exception. Even if an institution was to make GELT adaptations to its curriculum at the institutional, department or course level, teachers' viewpoints must be considered, lest they may not be delivered at the classroom level as envisioned.

GELT requires a new ontological stance, or understanding of language, and teachers may, for example, reject the change if it clashes with their beliefs. 'Research on individual beliefs, everyday contexts, and practices casts an instructive light on potential obstacles to policy initiatives and reforms' (Ramanthan & Morgan, 2007, p. 449). Indeed, the study presented in Chapter 7 highlights a number of context-specific barriers salient to the pre- and in-service TESOL practitioners involved in that study. Consideration of the beliefs of stakeholders, towards both English and ELT, is important, particularly given the pervasiveness of standard language ideology, which has been identified as a possible barrier to GELT (Galloway & Rose, 2015). As Kramsch (2014) notes:

> The purity ideal embodied in the authentic NS [native speaker] still remains intact for FL [foreign language] educators. For sure, they acknowledge the increasing variations and non-standard manifestations of the language as it is used in real life, but their teaching is pegged to the pure linguistic standard established by the national gate-keeping academies monitored by NSs. (p. 299)

Thus, if teachers' ideology does not match a new ontological stance, it is more likely that TESOL practitioners will reject the changes.

In Thailand, for example, the Education Ministry launched a Regional English Training Centres Project (British Council, 2018), following on from the success of a 'boot camp' intensive teacher development pilot programme in 2016. Thai English teachers were trained by British Council L1 English speakers, with an aim to boost teachers' confidence in English and their communicative teaching techniques via a thirty-seven day immersion where they communicated only with 'native' English speakers (Mala, 2016). The initiative followed a survey on the English proficiency of Thai English teachers conducted by the Ministry of Education that found that six out of more than 43,000 teachers in public schools could achieve native-like fluency or C2 level on the CEFR. These scores were used to select teachers for the boot camp. The three-week intensive course used

British Council course materials tailor made to the Thai context, although it is clearly questionable how much these materials were centred around Inner Circle norms.

Compatibility with Language Norms and Attitudes/ the Social System

The Quirk/Kachru debate on standards may have been more than two decades ago, but many TESOL practitioners may still consider teaching anything other than the so-called standard, a 'cheat' (Quirk, 1990, p. 6). Many studies have been conducted on practitioners' attitudes towards Global Englishes, some of which also looked at their attitudes towards ELT (see Galloway, 2017a; Galloway & Rose, 2015; Jenkins, 2007; Chapter 7, for an overview). These studies reveal that many TESOL practitioners, and other key stakeholders, including students, cling to 'standard' norms and have fixed ideas about how it should be taught (see Galloway, 2017a; Galloway & Rose, 2015; Jenkins, 2007 for an overview). Many ELF scholars have expressed concerns about these views and noted the need to raise teachers' awareness of ELF research (Blair, 2015; Dewey, 2012, 2014, 2015b; Dewey & Patsko, 2018; Mauranen, 2012; Seidlhofer, 2011; Sifakis, 2014, 2017; Sifakis & Bayyurt, 2015, 2016, 2018; Vettorel, 2016; Widdowson, 2012). However, of the studies on practitioners' attitudes, only Zacharias (2005) used mixed methods (questionnaires, interviews and classroom observations). His study of 100 tertiary-level teachers investigated beliefs about the use of teaching materials produced locally and in Anglophone countries (i.e. 'internationally published'). The study revealed a preference (86% and 87%) for materials produced in Anglophone countries.

However, several studies do provide insights into some of the underlying factors influencing positive orientations to native norms. Jenkins's (2007) questionnaire study with 326 English teachers in 12 countries, for example, highlighted the importance of preconceived stereotypes on attitudes towards English (p. 166). Unsurprisingly, respondents had positive attitudes towards 'native' accents. However, Swedish English was rated more unfamiliar than all of the non-native English accents, except Brazilian and Indian English, but more correct, acceptable and pleasant than other non-native English accents. Other studies have also highlighted the complexity of practitioners' attitudes, particularly differences in those manifested in theory and in practice. Sifakis & Sougari's (2005) questionnaire-based study of 421 Greek teachers once more revealed that attitudes are norm bound. There was a lack of awareness of English as an international language; more than 70% felt English belonged to native English speakers or to people with native English-speaker competence. However, for their own pronunciation teaching practices, the teachers revealed a need to focus more on communication, as opposed to rules and standards, when considering non-native English-speaker–non-native English-speaker communication. Teachers in this study could conceive ELF and the importance of intelligibility, but they did not consider it when teaching, preferring a native English-speaker model (Jenkins, 2007).

Similarly, Sasaki (2004, cited in Yoshikawa, 2005) found that 80% of the 97 Japanese high school English teachers surveyed recognised the necessity of touching on varieties of English in their classes, but only 7.8% did. Moreover, when these teachers did focus on variation, the emphasis was only on Inner Circle differences. Reasons included a lack of time and knowledge about World Englishes, both of which have been identified as possible barriers to GELT (Galloway & Rose, 2015). Seidlhofer and Widdowson (2003) examined essay responses to an article by House (2002), which challenged native English-speaker norms in ELT. The participants in this study were forty-eight students taking a teacher education option at the University of Vienna. The study revealed that the student-teachers' main concern was with teaching, and specifically with cultural aspects and pronunciation. Jenkins's (2007) interview study of seventeen L2 English-speaking teachers found that several claimed to support ELF pronunciation, but aimed at 'native' English themselves, and most referred to 'non-native' English as 'incorrect'. However, only two were entirely against the notion of ELF and many reasons were provided, such as pressure from government, schools and parents to teach native English, a lack of ELF pronunciation materials and teachers' traditional attachment to 'native' English. Several also thought that teachers need ELF experience to appreciate the irrelevance of the native English-speaker model for international communication, a finding that was used to prompt discussions on job recruitment sites for TESOL practitioners.

These studies highlight the complexity of attitudes, and from where they may stem. As Galloway and Rose (2015) state:

> It is not sufficient to simply state that teachers or students prefer native English, and to use this to justify the status quo. It is clear from these studies that a theory/practice divide exists. ELF is often accepted in the abstract by teachers, but rejected in the classroom. While the main and often-stated obstacle appears to be the lack of materials and research available, it is also possible that it is related to teachers' own investments in achieving native English-speaker competence, as well as a fear of replacing the status quo with something that appears to be a radical departure from the norm. (p. 189)

Cook (1999, p. 196) pointed out before the turn of the century that learners may well 'want to be native speakers', but such 'attitudes are the product of the many pressures on them to regard L2 users as failed natives'. Recent years have witnessed an increasing body of studies reporting on the positive influence that GELT instruction, language awareness and ELF experience has on attitudes.

Attitudes and the lack of support, discussed later, have also been identified as a barrier in the field of translanguaging. Weber (2014), for example, notes that there are 'major pedagogical and attitudinal obstacles' (p. 186) to implementing a more flexible multilingual education. Meier (2017), in her thematic decomposition analysis of Conteh and Meier (2014) and May (2014), both of which contain the phrase 'multilingual turn' in their title, notes that both books discuss the dominance of monolingual ideology and how there is a lack of support for practitioners in schools. Meier (2017) points out that this is based on misunderstandings (Ortega, 2014; Young, 2014), the widespread ideologically informed monolingual norm (Canagarajah, 2014; Ortega, 2014) and ingrained pedagogic and learning-theoretical traditions (García & Flores, 2014; Meier, 2014), as well as economic and political motivations (Leung, 2014; Norton, 2013), including the general acceptance of language hierarchies. There is the argument that pedagogic traditions and beliefs are largely built on a monolingual attitude, which is hard to shift (May, 2014a; Ortega, 2014; Young, 2014). This includes the native speaker myth and the language separation myth.

Previous Innovations

We are not the first to advocate the centrality of context and much has been written on the subject in the field of TESOL. Holliday (1994), for example, stresses the need to understand the innovation situation and warns against transferring methodologies from one context to another. GELT is not a new 'methodology' per se, nor is it a one-size-fits-all curriculum framework that can be transplanted from one context to another, but it is important to learn from the various studies that have been conducted on TESOL innovation, particularly with regard to communicative language teaching. 'The potential for such a mismatch has long been recognized in the TESOL literature' (Wedell, 2003, pp. 441–2) and many scholars have been critical of exporting Western methods and materials and the incompatibility of such methods and materials in contexts around the globe.

Many language curriculum change projects remain to be influenced by what Holliday (1994) calls the BANA (British, Australasian, North American) thinking (Wedell, 2003, p. 443). It is, then, no surprise that such policies can be an ill-fit for other contexts, and can even result in the expansion of BANA educational systems to non-BANA contexts. English-only policies, for example, perpetuate the monolingual orientation and require highly proficient teachers who are capable of not only teaching the subject of English but also teaching it through English. EMI policies similarly require human resources to be able to deliver highly specialised content knowledge through English, and the lack of a needs analysis for EMI provision has been criticised (Galloway et al., 2017). When BANA educational ideologies are transplanted to other contexts, this can also advantage L1 English speakers over L2 users in the adopted contexts, who may not have the necessary training in the associated methodologies. Western pedagogies are prioritised over local pedagogies, which may be better suited to the local teaching environments. A teacher's ability to use English to teach through English is prioritised over subject expertise and local knowledge.

Swan (2015) found CLT to be a major issue in some educational contexts, referring to a 'mismatch between what the student teachers have been taught, and what they have to face in their teaching environments' (p. 65). The students took exams that did not necessitate CLT and classroom time was too limited to develop communication skills, leading Swan to conclude that we should be wary about asking teachers to embrace a new teaching approach and to abandon 'practices that are part of their own educational culture, which is bound to be different to the Western cultural setting of CLT' (p. 65). This is an issue we are trying to avoid with our call for action research in Chapter 5. The topic of practitioner education will be returned to later in the chapter, and also more fully in Chapter 6, but it is important to note that GELT-related innovation places emphasis on providing practitioners with the opportunity to reflect on their own learning and teaching contexts when introducing GELT.

In Japan, Humphries and Burns (2015) looked at curriculum innovation in a school context, concluding that teachers did not have enough time to guide the students through the communicative activities or explain unfamiliar cultural issues. In Hong Kong, Carless (2004, 2007) found that secondary school English teachers experienced challenges implementing TBLT due to time, large class sizes and the mismatch with the examination system. Carless's (2009) interview study with twelve secondary school teachers and ten teacher educators in Hong Kong also found that secondary school teachers of English preferred the Presentation–Practice–Production (PPP) model, seeing TBLT as too complex. Deng and Carless's (2009) study in primary schools in mainland China, which included twelve observations and seventeen interviews, also found that activities did not reflect principles of TBLT, due to contextual factors, including examinations and teachers' limited understanding of how to implement TBLT.

It is also important to note that some studies have also been conducted with L1 English-speaking TESOL practitioners. Andon and Eckerth (2009), for example, examined the understandings of TBLT of four teachers of adult English learners using interviews and observations. The study found that they had a good sense of awareness of their own pedagogic practice and TBLT. Li and Edwards (2013) looked at the impact of a UK-based professional development programme on curriculum innovation and change in English-language education in western China, a context where much has been written about the traditional Confucian heritage culture, which values teacher-centeredness, which may seem at odds with GELT, and which promotes learner and teacher agency. They applied tenets of Roger's 'diffusion of innovation model' to examine aspects of the Chinese situation that are supportive of change and those that constrain innovation. The authors note that, while traditional pedagogical practices predominate, there is evidence of openness to experiment and a willingness to change. However, those returning to the Chinese context after overseas-based professional training adapted new approaches to their own context and did not adopt them uncritically, remaining attentive to their environmental constrictions, including the examination system, which has not kept pace with curriculum development. This highlights the importance of the notion of reinvention (Figure 4.1) for successful innovation in contexts with poor levels of resourcing, large classes, limited teacher proficiency in English and, in relation to GELT, an examination system that does not match.

Complexity

More complex innovations are clearly more problematic and, to increase the chance of GELT being adopted, we have to be wary of bombarding practitioners with new ideas and practices. Indeed, ELF researchers have always been wary of prescribing what to teach. In 2004, Seidlhofer noted that this would be 'premature' until 'certain prerequisites have been met' (Seidlhofer, 2004, p. 209) and Jenkins (2012) warns against providing 'specific pedagogic recommendations', noting that:

> ELF researchers have always been careful to point out that we do not believe it is our place to tell teachers what to do, but that it is for ELT practitioners to decide whether/to what extent ELF is relevant to their learners in their context. (p. 492)

Innovation is highly specific to institutional and contextual factors and their specific needs. In Chapter 2, we highlighted the complex nature of GELT-orientated testing. Despite arguments for change in language assessment practices, many international, standardised tests continue to focus on form for one simple reason: it is far more difficult and far more expensive to test the construct of strategic competence as opposed to the grammatical knowledge of a language. Due to this fact, high-stake tests continue to focus on prescribed English grammar, simply because they are easier to construct, cheaper to run and more systematically graded. As McNamara (2012) notes, changes to testing at this level would result in revolutionary consequences, which 'are likely to be as revolutionary as the advent of communicative language teaching some forty years ago' (p. 202). He notes, however, that such changes are necessary. Rose and Syrbe (2018) add that, even though testing Global Englishes constructs via a standardised test 'may prove more difficult, more expensive and more time-consuming, it should not detract from the importance of testing English proficiency against the "real-life" future use of the language' (p. 11).

Standardised tests do more harm than merely not capturing the appropriate constructs. Due to the power of the 'washback effect', poor fitting tests can disrupt the entire curriculum. Washback effect refers to the negative or positive impact that language testing can have on a curriculum, in terms of impacting on choices made by learners and teachers regarding what to prioritise (McKinley & Thompson, 2018). For example, if grammatical knowledge of standard language forms is likely to form the basis of important tests for learners, teachers may prioritise the teaching of such forms, even if, by doing so, they compromise other curricular goals. Thus, '[n]egative washback occurs when there may be a mismatch between the stated goals of instruction and the focus of assessment; it may lead to the abandonment of instructional goals in favour of test preparation' (McKinley & Thompson, 2018, p. 1). Testing practices are seen as a major barrier to curriculum innovation and form one of the six GELT barriers outlined by Galloway and Rose (2015).

Washback is also highly challenging to combat, as innovation in testing is difficult. Measuring test-takers on their intercultural strategic competence and their ability to use ELF, and its associated strategies, such as accommodation, in international situations may be daunting for those used to testing students on 'errors' or deviations from the 'standard' norm. It may also be time-consuming, labour intensive, costly and require an additional workload for practitioners. However, the misalignment in the curriculum caused by the focus on native norms in testing is something that urgently needs to be addressed. More research is also needed in collaboration with large-scale testing companies to address the negative washback effect on classroom practice. McKinley and Thompson (2018) offer a positive outlook on the future of testing by observing that, 'although the impact of TEIL [teaching English as an international language] in testing has yet to be seen, the impact of TEIL on testing is coming' (p. 11).

Trialability

While the GELT framework is presented within specific categories for change, not all dimensions will be relevant for all contexts, and some will likely be more important than others, depending on student needs and environmental constraints. In Chapter 7, for example, the study invited participants to comment on the proposals for change put forward by Galloway and Rose (2015), in order to consider their relevance for their own context. Students were invited to review the advantages and disadvantages, and the strengths and weaknesses, while suggesting ideas for adaptations to their local teaching contexts. Simple activities such as this allow early adopters to see GELT as being representative of options for innovation, rather than it being presented as something fixed, or in need of absolute compliance. Rogers (2003) points out that there is evidence that 'a higher degree of re-invention leads to a faster rate of adoption . . . [and] a higher degree of sustainability of an innovation' (p. 183), and, as we noted in Chapter 2, we see the curriculum evaluation process as something ongoing; once an innovation is in place, it is not a fixed entity. Rather, we wish to encourage those who introduce it to shape it and inform it continually as they integrate it into their context.

Thus, trialability is an important factor in the innovation process. *Trialability* refers to the degree to which teachers or curriculum planners are able to experiment with an innovation, in order to consider it for adoption (Rogers, 2003, p. 16). It is hoped that the increasing number of practitioners taking Global Englishes-related courses will lead to a growing community of practice interested in adopting this perspective into teaching practice. Robinson and Latchem (2003) identify two conditions necessary for new teaching methods to become established: they have to be 'proven in practice' and they should be adopted by 'a critical mass of teachers who, together, reinforce each other's beliefs, reduce the risks of innovation and eventually change the culture of teaching' (p. 239).

Observability

To 'prove' GELT, *observability* is an important factor, and, as noted above, the growing body of research that 'proves' the effectiveness of this curriculum perspective for learners today, or proves the relative advantage for the innovation, is helpful. Communities of practice will grow with the increasing presence of Global Englishes at TESOL conferences and with reported action research.

Institutional: Teachers (Qualifications, Skills, Experience, Education and Support)

Teachers are key players in the innovation process, and we recognise the importance of involving practitioners and giving them autonomy. As with McKay's (2003) notion of EIL, we draw on Canagarajah (1999), who argues that:

> If English teaching in Periphery communities is to be conducted in a socially responsible and politically empowering manner, the authority for conceiving and implementing the curriculum and pedagogy should be passed on to the local teachers themselves. (pp. 90–1)

As mentioned in Chapter 1, Canagarajah's early work inspired Galloway's (2011) first iteration of the GELT framework, so it is comforting to see calls for local teacher autonomy during innovation stretching back to this work. However, we have to be mindful of the importance of complexity in curriculum innovation, particularly since GELT requires new skills and understandings. Teachers will need time to understand GELT, and will also need support and training (Figures 4.1 and 4.2).

As noted above, Wedell (2003) criticised many of the twenty-first-century nationally planned TESOL curriculum change projects, which continue to be expressed in the same way as projects of the 1980s–90s, which assume that practitioners in diverse contexts are able to make cultural and professional adjustments to enable such changes. He adds that one of the reasons for the limited success of such projects was planners' failure to adequately consider the support that classroom teachers would need, including the time needed to make the required adjustments. It is imperative that any discussions on GELT involve the key stakeholders, as only this will ensure successful and sustained innovation. It is also important to highlight the need to give practitioners the opportunity to gain understanding of the innovation before implementation. We recognise the importance of teacher education with a study in Chapter 7, where we examine relevant studies and present our own study of the attitudes of pre- and in-service TESOL practitioners taking a GELT course within a postgraduate TESOL course.

Referring to problems encountered incorporating CLT into the Japanese school context in Japan, which again highlights the importance of examining previous innovation attempts, Humphries and Burns (2015) note that, 'if teachers gain understanding of an innovation, they can adapt it to their context in a principled manner' (p. 246). They also noted the importance of the expectations and beliefs of the teachers implementing the change, in addition to the training and ongoing support needed to 'accompany the gradual transition to new practices' (Humphries & Burns, 2015, p. 247).

Just as the global growth in EAP has led to a growing need for EAP-orientated teacher education programmes (Basturkmen & Wette, 2016), the growth in English as a lingua franca necessitates 'a need for a new kind of teacher training, one more attuned to the diverse linguistic reality of the 21st century with less prescriptive and with more context specific goals' (Nero, 2012, p. 151). Nero (2012) further claims that TESOL programmes should require courses in such topics as Global Englishes for pre-service and in-service teachers, in order to challenge their thoughts on standard English and 'correct versus incorrect' grammar. Many ELF researchers have discussed the need to work with teachers and have explored the implications of ELF for teacher education (e.g. Blair, 2015; Dewey, 2012, 2014, 2015, 2015, 2017; Seidlhofer, 2011; Sifakis, 2014; Sifakis & Bayyurt, 2015, 2018). As noted by Borg (2018), it is during teacher education that the teachers' prior expectations and professionally and personally held beliefs can be transformed, the effect of which can last throughout teachers' entire careers.

In the field of teacher education, research is varied on whether teacher education influences beliefs (for an overview of studies in the field of foreign- and second language teaching on teacher cognition and teacher education, see Borg, 2003), teacher cognition and language education in general (Borg, 2006, 2009) and on the relationship between teacher beliefs and their actions (Borg, 2018). Busch (2010), for example, who conducted a mixed methods study of the influence of an SLA course on the beliefs of 381 pre-service teachers enrolled at a Californian university over three years, found significant changes in beliefs from the course and also their experiences tutoring whilst studying. In contrast, Tang, Lee and Chun (2012) found that pre-service teachers in a TESOL programme did not always make pedagogical decisions based on TESOL concepts and theories introduced in their programme, but in ways that reflected their own experiences as students.

However, teacher education provides a direct opportunity to engage with teachers and to challenge their ideas. Dewey (2012) notes that change must come from working with teachers themselves and, along with Widdowson (2012), he notes the need for teachers to reconceptualise the notion of language. In Rose and Montakantiwong's (2018) duoethnography of experiences of teaching English as an international language in Japan and Thailand, Montakantiwong explicitly mentions teacher education as being the catalyst for change in her curriculum. Both authors describe teacher education as being the 'seed' for curricula innovation. Headway in teacher education has been made in this area, evident in such publications as Matusda (2017) that provide an overview of teacher education programmes to teach English as an international language. A number of postgraduate TESOL programmes now include Global Englishes components (Galloway, 2017b) and the University of Southampton now has an entire graduate programme on the topic.

Teacher education has also been discussed within the field of translanguaging and multilingualism. Meier (2017) notes that in both Conteh and Meier (2014) and May (2014b) the topic is discussed. Both books argue for a reconceptualisation of the teacher and propose the use of web-based and research-informed teacher resources and critical reflection on student teachers' own language ideologies, power, and status, in order that they can develop as agents of change in their multilingual classrooms (Young, 2014). It is important, however, that these courses do not merely include a superficial coverage of the topic, but offer the opportunity to gain 'a meta-understanding about EIL – its forms and histories' (Dogancay-Aktuna & Hardman, 2012, p. 103). Practitioners require more than a surface-level understanding; they require the opportunity to critically reflect on current practices and norms, in order to evaluate the relevance of Global Englishes in their own teaching contexts.

The inclusion of GELT on practitioner education programmes is also important, due to criticism of the shortcomings of ELF when it is related to pedagogy and also the ambivalence present in many practitioners' attitudes. Godó's (2014) study in Hungary, for example, found that teachers thought that ELF was a variety to replace, or threaten, standard English. Blair (2015) also found many tensions and uncertainties about such aspects as error correction and participants referred to a lack of teacher training to deal with 'new' models. There are many critics of the pedagogical implications of Global Englishes research (Kuo, 2006; Maley, 2010; Sewell, 2013) and we propose a critical approach to this topic on such courses. Courses should incorporate aspects of reflective practice to challenge the hegemony of Western TESOL programmes, encouraging student teachers to reflect and engage critically with key theories introduced on other courses, as well as to reflect on their appropriateness to their own teaching contexts. As outlined in the next chapter, we also propose that such courses should foster opportunities for action research.

Resources and Materials

A further 'barrier' to GELT identified by Galloway and Rose (2015), and an important factor when considering innovation complexity and compatibility, is the availability of GELT resources and materials (Figures 4.1 and 4.2). As Matsuda (2012, p. 169) notes, due to teachers' lack of awareness of the diversity of English, they often have to rely on current materials. However, the majority of TESOL materials currently focus on native English (Galloway, 2018b). As Chapter 6 will show, while some textbooks claim to have a global English focus, at times this is provided at a tokenistic level. GELT requires more than merely a few token 'non-native' English speakers on the accompanying audio.

A native English bias is also evident in TESOL practitioner materials (Galloway, 2018a) and, while some recent texts do at least acknowledge Global Englishes, it is unfortunate that they do not fully integrate the ideals in the rest of their books. In *A Course in English Language Teaching*, for example, Ur (2012) notes that, 'Since English is today being used for all sorts of purposes worldwide, it is important for our students to know that there is not just one "English style". There are, in fact, an enormous number of them' (p. 2).

Closer examination of this text also reveals several things/factors/content that fit well with GELT. The section on 'English as an International Language' makes reference to the fact that:

- non-native English speakers outnumber native English speakers
- English is not a 'foreign' language for the majority of learners
- English is a globally owned language
- such factors have implications for ELT

- global intelligibility, rather than a focus on native English, should be prioritised
- importance of the non-native English speaker
- non-native English-speaking teachers are in the majority, and may have better insights into the learning processes of their students and can function as good role models.

However, there is no mention of ELF research and it is unfortunate that the examples used in this book are not based on empirical research from ELF. We are also unclear why it is 'more useful to teach the spelling *organize* than *organise*' (Ur, 2012, p. 4). Further, while we agree that 'non-native speakers' can be good models, we would question whether the English spoken by them 'is also likely to be a better model of international English for their students than any "native" variety' (p. 5). As discussed in Chapter 1, GELT is not about replacing one norm with another. Teachers should be valued according to their professional qualifications, and their multilingual competence, rather than whether they are L1 or L2 English users.

Nevertheless, such texts are promising, as is the increasing body of Global Englishes texts that include practical suggestions and ideas (e. g. Alsagoff et al., 2012; Bayyurt & Akcan, 2015; Cogo & Bowles, 2015; Galloway, 2017a; Galloway & Rose, 2015; Matsuda, 2012). Matsuda (2012), for example, includes chapters on syllabi (e.g. Bayyurt & Altınmakas, 2012; Lee, 2012; Matsuda & Duran, 2012) and Matsuda and Duran (2012) include example activities for teachers, albeit with a World Englishes focus. Matsuda (2012b) focuses on evaluating teaching materials in relation to EIL, encouraging practitioners to ask questions related to the variety of English speakers presented and the cultures represented.

Alsagoff et al. (2012) cover such topics as curriculum, assessment and learning strategies from an EIL perspective. However, as discussed in Chapter 2, despite the impressive inclusion of chapters on curriculum, assessment and learner strategies, which aim to 'guide critical and informed practice and reflection in teaching, and, more importantly, to raise questions whose answers can only be discovered by teachers and learners of EIL in each of their unique contexts' (Alsagoff, 2012, p. 5), it is overly theoretical and does not offer teachers any practical suggestions for incorporating an EIL perspective into their classroom. Nor does it explore the various barriers to implementing change, or research projects directly investigating this topic (Galloway and Rose, 2015).

In McKay's (2002) *Teaching English as an International Language: Rethinking Goals and Approaches*, teaching the language is discussed only in the last chapter. Further, the first half is devoted to looking at CLT and only a small section focuses on the methodology for teaching English as an international language. Nevertheless, we agree with many of the points made by the author about the principles that should inform the pedagogy of an international language, including:

- giving the local practitioners control over how English should be taught
- placing priority on a context-sensitive methodology, as opposed to a Western-centric one
- entering learning on the needs of the students
- recognising that bilingual users of English may not necessarily want, or need, native-like competence
- learners should be taught in a way that respects the local culture of learning (p. 129).

Overall, the dominance of TESOL materials that orientate to native speaker norms is problematic and we have to acknowledge that, until the creation of more materials, many will have to create or adapt existing materials.

Of course, support mechanisms are also needed and institutions would benefit from a collaborative atmosphere. Bayyurt and Sifakis (2017, p. 11) warn that unassisted innovation requires a 'substantial amount of autonomy and maturity', thus collaboration with other teachers (in groups, or under the mentorship of more experienced teachers) can help in the development of EIL-aware lessons. Recent studies have shown that collaborative reflective practice, in particular, can aid teachers in 'jointly constructing new meanings about their practice' (Burhan-Horasanlı & Ortaçtepe, 2016, p. 380). Thus, this brings us back to the importance of the user system (Figures 4.1 and 4.2) influencing change. School culture may prohibit and facilitate innovative practices.

Reporting on Innovation via Communication Channels

Our figures (Figures 4.1 and 4.2) outline the different people involved in the innovation process, in terms of when they adopt the innovation, borrowing from Roger's (2003) terminology: the innovators; the early adopters; the early majority; the late majority; and laggards. People will vary in the innovation-decision period, and methods used for reporting practice by these people may vary, which is discussed further in Chapter 5. The innovators may be more likely to report ideas in conceptual pieces, or via analysis of the relative advantage of the innovation. The early adopters are more likely to report on implementation via experimental methods, or action research. Once an innovation reaches a stage where there is an early and late majority, more comparative work can be carried out. Teachers are the glue to ensure an innovation sticks and, thus, GELT treats them as important autonomous agents for change in the innovation process. The role of teachers, therefore, is essential in communicating innovations with each other.

Conclusion

This chapter has shown that in order to achieve macro-level change in TESOL, it is important to recognise that the implementation of curriculum innovation is complex in itself and even more so with regard to GELT. The process has to be planned properly and planners have to take into account various factors that may influence successful implementation. Careful consideration of the various factors outlined in this chapter will enhance the potential for successful and sustained long-term innovation. It is also crucial not to alienate experienced teachers by telling them that their current teaching practices are irrelevant and out of date. By giving adequate consideration to these factors, and also the context within which they are working, we aim to reduce the possibility of practitioners being resistant to change.

GELT aims for a bottom-up approach to curricular innovation that values both teacher and learner agency in the curriculum innovation process. However, we do not wish to be idealistic and recognise that change will require time and support. It is further important that calls for change are grounded in classroom-based research, and are not merely based on theoretical arguments. In order to bridge a theory–practice divide, we call for more research carried out by practitioners, so that on-the-ground innovative practices can feed back to our knowledge of how Global Englishes is best integrated into various curriculums and contexts.

Part I Conclusion

This concludes Part I of this book, which has laid a foundation for Global Englishes for language teaching, including an overview of its theoretical foundations, pedagogical implications and pathways to innovation. Chapter 1 collated relevant literature in applied linguistics in order to show that calls for change in TESOL practices are emerging from a variety of interrelated fields. These calls have emerged from the rapidly changing sociopolitical landscape of English use around the world. We have shown how World Englishes scholars have lobbied for more inclusivity of global varieties of English for decades (e.g. Kachru, 1990). We have shown how ELF scholars (e.g. Seidlhofer, 2001) seek to challenge native speaker hegemony in TESOL in order to prepare learners to use the language in fluid lingua franca settings that are not be bound by native speaker norms. We have shown how critical applied linguists (e.g. Canagarajah, 2007, 2016; Pennycook, 2010) challenge the very foundations of our views of the English language, and how it is used in today's global society but a global community. Translanguaging research has challenged the linguistic boundaries between languages and their use in multilingual contexts. We have further shown in Chapter 3 how SLA researchers (e.g. May, 2014c) are challenging the prevailing monolingual orientation to SLA theory by calling for a multilingual turn, which has clear implications for TESOL (e.g. Canagarajah, 2014; Leung, 2014; Norton, 2014).

It is clear that English has a complicated relationship with globalisation and has emerged as the world's foremost lingua franca. Further, it is clear that so-called second and foreign-language users of English have outnumbered L1 users of English for some time – a position likely to strengthen in the future as L2 users of the language continue to grow in numbers.

By taking a curriculum perspective, as outlined in Chapter 2, we have teased apart the various facets of English language teaching practice that are in need of innovation. This perspective has shown that as the needs of our learners have changed, so too must the other elements in order that the curriculum is properly aligned. In order to match learners' needs to use English as a global language, we may need to reconsider our curriculum objectives, syllabus design, assessment and evaluation practices, and possibly even our teaching methods. However, students in global contexts have vastly different needs depending on their future use of the language; thus, innovation is complex and likely to be highly context-dependent. In order to achieve macro-level change in TESOL, it is important to recognise that the implementation of curriculum innovation is complex in itself and even more so with regard to GELT.

Chapter 4 furthers the discussion of curriculum innovation, exploring the multiple facets of the process, as well as the potential barriers that can cause institutions to reject innovation. Central to this process is for innovators and early adopters to report on their innovations so that this knowledge can feed back into the innovation cycle. Thus, in order to stimulate widespread GELT innovation, we call for more research carried out by practitioners or researchers who work very closely with practitioners. This leads us to the second part of the book, which outlines research directions in GELT, and is accompanied by three example empirical studies.

Part II

Researching Global Englishes for Language Teaching

5 Research Implications for GELT

Part II of this book takes a departure from the theories underpinning, and issues surrounding, a Global Englishes approach for language teaching. Part II turns to Global Englishes-informed pedagogic research by showing how the GELT framework can be applied to empirical studies. The previous chapter outlined a number of barriers to implementing Global Englishes into language teaching, many of which stem from a need to investigate: the relative advantage of a GELT pedagogy; the processes of incorporating pedagogical innovation into diverse educational contexts; and the successes and failures of GELT innovation. In order to gather evidence of what good GELT pedagogy should look like, there is an urgent need for research on Global Englishes in practice, so we are able to learn from early adopters. In short, there is a need for practice-based research, in order to better understand what GELT looks like in practice. This can complement the growing amount of theory-led research, which builds on our conceptual understandings of the various facets of GELT, and lays the foundation for understanding its relative advantage over current teaching approaches. The researcher–practitioner is in the ideal position to conduct future research.

Therefore, this chapter examines pathways forward for researchers and researcher–practitioners to examine the applications of Global Englishes within language learning contexts. It first examines calls for research, which have emerged from the literature explored in the first part of this book. It then examines the necessary research methodologies for addressing these gaps. Finally, the chapter outlines previous and current research projects occurring within GELT, in order to illustrate the types of research that are driving the field forward. This chapter also acts as a segue to the next three chapters in Part II, which provide examples of original research on Global Englishes in classroom materials (Chapter 6), teacher education programmes (Chapter 7) and English-medium classrooms (Chapter 8).

Calls for Further Research

It is impossible to compile a complete list of all calls for research in the expansive field of Global Englishes, as the umbrella term covers topics as diverse as linguistics (exploring morphosyntactic and phonological diversity in English), sociolinguistics (exploring a language in use, including societal beliefs about English), second language acquisition (exploring a language that is acquired and learned in increasingly diverse contexts and for increasingly diverse purposes) and TESOL (exploring pedagogical implications of the spread of English). Nevertheless, when confined to implications for language teaching, there are a few topics that emerge as key areas of research interest. While not exhaustive in coverage, we posit six areas in need of urgent review.

Classroom-Based Research on Implementing GELT Innovations

The first call for research involves a need for classroom-based research into the implementation of GELT innovations into language curricula. While some work has been done (see Galloway, 2011, 2013, 2017a; Galloway & Rose, 2014, 2018; Rose & Galloway, 2017; Shim, 2002; Sung, 2014c, 2018), more is needed. In one of the three studies reported by Shim (2002), twenty-seven students in the researcher's own class were exposed to World Englishes through TV (a programme called *Crossroads Café*). Effects were somewhat unpronounced with twenty-three wanting an internationally accepted teaching model (although this is not fully explained in the article, nor are benchmarks of attitudes before the exposure was properly reported in order to understand change). However, all twenty-seven participants felt a need to understand non-native English speakers, and all twenty-seven stated they would be willing to participate in an ELT programme that introduced non-native English speakers. Further work is needed on the exposure of varieties of English in the classroom, including more stringent measures of attitudes and measures of change before and after exposure.

In Galloway's studies (2011, 2013, 2017a), she reports on the creation and implementation of a specialised Global Englishes course at a Japanese university. The course included a number of activities surrounding Global Englishes topics, including ELF, variation in English and standard language ideology. In addition to questionnaires and interviews, she used focus groups with students, and pre- and post-course questionnaires to examine changes in attitudes to the issues surrounding the spread of English as a global language. She used a comparison group of students studying a module on tourism, which revealed a significant broadening of the Global Englishes students' views towards English, including raised confidence in students' self-identity as English users.

In Galloway and Rose (2014) listening journals were used with 108 students in Galloway's own English classes at a Japanese university. The journals were attached to an activity that exposed learners to samples of self-selected varieties of English or samples of ELF interactions, by having them reflect on their reasons for choosing the sample, and their reactions to it. We found that, while the listening journals raised awareness of variation in English, the superficial nature of the task also reinforced stereotypes in some students and saw them see some non-standard varieties as 'strange' compared to the models they had received in class. While this activity was more prolonged and student-centred than the one used in Shim (2002), and collected a richer set of attitudinal data, it, nevertheless, suffers from a lack of a stringent measure of attitudinal change; hence, the long-term effects of the type of superficial exposure remain unknown.

In response to our first article on listening journals, Sung (2014c) called for more research on how to incorporate Global Englishes into ELT, which he responded to in his own pilot study involving the incorporation of a range of Global Englishes-orientated activities into a course in Hong Kong, in which twenty-five students from different disciplines had enrolled. Tasks included a discussion on standard language ideology, a listening task that involves listening to Chinese accents of English, an accent identification task involving different accents of English from Kirkpatrick's World Englishes (2007); a comprehension task on understanding global English, and a group discussion on ELF communication. We responded to Sung's call in agreement 'that such work is needed to help practitioners raise learners' awareness of the diversity of English and prepare them to use English in lingua franca contexts' (Galloway & Rose, 2018, p. 1).

Answering Sung's (2014c) call, we further reported on data from the same teaching context as our 2014 study in two separate studies (Galloway and Rose, 2018; Rose & Galloway, 2017). In the first study, we used a presentation task to have students select a single English-using community and research the Englishes used within the community to better understand the sociolinguistic forces that shaped them (Galloway & Rose, 2018). This task saw students engage with the English variation at a deeper level, and to present their findings and reflections to their peers, further creating an opportunity to discuss a diverse range of Englishes. This task yielded more positive results than our 2014 study, with many students reporting positive viewpoints on non-standard Englishes in their reflection papers. The study also reported that the task had an added benefit of eliciting some interesting post-presentation discussions on language norms. In Rose and Galloway (2017) we reported on a classroom activity, where students in the same context engaged in a debate over standard language, using the Singaporean Speak Good English Movement as a case study (for academic debates surrounding this movement, see Bokhorst-Heng, 2005; Lim et al., 2010; Rubdy, 2001). Other work has recently emerged from Sung (2018), where he reports on an out-of-class activity requiring Hong Kong learners to engage in ELF communication. Sung analysed students written reflection, which was similar to the methodology of our 2018 study on presentations, in order to elicit students' unprompted reactions to the experience. The author concludes that the activity raised student awareness and critical consciousness of the use of English as a global language.

Despite consistent calls for pedagogically situated research, little has been done beyond the studies described above. Apart from Galloway's longitudinal study (2011, 2013, 2017a) and Marlina's (2018) study of an EIL programme at a university in Australia, research has been confined to a single classroom context or a single activity, rather than examining the implications of wide-sweeping innovations throughout a language curriculum.

There is also a notable lack of pedagogy-focused research emerging from the ELF paradigm, where there are continued calls for more ELF-aware language teaching, accompanied by an imbalance of pedagogical research. Except for a handful of classroom-based ELF studies (e.g. Baker, 2009, 2012b; Sung 2017; Vettorel, 2013), we have a paucity of research into what ELF innovation in classrooms looks like. A recent example is the *Routledge Handbook of English as a Lingua Franca*. While there is one chapter in the handbook dedicated to the topic of teaching, even this focuses on teacher education rather than actual classroom practices. Thus, we call for more ELF classroom-based work in the vein of Baker's and Vettorel's, more EIL research in the vein of Marlina's (2018) and more Global Englishes work in the vein of Galloway (e.g. 2017a), in order to better understand on-the-ground challenges of GELT innovation. The previous chapter highlighted the necessity for early adopters of an innovation to report on their practices, in order for the innovation to be adopted more widely. This classroom-based research is essential for the innovation process.

ELT Teaching Materials Research

A lack of materials has been noted by numerous researchers in the past as a major barrier to implementing change in language teaching classrooms (see previous chapter for discussion). ELT materials play a crucial role in not only dictating teaching input, but also in structuring a syllabus, and even suggesting appropriate teaching approaches. Thus, they are a core part of a language programme and the learning and teaching process (McDonough et al., 2013).

As ELT materials remain undoubtedly orientated around Inner Circle norms (Galloway 2017a, 2018a; Jenkins, 2012), research is needed to understand how Global Englishes can be integrated into them. Research work has begun to investigate the linguistic, sociolinguistic and cultural norms that current materials communicate to learners, in order to highlight what needs to be changed (Galloway, 2018a; Vettorel, 2018). Research into what materials are used, and what they communicate about norms, is needed to ensure that twenty-first-century ELT is effective in preparing learners to use English in global contexts (Galloway, 2018a). While some research has been conducted in terms of investigating the linguistic and cultural diversity presented in textbooks (Chan, 2014; Syrbe, 2017; Syrbe & Rose, 2018; Tajeddin & Teimournezhad, 2015), there is a dearth of published studies of materials research (see Chapter 6, this volume, for an overview). Considering the vital role that ELT materials play, we simply need more research into materials evaluation and analysis on how key GELT constructs (the target interlocutors, role models, norms, cultures, ELF strategies) are construed in textbooks.

The next step after this would be to begin to investigate what Global Englishes materials look like, and their effects on learners and the learning process. Currently, many GELT materials are 'home-grown' in-house materials used additively to the curriculum, and are not made widely available in the public domain. An exception is the materials in the appendix of Galloway (2017a) and on the companion website of Galloway and Rose (2015), although the latter are not aimed specifically at the language learner, and are not part of a uniform curriculum.

Leading on from the creation of new materials is the need for reporting on their development and implementation. While some frameworks have been proposed (e.g. Galloway, 2018a), but more work is needed to trial them with a range of materials. Many authorities in materials development have noted a need for materials to better reflect Global Englishes constructs. *Materials and Methods in ELT: A Teacher's Guide* (McDonough et al., 2013, p. 48) explicitly comments on the global spread of English, pointing out that World Englishes and English as a lingua franca see a need for teachers 'to be able to evaluate, and adapt and develop, their own approaches in the form of principled materials based on their own judgement and experience'. Similarly, *Teaching Materials and the Roles of EFL/ESL Teachers: Practice and Theory* (McGrath, 2013) states it is difficult to justify the use of textbooks that orientate learners towards specific native speakers and Inner Circle cultures, when used in contexts where learners will use English predominantly outside such contexts and with other L2 speakers. The book also states that it is unclear how to translate calls for exposure to a diverse range of models into materials development, but encourages publishers to 'dare to be different?' (p. 198). Chapter 6 evaluates some textbooks that claim to be different, and we compare these alongside some examples of general English textbooks and business English textbooks to evaluate whether there is substance in these claims. While Chapter 6 presents GELT-informed materials research, its main aim is to provide a model for further research into both commercial and novel teaching materials.

An Examination of the English in English Medium Instruction

A third area of much needed research is the role of teaching English language in emerging contexts where it is being used as an academic lingua franca.

English as a medium instruction is in a state of boom, as evidenced from the oft-cited statistics on the growing number of English-taught programmes in Europe that show a 1,115% increase in English-taught programmes in Europe from 2001 to 2014 (Wächter & Maiworm, 2014), with particularly pronounced growth at the taught Masters level (Brenn-White & Faethe, 2013). While much research attention on EMI has focused on Europe, the EMI boom is also occurring across the globe, with noted growth throughout East Asia and South-East Asia: 'Now, English as a "medium" of instruction (EMI) (as opposed to English as an "object" of instruction) is becoming a new "normal", and a key site for this change is higher education, and nowhere more so than in the Asia-Pacific' (Walkinshaw et al., 2017, p. 2). Such trends raise questions about norms in EMI and the need to reconceptualise the 'E' in EMI (Galloway et al., 2017).

Links to English as a lingua franca are clearly relevant in a context where English has become a lingua franca in an academic setting; however much ELF work has centred on an analysis of a language in use in academic settings (e.g. ELFA corpus), rather than as a language being learned. This may be due to the fact that much ELF research has occurred in Europe, where English-language proficiency tends to be much higher, and the switch to English as a medium instruction has occurred independent of trends in English language teaching. In many Northern and Western European contexts, EMI has occurred as a result of internationalising higher education in response to catering for a mobile student population in need of a lingua franca of education. As most academic sources are in English – more than 90% according to some sources (Montgomery, 2013) – English seemed to be the logical choice. In other Expanding Circle contexts, English proficiency tends to be lower, so movements towards EMI are not independent of English-language learning aims. For example, while Swedish students may not feel that learning in English affects their ability to understand content matter (Airey, 2011), less than a third of Korean students studying through EMI feel that they can understand 80% of the subject matter (Kim, 2017). Thus, EMI puts demands on students, particularly if Inner Circle standards are enforced.

In EMI contexts emerging in the Middle East and East Asia, English language teaching still clearly needs to play a central role to models of EMI (see Chapter 8, this volume). Thus, language teaching in these contexts warrants a lot more attention, in terms of how ELT meets its goal of facilitating learners to use English as an academic lingua franca for the purposes of subject-specific study. EMI students are, by definition, those who are most likely to go on to use English in global contexts, being the business leaders, engineers, medical personal and scientists of a global marketplace, and, thus, GELT seems intensely relevant.

Currently, EMI is under-researched, and there have been recent calls for an examination of the challenges faced by students in EMI contexts (see Macaro et al., 2018). A GELT perspective can add to this research agenda by calling for more research on the 'E' in 'English medium instruction' – that is:

1. What English is used in EMI? (An opportunity to explore language variation in EMI.)
2. How is English being used alongside other local languages? (An opportunity to explore fluidity and translanguaging in EMI.)
3. How can English-language curriculum better prepare students to use English as an academic lingua franca? (An opportunity to explore the nexus of TESOL and EMI.)

These are ambitious questions that cannot be answered by a single study, but create an opportunity for context-specific case studies, in order to fully comprehend the impact of EMI on language development through a Global Englishes lens. As Galloway (2017a) notes:

> With the global spread of English medium instruction (EMI) in Higher Education institutes in non-Anglophone contexts and the lowering of the age for English instruction in many contexts, there is an ever-increasing demand for ELT practitioners . . . The mismatch between the languages taught in the classroom and the increasing evidence of how it functions in real life calls for an urgent need for a critical examination of ELT. The monolingual approach does not permit the use of ELF strategies or translanguaging and anything that deviates from the 'standard' is seen as a sign of a lack of proficiency. (p. xiv)

Chapter 8 introduces some research in this vein and presents data on attitudes towards deviations from language norms within several EMI programmes in Chinese and Japanese universities.

Learner and Teacher Attitudes Towards Global Englishes

Attitudes are an area that has been explored quite thoroughly through a World Englishes lens, but there is a need to re-examine attitudes via new ideas that have emerged in the multilingual turn. Traditionally, studies that explore attitudes towards variation and diversity in English have opted for indirect or direct measures. Examples of indirect measures have included widely used verbal guise and matched guise techniques. These measures involve participants listening to samples of speech in different language dialects. While the former technique uses the same speaker, who adopts different accents (or guises) to minimise confounding variables, the latter uses different speakers to increase authenticity (for further discussion of these techniques, see Galloway & Rose, 2015). An example of a direct measure is perceptual dialectology, which involves rating languages without having any exposure to them and, thus, examining 'people's (more conscious) beliefs about language use' (Jenkins, 2007, p. 75). The technique sometimes makes use of detailed maps for participants to mark out speech zones and record their perceptions of accents within each zone. This technique was also used in Galloway's (2011, 2013, 2017a) studies.

Global Englishes sees measures that encourage hard boundaries around 'varieties' as problematic for researching attitudes in the twenty-first century, where populations are mobile, and geographic boundaries no longer accurately dictate the way English is used within and across historical speech communities. These ideas are also incompatible with research in the multilingual turn, which calls for a reconceptualisation of the relationship between languages and language varieties. We have previously argued that the field needs to move beyond geographic descriptions of language, which constrain much World Englishes research (Galloway and Rose, 2015), echoing the opinions of other Global Englishes scholars (e.g. Pennycook, 2010).

How, then, do we better examine attitudes towards diversity in English, as well as answering the more important question of where attitudes come from? A Global Englishes research highlights a need to investigate how attitudes are formed, as this is essential to understand how innovations in the curriculum can change them. Galloway's (2011, 2013, 2017a) study was seminal in using in-depth qualitative techniques to more fully understand learners' attitudes in Japan. She was one of the first researchers to apply focus groups to explore attitudes to English as social constructed, rather than individual manifested. Focus groups allowed the participants to discuss attitudes within their peer groups, which more accurately reflects how attitudes are formed and solidified. Attitudes do not emerge in a vacuum but are created in social circles, of which peers are an important part. Galloway's study also applied a quasi-experimental design as a means to examine how attitudes can, if at all, be influenced by the English-language curriculum. Thus, this study not only examined what attitudes were, but how they are formed, and how they can be changed. Future GELT research needs to explore this more complex view of learner attitudes. In order to fill the gap created by the departure from matched and verbal guise techniques, new instruments to measure attitudes need to be developed. These instruments should transcend static depictions of varieties, and tap into speakers' underlying openness for variation in general.

If engaged in GELT-like practices, such as those reported in Galloway (2011, 2013, 2017a), quantitative attitude measures could be used in a pretest/post-test design to examine the effects of GELT on learner attitudes. Such measures could also be used to compare the orientations of learners in different contexts to examine whether proficiency, context or teaching and learning experiences have an effect on learner attitudes. However, in order to fully understand attitudes, questionnaire measures should not be used in isolation. In-depth qualitative measures, such as focus groups, learner diaries and written reflection, are much more powerful in providing a more nuanced understanding of the complexities of attitudes. Instruments will be discussed later in this chapter.

Students' Specific Needs in a Global World

Building on from Chapter 2, we also see a need to explore the needs of students learning English for use in global contexts. When conducting needs analysis, it is important to consider who to involve, the purpose of the needs analysis and how to carry it out. Those involved may include the target group, the audience, the needs analysts and the resource group (Brown, 1995). The target group for GELT may not be all learners. GELT, as a type of ESP, is intended for the specific purposes of use in global domains, where linguistic speech communities meet, and linguistic boundaries blur. Needs analysis is essential, informed by the type of rich research from which other realms of ESP have benefited.

An ideal needs analysis team for GELT should include all stakeholders involved: Global Englishes researchers have an important voice, yet it is practitioners who are working in the classroom, the learners whom they teach and the graduates who enter global communities who are in the best position to understand these needs. A lot of approaches to needs analysis stem from Munby's (1978) needs analysis model; however, current approaches are largely flexible in design, seeking knowledge of needs from all available sources. Richterich and Chancerel's (1977) approach was also influential in identifying the gap between what students can currently do and what they need to know. Much ESP needs analysis centres on identifying the gaps between current abilities and students' needs and wants, thus moving away from just studying the situation and producing long lists of language items.

While traditionally surveys and studies of corpora to identify domain-specific vocabulary have been used, other approaches include interviews and observations. Swales (1985b, p. 219) advocated early on for an ethnographic approach in ESP, for example, by going into target communities in order to identify the language used. This tradition has continued to the present day with scholars like Starfield (2016) calling for a richer exploration using multiple methods:

> These draw on insider understandings and triangulate multiple perspectives through observation, in-depth interviewing and other forms of data collection (see, for example, Bosher and Smalkoski, 2002), although, as Cowling (2007) points out, real-world constraints, such as limited time, often complicate the carrying out of more in-depth observation. (p. 154)

Starfield (2016) argues that researchers should be encouraged to collect data in the workplaces into which their students are likely to go after graduation, and to use multiple methods to collect data on the language the students will likely need. As an example, she highlights Handford and Matous's (2011) study at a Hong Kong construction site, which combined a corpus-style analysis of spoken discourse used at the site with ethnographic observation. She also illustrates her point with Gimenez's (2014) study of the multi-communication practices in four multinational corporations, via a number of ethnographically orientated methods.

Curriculum designers who want to incorporate GELT into their syllabus, then, need to venture out in the social realms where their students are likely to use English to more deeply understand how they will use English in the future. Here, a lot of groundwork has been carried out by ELF researchers, who have, by and large, focused on exploring how English is being used as a lingua franca in a range of settings. Business English as a lingua franca is a good example, which has been accompanied by recent research (e.g. Kankaanranta & Louhiala-Salminen, 2007, 2010; Kankaanranta & Planken, 2010; Louhiala-Salminen et al., 2005). Such research has focused on the use of English in a range of business settings, so their work may be highly relevant to needs analysts of business-focused ESP courses. However, one caveat is that much ELF corpus-based work shows ELF to be highly variable, making it difficult to apply to the pedagogical purposes of needs analysis. Thus, it is questionable how much of ELF research findings can be used to directly inform classroom practice, where needs of students differ from context to context. For example, ELF research based on European speakers in a multinational corporation in Europe may prove to be of little relevance to learners who aim to use English in multinational corporations in China. Thus, specific examination of needs is essential, as a one-size-fits-all model is likely to be an ill-fit for most.

Global Englishes in Teacher Education

A further area of needed research is in the realm of teacher education, discussed further in Chapter 7. As the previous chapter has illustrated, teacher education is described as being both a barrier, due to a professional resistance to change, and a catalyst for innovation when those in charge embrace Global Englishes ideology. While there are positive movements in the field, such as those reported in Matsuda (2017), many scholars lobby for more change (e.g. Nero, 2012), while others argue that change must come from teachers themselves, in joint consultation with new ideas for innovation (e.g. Dewey, 2012).

While the pace and amount of change needed in teacher training is somewhat context-dependent, it is important for teacher educators to have a clear understanding of what GELT-informed teacher education could look like. The 2017 edited book by Matsuda (2017) offers considerable headway into teacher education, with its collection of narratives from researchers working around the world, who report on their own incorporation of EIL ideology into in-service and pre-service teacher training programmes. There is a clear worth in reporting on innovations vis-à-vis the thick descriptions of programmes in Mora & Golovátina-Mora (2017), Galloway (2017b), Selvi (2017), Rose (2017) and Vettorel and Lopriore (2017). These descriptions help to communicate to other teacher educators the state of the art practices occurring globally, as teacher education programmes, courses and units turn to more Global Englishes content.

However, while books such as Matsuda's help to disseminate teacher education practices, it is also important that research monitors the impact of such change on teacher beliefs, teacher attitudes and teacher practices. Even if global perspectives are integrated into existing programmes, this does not mean these ideas will be adopted by teachers or will manifest as change in the classroom. Thus, the field also needs research into the implications of these programmes on the teachers themselves and on their pedagogies. Hino (2017) conducted some work in this vein, observing the teaching practices of two alumni of his EIL course, and conducting interviews with them. This small amount of data collection revealed that 'the graduate class helped them, among other things, to be aware of the legitimacy of showing the teachers' own non-native English to the students as one possible model' (p. 95), and gave the teachers confidence as so-called non-native teachers of the language.

Hino's observation was not part of a structured study and, therefore, only serves as anecdotal evidence that teacher education of Global Englishes can affect actual change. One area of further research would be to examine in what ways Global Englishes content in teacher education programmes result in a change in teacher cognition (i.e. the attitudes or beliefs of teachers, which underpin and inform their pedagogical practices). A second area of research could further investigate whether Global Englishes content in teacher training programmes leads to real innovation at the classroom level, such as the incorporation of Global Englishes constructs into taught syllabi.

A potential study, therefore, could measure the attitudes towards (and awareness of) Global Englishes before and after the teacher education course. If a change in attitudes is evident, the course could be said to influence teacher cognition. An extension of this study could include an investigation of whether this change in teacher cognition manifests into future classroom practices. Chapter 7 aims to investigate the first part of this research gap in an investigation of a Global Englishes course in a TESOL master's programme at the University of Edinburgh.

Identity

There is a further need for research at the nexus of the English-language curriculum and global migration, particularly looking at issues connected to identity and transculturalism. As Guo & Maitra (2017) note:

> A transnational and transcultural framework would align curricula with the shifting ideas of culture, language and identity. By going beyond the "border-centered" conceptualization of culture, language and identity, such a framework would move the curriculum from a "mere celebration of differences" toward an understanding of how, within transnational and transcultural social spaces and, despite their mobile identities, migrants remain implicated within unequal power relations of gender, race, ethnicity, class and occupy a range of dominating and dominated positions. (p. 88)

They further argue that curriculum innovation 'will nurture students toward becoming well-informed, engaged, cosmopolitan citizens dedicated to the cause of building a just and equitable world order' (Guo & Maitra, 2017, p. 88). GELT also aims to create a democratic space for learners to reflect on dominant discourses and stereotyping and injustice.

Further, Rizvi and Beech (2017) also note that, today, 'students (and teachers) are involved in everyday experiences of cosmopolitan encounters and that these can, and should, be used as a starting point for the development of a cosmopolitan curriculum aimed at steering the cosmopolitan outlook of students towards morally open but productive directions' (p. 125). The authors observe that global mobility has changed people's sense of local communities and identities, because

> they bring diverse cultural traditions and practices into contact with each other as never before, both within and across national borders. Such contact of course creates a range of new challenges for living together, giving rise to a new politics of difference that is often globally stretched. (p. 125)

Such ideas very much resonate with Global Englishes, which also explores the implications on the language of a mobile global community. Transnationalism, however, makes an important point, in that language is so inexplicably intertwined with identity and cultural politics that these topics are in need of research, in terms of their positioning within the curriculum and in curricular research. Thus, future research could explore the implications of topics such as transnationalism and cosmopolitanism within a GELT curriculum, as these fields also problematise the traditional nation-centric notions of identity and citizenship (Thiel & Friedman, 2016).

Native Speakerism

Finally, there is a need for different research within the study of native speakerism within English language teaching – which is already a thriving area of research in itself. However, future research in this area needs to stop comparing two groups based on the 'native' dichotomy of 'native' versus 'non-native' speakers. As Holliday (2015) notes:

> The terms have become commonplace in the field and we use them without thinking and all the research that is done on comparing the two types of teachers just reinforces the terms and suggests that there is a difference. There is nothing to prove; nobody would think of doing research about the value of the 'native speaker'. (p. 18)

Future research needs to take a postmodern view in exploring ideological and discoursal underpinnings of native speakerism and the terms associated with it, rather than taking a differences perspective (Holliday, 2015).

A Framework for GELT Research

The second part of this chapter explores the frameworks necessary to research Global Englishes for Language Teaching. While we have already posited GELT as a framework for teaching in this book, as well as a framework for innovation in our previously published research (Galloway, 2011, 2013, 2017a; Galloway & Rose, 2013, 2014,2015, 2018; Syrbe & Rose, 2018), we need some discussion on how constructs can be operationalised for the purposes of data collection and analysis.

Operationalising GELT as a Quantitative Research Measure

If 'GELT' and 'traditional ELT' are positioned as labels at either end of a continuum, the various constructs of the GELT framework can be operationalised so that they can produce data for quantitative analysis. Syrbe (2017) has done some groundwork in this regard, with her analysis of ELT textbooks, which she analysed via the GELT framework. An important conclusion Syrbe (2017) drew from her analysis is that evaluations made through the GELT framework should be done so on a continuum, rather than in distinct dichotomous categories, and this is in keeping with our suggestion. Syrbe (2017) argues that 'a move away from this dichotomy and towards an approach that conceptualises the relationship between the two approaches along several scales seems more appropriate'. She offers a framework in order to measure five facets of textbooks on a five-point scale. She further recommends that measurements be conducted on a five-point scale, with descriptions of items at each point (see Figure 5.1 for a sample item). This framework should be

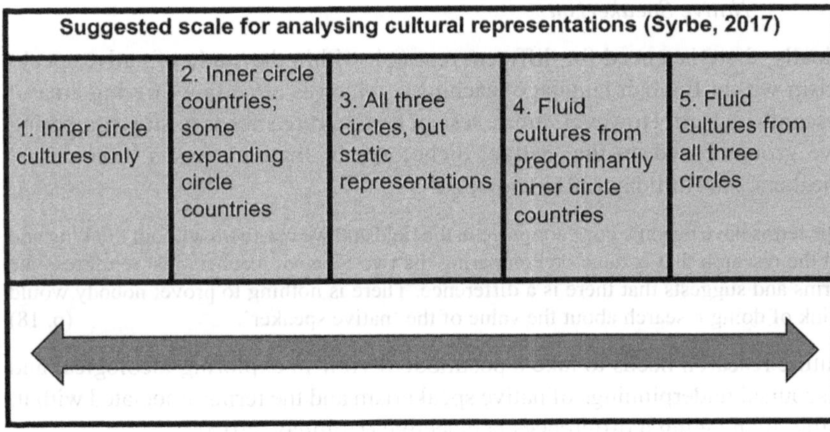

Figure 5.1 A GELT construct operationalised on an ordinal scale (Syrbe, 2017).

commended on a conceptual level but falls short in terms of being a truly usable framework for quantitative analysis.

While this results in an easy-to-use framework for teachers, it is more problematic as a framework for researchers. The recommended scale is on an ordinal scale, rather than a nominal scale, which would exclude opportunities to analyse continuous data via parametric tests, should one wish to use the framework in such a way. Additionally, the scale labels are somewhat arbitrary, and one might argue that point three on the scale is not in an ordinal position to point four on the scale, and, thus, produces categorical data. Nevertheless, the point Syrbe (2017) makes remains important: the labels used within GELT should not be seen as dichotomous, but as a means to measure movement *away* from traditional models of ELT *towards* global-orientated models.

Although not explicit in our 2015 description of GELT, we have always conceptualised the framework labels as being at either end of a continuum, with descriptions of traditional ELT at one end and GELT at the other. We never intended the GELT framework to be perceived as a 'one-or-the-other' description of language teaching (while this was always our intention, it may not have been communicated effectively in our arrangement of the paradigm into a two-columned table). Figure 5.2 reimagines the cultural dimension of GELT on such a scale. Even from a pedagogical point of view, rarely would practices fall neatly within either description in a black-and-white manner. That is, many practices could loosely be placed within a 'grey' area. Practices embodying a traditional approach might still prepare students to use English as a global language in a small way. Similarly, some of the practices that embody a global

How are cultures positioned in the curriculum?		
Traditional ELT	Scale	GELT
1. Static native English cultures	←--→	5. Fluid, diverse cultures

Figure 5.2 A GELT construct operationalised on a nominal scale.

approach to ELT might still incorporate some traditional ideologies. Thus, when conceptualised as a continuum, we are better able to report on where an observed, or reported, practice lies on the spectrum.

Operationalising GELT as a Qualitative Research Measure

The GELT framework can also be developed to create qualitative measures used to explore various orientations within the English-language curriculum, or the learners and teachers themselves. Galloway (2017a), for example, used concepts from GELT to construct her focus group prompts in her investigation of learner attitudes in a university in Japan. The constructs were also used to help organise and inform her qualitative data analysis.

A recent study by McKinley (2018) used constructs from an adapted GELT framework to review three language-related programmes in Japan. First, using interviews with lecturers and observation data, he used constructs from GELT to deductively code data, looking for examples of reported and observed practices within each construct. While the data was reported thematically in a tradition typical of content analysis, he also qualitatively summarised the data according to whether aspects of GELT were present in the curricula of the three programmes. He used symbols to condense a lot of qualitative data in his cross-examination of the programmes: a tick indicating the construct was present; a cross indicating that the item was not present; and a triangle indicating some elements of the construct were present. An example is provided in Table 5.1. While reductive in presentation, the study explored each element in greater detail in its findings. This table importantly highlights the GELT framework to be linear, rather than dichotomous, in nature.

Table 5.1 *A cross-tabulation of summarised qualitative data using GELT-inspired coding (adapted from McKinley, 2018, p. 245)*

Did the curriculum value:	Program A	Program B	Program C
a difference perspective?	✗	✗/ ✓	✗/ ✓
a movement away from a monolingual bias?	✗/ ✓	✗	✗
code switching and mixing as a resource?	✗	✗	✗
L2 target interlocutors/cultures?	✓	✓	✓
both NESTs and NNESTs?	✗	✗/ ✓	✗/ ✓
L2 English-using role models?	✗	✓	✓
the first culture and language as resource?	✗/ ✓	✗	✗

GELT Research Methodologies

Research methods span topics and disciplines, thus it is impossible to provide an overview of all appropriate research methodologies that could be used to conduct GELT research. However, in terms of our call for research in the first half of this chapter, we see clear opportunities for needed types of research: action research, field research, corpus studies, attitudinal surveys and content analyses of curriculum-related documents. Further, just as the multilingual turn has necessitated the need to explore new and alternative research methods (Meier, 2017; Ortega, 2014), so, too, does GELT.

Action Research

Reflecting on the last paradigm shift of communicative language teaching, Medgyes (1986) notes a high level of resentment from teachers, in that their own experiences and wishes in the classroom were not considered when outside researchers decided what was best practice in their classrooms. There was a sense that communicative language teaching was forced on teachers without their participation in the research process, which perhaps contributed to the slow uptake of the approach in many parts of the world. In order to involve teachers in the GELT paradigm shift, it is essential that they take a front and centre role in researching how GELT might be best manifested into classroom practice. As we have said previously (Galloway, 2011, 2017c; Galloway & Rose, 2015), action research appears to be an excellent methodology to fulfil this urgent need.

Action research is defined as 'a process in which participants examine their own educational practice systematically and carefully, using the techniques of research' (Ferrance, 2000, p. 1). According to Kemmis and McTaggart (1988), who were the early advocates and formulators of action research:

> A distinctive feature of action research is that those affected by planned changes have the primary responsibility for deciding on the course of critically informed action which seem likely to lead to improvement, and for evaluating the results of strategies tried out in practice. Action research is a group activity. (p. 6)

This sentiment is echoed more than twenty-five years later: 'For action researchers, a key concept is a dual commitment to both participation and action. Action research is done with, rather than on, the participant' (Dick & Greenwood, 2015, p. 195).

In action research, 'teachers apply a manageable process of planning, enacting and reviewing change in their classroom practices' (Mickan, 2013, p. 125). The process is typically illustrated as cyclical, or as a series of trials, because adjustments are necessary in order to improve the teaching innovation or resolve any issues emerging from the previous cycle.

GELT research requires more practitioner-driven trials of classroom implementation. Moreover, it is imperative that teachers report on this research in practitioner-orientated journals, newsletters, blogs and other publications, in order to share the practices that worked and did not work for them. These innovations do not need to be large. For example, in the late 2000s, one of us (Galloway) identified a problem in our English-language class in Japan, where the Japanese students we were teaching were not being exposed to a selection of English accents that were salient to their planned future use. In order to innovate ways to expose students to other languages, Galloway trialled a listening journal task and later a presentation task, which we disseminated years later in an ELT journal (Galloway & Rose, 2014, 2018). Both of these trials were small and aimed at innovating just one of GELT's constructs for change, exposure to a greater diversity of English, but were, nevertheless, worthy of dissemination. (For a detailed description of Galloway's approach to GELT innovation via action research, see Galloway, 2017a, 2017c)

Vettorel's (2013) action research project was considerably larger in its exploration of the efficacy of an ELF interaction exercise between school-aged children in Italy and peers from European countries. The project involved primary school pupils aged 9–11, who participated in a multi-stage project, which first raised awareness of English as a lingua franca, before introducing a series of activities over two years, where 540 students from Italy, Poland, Latvia and Slovakia interacted first via written correspondence and, in later cycles, via online communication (both written and spoken). The project used corpus research methods to analyse the data to examine language use; however, the findings also have pedagogical value in their evaluation of the activity itself. Vettorel's (2013) meticulous reporting of, and reflecting on, the activity provides opportunities for other teachers to implement elements of the project within their own teaching contexts.

Galloway and Rose's studies (2014, 2018) used a methodology of a single-shot innovation (the equivalent to just one cycle of action research), and Vettorel's (2013) study reported on pooled data from all implementation cycles, thus none of these studies fully mirror an action research design. Upon reflection, a better-planned, cyclical action research design may have yielded better results in our own studies. The listening journals reported on in Galloway and Rose (2014), for example, showed a lot of promise, but we retrospectively noticed problems with their implementation and we were dissatisfied with some of our findings. With just one cycle of innovation, we did not have the opportunity to improve on the task and report on enhanced implementation of this activity. Similarly, as Vettorel (2013) did not report on each cycle of implementation, it is difficult to assess which of the ELF interaction activities students got the most value from. Thus, there is still a strong need for carefully planned and executed action research to delve deep into the issues of implementing Global Englishes into classroom pedagogy.

Quasi-Experiments

We are hesitant to recommend quasi-experimental designs, due to both the difficulties of conducting them and the difficulties in having them published, as they are often held up to the standards of the so-called true experiments, which are devoid of the contextual factors that make for authentic learning environments. Nevertheless, quasi-experiments have a strong history in educational research, and are an important method if researchers wish to directly measure the effects of GELT practices on the learners they teach.

One caveat of quasi-experiments in yielding conclusive results on innovative teaching approaches is a lack of control. Unlike experiments, quasi experiments do not involve a strict random assignment of participants, although they strive to give treatments to roughly matched classes. Class groups, however, may never be exactly the same. Additionally, while true experiments aim to isolate all confounding variables, quasi-experiments conducted in the real world outside controlled environments cannot claim to exert full control over the magnitude of variables impacting learners' everyday lives.

Because of a lack of control over confounding variables, quasi-experiments are generally weak at measuring the effects of teaching approaches. For example, a quasi-experiment that aimed to compare a GELT syllabus with an existing syllabus would inevitably encounter issues of controlling for all other variables. Breen (2001) writes:

> Very little research has been undertaken to evaluate the relative effectiveness of syllabus types. Since a syllabus is implemented in a classroom and operates within

the wider process of teaching and learning, this would be difficult to do. Just as it has proved virtually impossible to show that one teaching method is more effective than another (Stern, 1983; Allwright, 1988), variations in teacher interpretations of a syllabus during the course and variations in what students actually learn from the teacher intervene between the syllabus as a plan and the actual outcomes which learners achieve. (p. 154)

However, the difficulty in conducting meaningful quasi-experiments should not dissuade such research from being undertaken, especially as many English-language teachers are often well placed to conduct them using their own classes. English-language teachers often teach multiple classes of a similar level within the same student body, which provides opportunities to conduct more robust quasi-experiments with similarly matched students, controlling for both the educational context and the teacher.

Galloway (2011, 2013, 2017a), for example, conducted a quasi-experiment comparing a class of learners taking a content syllabus on Global Englishes to a comparison group who studied an existing content syllabus on an arbitrary topic. Galloway was the teacher of both classes of learners at the same university of a similar proficiency, which minimised many confounding variables. In cases where matched classes cannot be found, or ethical requirements limit one's ability to offer different experiences to groups of learners, quasi-experiments can be conducted without the use of a control group. Baker's (2012b) study involved pre- and post-course questionnaires and interviews with learners undertaking an online course on intercultural communication. Although this study did not have a comparison group, its findings, nevertheless, revealed important conclusions and pedagogical implications.

We need more work of this nature to fully understand the effect of GELT on learners, and to understand whether GELT equips learners for global English use better than existing pedagogies. While one cannot draw definitive conclusions from a single study (because of confounding variables), the findings can build on a body of research that contributes to knowledge building in the field. The field of research of written corrective feedback – the efficacy of which had been debated for decades – is moving closer to a definitive answer on what feedback works in certain educational contexts, due to the growing volume of quasi-experiments over the years that collectively inform best practice.

Document Research of Curriculum: Syllabus, Textbooks, Tests and Policy

A further method of research, which could prove useful to GELT, is document analysis of curricula, textbooks, tests and policy documents surrounding English language teaching. Document research can also be extended to other artefacts, such as job advertisements for language teachers, or linguistic landscapes of learning environments. In order to challenge the status quo, we must first understand what the status quo is and identify areas that are already changing or are most resistant to change. Because many teaching practices centre on written documents in the form of the materials teachers use, the tests learners take and the policies and curriculum they teach within, document analysis can be a powerful research method to investigate such practices.

When analysing documents for GELT constructs, there is a need for both quantitative and qualitative content analyses. Quantitative content analysis can help identify *what* ideologies exist in documents, and qualitative analysis can identify *how* these ideologies are manifested. While both qualitative and quantitative content analyses are similar, in that both follow replicable procedures (Mayring, 2000), there are fundamental differences. While quantitative content analysis explores textual meaning through frequency counts, qualitative content analysis explores meaning as it is constructed throughout the text, providing a richer description. Both types of analysis offer a systematic description of data through coding and categorisation. Kuckartz (2014) summarises the differences as follows:

> While the atomizing manner of quantitative analysis aims to convert the verbal data into precise categories (represented by numbers) and then to statistically evaluate the resulting data matrix, qualitative text analysis is interested in the text itself, notably based on the text in its entirety. Even after categories have been assigned, the text itself, i.e. the wording of the statements, is relevant and also plays an important role in the preparation and presentation of results. (pp. 65–6)

Thus, the aim of qualitative content analysis is to comprehend meaning in the text itself. Rather than equating coding frequency with the relevant importance of a particular theme, qualitative content analysis provides detailed descriptions of the themes in a text and requires the researcher to focus on aspects of meaning related to the research question (Mayring, 2000; Schreier, 2014).

In Syrbe's (2017) analysis of major English-language tests and textbooks, she mainly adopted a qualitative analysis of the documents in her sample. Although some quantitative data is provided in her study, this is generated via a process of data reduction, rather than an analysis of quantitative data via statistical procedures. For a good example of quantitative content analysis, see Evans and Davies's (2000) content analysis of the representation of masculinity in elementary school reading textbooks. Although this is not a study of Global Englishes, its approach to analysing the data provides a robust procedure that a Global Englishes analysis could be based upon. For example, a GELT study could replicate the procedures of this study, but, instead of exploring masculinity in textbooks, a researcher could explore the representation of Global Englishes according to a number of the dimensions within the GELT framework.

Language-policy research offers a further approach to research that is needed in Global Englishes. As Global Englishes is tied to ideologies, such research may need to take a broad research lens, where policy is considered in not only what is written in top-down documents, but also in the norms and beliefs expressed through practice. Such perspectives would require an examination of language policy via a variety of de facto practices, in keeping with Shohamy's (2006, p. 50) view that 'language policy is more difficult to detect, as it is subtle and hidden from the public eye'. Thus, policy research could examine an educational context, exploring the way Global Englishes is presented in national (macro), institutional (meso) and classroom (micro) policy and practices, which underpin a language course. This type of richer document analysis would require examination of educational policy, institutional policy (in the form of course descriptions, website materials and syllabus) and classroom-based policy (in the form of curricula and classroom practice-based norms) to fully develop an understanding of how English is positioned in such educational contexts. An example of a 'wide-lens' approach to policy analysis is Jenkins's (2013) book on the international university.

Ethnographic Field Research

Ethnographic field research has a long tradition in educational research, and it has clear applications for investigating Global Englishes in language teaching contexts. This method is very useful to explore on-the-ground practices, where Global Englishes may be making inroads into educational contexts. This type of research is currently underrepresented in research papers.

While field research in itself is an adaptive research design, there are, nonetheless, standard features that constitute good ethnographic research (Dörnyei, 2007; Fetterman, 2010; Wolcott, 2008). Ethnographies focus on obtaining a rich description of the shared and learned patterns of values, behaviours, beliefs and language of a culture-sharing group, which is sometimes referred to as a 'bounded unit' (Harklau, 2005). Thus, ethnographic research could involve the investigation of teachers, students, intact classes or entire institutional cohorts. It involves extended study of a group interacting in a natural setting, usually obtained through direct observations, interviews, field notes, journals and the analysis of documents. It is a flexible method that can include almost any evidence collected in the field that would help to inform the research of the object of study. Ethnographic researchers seek to understand patterns of behaviours, beliefs and practices of single cases or communities of people to produce a holistic interpretation via a thick description of the constructs under investigation.

The objective of field research in the case of GELT would be to understand current classroom practices, in order to comment on areas of change and to identify areas of pedagogical practice that could benefit from change. Field research could also reveal cases of good practice in classrooms where Global Englishes innovation is already taking place. In order to make recommendations for classroom change, researchers must first fully evaluate what is happening in the classroom. In recent years, when giving talks on Global Englishes in various parts of the world, we have heard directly from teachers that many of the proposals for change within GELT are already being enacted in many teachers' classrooms. Recently, anecdotal evidence from a group of Finnish teachers undertaking professional development in the United Kingdom indicated that teaching approaches in some Finnish English-language classrooms had embraced a lingua franca perspective. In particular, the GELT proposals calling for a shift in ownership and target interlocutors in curricula were already well underway. Field research would be a useful method to examine such practices, to learn from innovative educational contexts and to understand how they relate to other facets of language learning.

Despite the clear benefits of ethnographic field research in language classrooms, very little has taken place. There are, however, a few noteworthy exceptions, most of which involve examinations of wider topics, such as English medium instruction, where notions of Global Englishes are touched upon. Galloway et al. (2017), for example, explored universities in China and Japan, collecting data from students and teachers via observations, interviews and focus groups.

Surveys

The field of Global Englishes has generally suffered from poorly constructed questionnaires. Prodromou's (1992) survey study investigated students' attitudes towards bilingual and bicultural teachers, native English-speaking models and the cultural content of lessons, and was used to collect data from 300 students in Greece. The survey as a research instrument was quite problematic, due to its simplicity (only five questions in length, with an unclear scale), and would not be suitable to dissect the complexities of views surrounding Global Englishes. Kirkpatrick and Xu (2002) used an attitudinal survey to collect attitudinal data on World Englishes in China with 171 university students. The questionnaire included fourteen items with responses recorded on a Likert scale; however, the results were only descriptively presented as percentages, with no attempt to use this instrument for deeper investigations of the answers given. Furthermore, no data was provided in this study on the internal reliability of the instrument. Murray's (2003) study of 253 Swiss teachers from private and state schools on their attitudes to 'Euro-English' has similar issues. While this survey was more complex in design, its complexity was not matched in the analysis of its data. We need to examine variables that have been suggested to influence attitudes (proficiency, language exposure, learning context) against the data, rather than seeing results presented as the raw percentages of a homogenous group.

Despite a problematic history, recent years have witnessed the emergence of slightly more robust instruments. Buckingham (2014) used an adapted questionnaire with 347 university students in the Middle East. While this survey is reminiscent of the attitudinal work carried out in previous decades, the study shows good control over data analysis, going through the necessary steps to ensure robust dissemination of descriptive statistics, which the aforementioned studies fail to do. Galloway (2011, 2013, 2017a) uses a more complex survey with her participants at a Japanese university to directly explore their attitudes towards Global Englishes, as well as a Global Englishes pedagogy. Galloway et al. (2017) further use surveys to explore beliefs and practices in EMI settings in China and in Japan, which is a context also explored in Chapter 8. This study conducted statistical analysis between groups using independent sample t-tests, illustrating avenues for more detailed survey research for the purposes of not only descriptively reporting on attitudes, but to compare attitudes across variables of interest. Due to the scales used in this questionnaire, we reflect that non-parametric tests may have been more appropriate for data generated via these instruments.

A further limitation of previous research is that, while many surveys have been conducted in the area, very few reported studies share the questionnaires used, and even fewer report on any validation process in the development of their questionnaires. This means that most researchers who wish to build on past work are left with no choice but to build their own questionnaires from the ground up, rather than to build on existing work in the field. We also find that, of the better-reported and analysed surveys (e.g. Buckingham, 2014), many still need to rely on adaptations of the matched guise technique. Thus, the field currently lacks a reliable survey that can be adapted to a range of teaching and learning contexts. In short, what the field needs is carefully constructed questionnaire items that can be used for more interesting analysis.

Alternative Methodologies

Just as the multilingual turn has necessitated the need to explore new and alternative research methods to match emerging ideas and concepts (Meier, 2017; Ortega, 2014), we feel that GELT necessitates a certain degree of research innovation. For example, while action research provides a clear methodological blueprint to report on classroom innovation, the design indicates the 'solving' of an issue through careful planning and reporting. GELT innovation – particularly at the early adoption stage – will be at a trial stage for decades to come, and thus, may require more flexibility and reflexivity, before best practices can be found. Alternative methods to action research may be required, which will allow for more freedom of reporting on classroom-based trials. The reporting of reflective practices and autoethnographies are promising alternative methods via which teachers can report on their own practices within a freer, and more personal, research style.

Instead of ethnographic field research, which requires intimate access to classrooms and learners, other less direct methods could provide a window into others' practices. Narrative inquiry, for example, allows for an in-depth understanding of not only what can be seen in terms of learners' and teachers' actions surrounding innovation, but also their ideologies and thoughts which inform or underpin them. Instead of surveys, which capture a somewhat distanced and detached snapshot of a phenomenon, focus groups and interviews can allow for a more nuanced understanding. Critical incident techniques allow for deep introspection on critical episodes, which may help to report on precise areas of conflict or success in an innovation. Bruster and Peterson (2013) used reflection journals with twenty student teachers to capture critical teaching incidents. This methodology could be very useful for teachers implementing GELT innovations within their own classrooms, by providing an insider account of the changes in practice. The technique allows for the collection of a large amount of data that focuses on the crucial moments of implementation, without the required presence of a researcher in the classroom.

Innovative methods can further explore issues connected to identity and cognition. Kelly (2018) conducted a study with twelve pre-service teachers in a community college, where they drew pictures of ESL teachers with accompanying descriptions at the beginning and end of a TESOL methods course. These drawing were then used for content analysis, as the article explains:

> The researcher analyzed the drawings and descriptions with respect to the role of the teacher, the role of the students, the teaching strategies shown, the instructional content, and how the drawings changed over the semester. (Kelly, 2018, p. 110)

The research explained that the innovative data collection technique allowed an analysis of both visual and linguistic data, which facilitated a more thorough understanding of teachers' beliefs. Other techniques are making their way into applied linguistic research, which add new opportunities for research. These include research techniques such as repertory grids, which Borg (2015) argues can be used instead of traditional interviews to explore teacher cognition. They also include data analysis methods, such as Q methodology, which can be used for the systematic study of learners' and teachers' viewpoints.

Future Directions in GELT

This chapter has suggested areas of research in the exploration of Global Englishes, as it pertains to language teaching. We see a clear need for classroom-based research in terms of an exploration of attitudes, classroom practices, materials and teacher education. If researchers are not engaging in the groundwork that is needed to investigate how to link theory and practice, we make a call to arms for researcher–practitioners to do the work that is desperately needed. What is needed is on-the-ground research that reports on current practices and evaluates the efficacy of putting Global Englishes ideas into pedagogical practice. Without such research, the theory–practice divide will only deepen, and calls for innovation will continue to lack the empirical evidence of how this change can be operationalised.

This chapter has also outlined how GELT can be used as a research framework, and has suggested a number of research areas and accompanying methods that can drive future research. Of these methods, we see quasi-experimental and action research as essential avenues to evaluate curriculum change in real-world classrooms, although we also point to the potential of more reflexive alternatives. We also see fieldwork (including observation, interviews and focus groups), document analysis and surveys as powerful methods to investigate the current level of Global Englishes within curricula in various teaching contexts to benchmark practices in order to measure future change.

The second section of this book turns to putting some items on this GELT research agenda into action. Chapter 6 explores Global Englishes in classroom materials, by examining six textbooks that have been purposively sampled to represent a range of English language teaching contexts. Chapter 7 investigates a teacher education (MSc TESOL) programme at a UK university, in order to examine the effects of Global Englishes content for pre-service teachers. Chapter 8 explores some constructs of Global Englishes within emerging English-medium programmes in East Asian universities. While these three chapters represent a small subset of needed research in the field, we aim to illustrate how research can be conducted in the area by providing a blueprint of how constructs within the GELT framework can be operationalised for future research.

6 Global Englishes and Language Teaching Materials

Introduction

English language teaching materials can be broadly defined as any tangible object of language presentation that can be utilised for the purposes of language learning. Materials, therefore, can include anything from highly artificial textbooks to unaltered authentic sources of language. Gray (2016) states that 'the most significant and widely disseminated type consists of published materials, which includes an ever-growing array of items, such as textbooks, ancillary audio-visual accompaniments, workbooks, learner dictionaries, guided readers, online courses and online supplements to traditional textbook-based courses' (p. 95).

Although textbooks only provide one perspective into classroom practices, they remain the most prevalent sources of teaching and, as such, assert a major influence on the way language is taught and the way students view the language (Matsuda, 2012b). English language teaching materials also play an important role in the language-learning process, serving 'as the basis of much of the language input that learners receive and the language practice that occurs in the classroom' (Richards, 2001, p. 251). A reality of English language teaching is that commercial textbooks are often at the core of a programme (McDonough et al., 2013).

As a lack of suitable materials has been noted as a barrier to the implementation of a Global Englishes approach to ELT (see Galloway, 2017a, 2018a; Galloway & Rose, 2015), many teachers who want to present a global depiction of English to their students may be limited by a practical need to rely on commercial materials, which centre towards standard Inner Circle norms. Gray (2010) has argued previously that most of the listening components of published materials still promote a limited range of Inner Circle standard Englishes, with a dearth of exposure to authentic samples of English from Outer- and Expanding Circle countries. Because materials constrain innovation, we see materials research as a vital area for in-depth study, as it is currently under-researched. Therefore, we need to fully evaluate what current materials say about the language they teach if we are to make appropriate amendments to better incorporate Global Englishes into language teaching practice.

This chapter firstly outlines previous research on textbook analysis in general, in order to examine the methodologies used and our current understanding of textbooks in English language teaching. We then suggest appropriate frameworks for using GELT as a research tool to analyse materials before applying it to examples of popular textbooks. Following this illustration of materials research, the chapter outlines suggestions to supplement materials to incorporate a Global Englishes perspective. There is then a consideration of the challenges practitioners may face, including the perceived need for standardisation, exams and the financial motives of textbook writers. Finally, given that responsibility for what to use and how to use a textbook lies with the teacher (McGrath, 2016), it ends with a discussion on teacher education.

An Overview of Global Englishes-Related Materials Research

English language as depicted in many textbooks has been criticised as being contrived and not representative of English spoken in the real world (Widdowson, 1998). This rhetoric has given rise to considerable debates in both academic and professional circles over the importance of authenticity in textbooks and the use of authentic texts in the classroom. An oft-cited definition of authenticity comes from Morrow (1977), who stated that 'an authentic text is a stretch of real language, produced by a real speaker or writer for a real audience and designed to convey a real message of some sort' (p. 13). Scholars since this time have clarified that material designed for classroom purposes should not be considered authentic (e.g. Lee, 1995) – a point which McKay (2013) argues could alienate learners. Day and Bamford (1998) famously discussed a 'cult of authenticity', where authentic texts are being inappropriately used for pedagogical purposes for which they were not made or intended.

As far as Global Englishes is concerned, the element of authenticity we are most concerned about is not the purpose within which a text is used, but whether the language in textbooks is truly an authentic depiction of the English that learners are most likely to encounter outside the classroom. While some textbook approaches have aimed to increase authenticity through the use of corpora to select natural English language, including idioms, many of these approaches use corpora that capture English as an Inner Circle language. *Touchstone* (McCarthy et al., 2005), for example, is informed by a subset of samples of North American English in the *Cambridge English Corpus*. Thus, even though corpus-informed, the chosen corpora do not represent authenticity in terms of how English is used outside the North American context. In a study by Gray (2010), where he interviewed a number of teachers, he found a pervasive view that so-called native speaker idiomaticity was not a high priority when teaching English as an international language.

A study by Syrbe and Rose (2018) investigated three main textbook series in the state of North Rhine-Westphalia in Germany, a region of political and populous clout. The state-set English-language curriculum argues that it aims to develop learners' communicative and intercultural competence to use English as a lingua franca, as well as developing students' repertoire of linguistic resources [Verfügbarkeit sprachlicher Mittel] and multilingual profiles [Mehrsprachigkeitsprofil]. The study used an adapted GELT framework, focusing on representations of ownership, users, models and target interlocutors of English. The study found that, of the twenty-nine authentic excerpts used across the three books, twenty-six involved only native speakers of English, mostly dominated by American and British English users communicating within their own context, one involved communication between an Outer Circle speaker and an Inner Circle speaker, and another involved an Expanding Circle speaker communicating with a so-called native speaker from the Inner Circle. There were no examples of lingua franca communications of Expanding Circle speakers communicating with other Expanding Circle speakers. In a further examination of target interlocutors across all three textbooks, the authors found only two tasks where the target interlocutor was not a native English speaker. An analysis of audio materials saw Received Pronunciation as the dominant accent, with some representation of other Inner Circle varieties of English, but only one conversation between two speakers from Expanding Circle countries. The authors argue that this is unrepresentative, in considering that data shows that Germans use English most when they travel, and in greater numbers with people from Spain, Italy and Turkey than with people from the United Kingdom or Ireland.

A study by Chan (2014) evaluated the implied pronunciation target in the educational system of Hong Kong by triangulating information from the new ELT curriculum, examination papers and commercially published textbooks, with particular reference to World Englishes and English as a lingua franca. Results of an analysis of the new ELT curriculum showed that the curriculum took into account World Englishes and ELF perspectives in the choice of contexts, whilst downplaying the importance of conforming to 'native' pronunciations, but still being conceptually guided by them. The examination analysis observed that the listening examination included local Hong Kong English speakers, even when most of them had a 'native' accent. However, the assessment criteria seemed to implicitly stigmatise these speakers' phonological features. An analysis of ten commercial textbooks observed an inclusion of language-using contexts that involved English speakers from around the world; however, RP remained to be the main choice of accent in most recordings.

Tajeddin and Teimournezhad (2015) examined two intermediate-level textbooks: one localised textbook from Iran and one popular international textbook. They used a framework to categorise cultures into the target culture (American or British), the source culture (Iranian), international cultures or culture-neutral. The authors also quantified occurrences of intercultural interactions within the texts, including ELF interactions. Their results indicated that the localised textbook stressed *culture-neutral* representations while the international textbook contained a greater number of intercultural interactions, which included ELF interactions.

A study by Naji Meidani and Pishghadam (2013) investigated the extent to which four major English-language textbooks demonstrated the international status of English. Their analysis examined references to Inner Circle, Outer Circle and Expanding Circle countries, as well as an analysis of accents, places of cultures and people in the texts. The study tried to introduce a temporal element to the analysis, by choosing four different textbooks published over a twelve-year period. The analysis revealed differences among the selected books with a gradual tendency for later textbooks to show more recognition of the international status of English. Due to a lack of control for confounding variables besides time, which might also explain differences (e.g. the textbooks have different writers or publishers and may be aimed at different audiences), it is difficult to accept the results at face value. Nonetheless, the study does add evidence of a greater attention to EIL in some textbooks.

Galloway (2018a, p. 474) provides an overview of a number of textbooks in her chapter on ELF in language materials. In this review, she notes that, at first glance, Macmillian's *Global* series (Clandfield et al., 2011) states that the 'ground-breaking' course enables learners 'to learn English as it is used in our globalised world . . . and to learn about English as an international language'. While the blurb seems promising, a closer examination revealed a focus on native speaker norms, literature embedded in the Anglophone world. She observed that the text payed lip service to a small selection of Englishes outside the Inner Circle while ignoring lingua franca contexts and usage. Galloway (2018a) also reviews Cambridge University Press's *English for Business Studies* (MacKenzie, 2010), which includes native and non-native English recordings, where the editors note that 'Listening to non-native speakers of English is important, as much of the English you will hear in your professional life will be spoken by people who don't have English as their first language' (p. 6). Again, while this was promising, Galloway (2018a) observed that the texts mainly deal with variation at a superficial level with the inclusion of some non-native English speakers on the accompanying audio. While these may be tokenistic examples of inclusion, they are, at least, indicative of small changes being introduced. Importantly, changes occurring in business textbooks indicate that this may be one field where faster progress may be occurring.

Other recent textbook analysis studies include: Caleffi's (2016) investigations of ELF in the speaking and listening activities of recent English-language coursebooks; Cavalheiro's (2013) exploration of language and teaching materials from an EIL perspective; Siqueira's (2015) discussion of ELF in materials; Vettorel and Lopriore's (2013) investigation of ELF in coursebooks; Takahashi's (2016) study of attitudes of learners and teachers towards ELF-orientated materials; Xu's (2013) discussion of globalisation and culture in relation to ELT materials used in Chinese secondary education; Yu's (2015) critical evaluation of ELF materials in the Taiwanese context; and Vettorel's (2018) examination of communication strategies with a focus on ELF in Italian secondary school materials.

Methods of Textbook Evaluation and Analysis

Textbook analysis is an important area of study in English language teaching, serving both a pedagogic purpose (in investigating the suitability of certain textbooks for specific teaching contexts) and a research purpose (in investigating the suitability of a textbook for English language teaching in general), to uncover its strengths, limitations and hidden ideologies. This distinction between two types of materials research was made more than twenty-five years ago by Littlejohn (1992), who compared materials evaluation (materials research for the purposes of development and implementation into the classroom) to materials analysis (research for the purposes of analysing features of a textbook).

In terms of pedagogical frameworks of evaluation, there are a number of good resources that teachers can use (see, e.g., McGrath, 2016) to draw upon general analytic approaches. While some practical evaluation frameworks exist to provide structure to an evaluation, they tend to lack the scholarly robustness we are accustomed to seeing in other areas of applied linguistics research. This may explain the general lack of published findings of materials evaluations for the purposes of informing teaching, which tend to be relegated to review sections of scholarly work rather than being positioned as research within their own right. All of this is a shame, of course, in considering how vital materials are to the teaching profession, and how important a critical evaluation of these materials is for the field.

Two popular methods of evaluation are the CATALYST method (Grant, 1987) and a checklist method, detailed by Tomlinson (2010) as being useful to use for both first-glance evaluations and close-up evaluations (McGrath, 2016). Both methods involve an evaluator examining the textbooks, according to a set list of items, such as the textbooks' suitability to the students' level, the students' potential interests in the content matter, the communicative nature of the tasks, the textbooks' layout and the teachability of text. A first-glance evaluation requires the evaluator to take a holistic approach to evaluation based on the evidence from their impression of the textbook as a whole. A close-up evaluation is similar to the first glance but requires a little more systematicity, where criteria that are important to the teaching context are first identified and the textbooks are evaluated according to these criteria, usually using a simple rating system (e.g. scores of 1–5). McGrath suggests that, for a further depth of evaluation, criteria that are more important to the teaching context be weighted more than those of less importance.

While checklists are convenient and quick tools for practitioners, they encourage superficial judgements (McGrath, 2016). To provide a more in-depth examination of textbooks, some scholars advocate for a more fine-grained analysis. Breen and Candlin (1987) propose a two-phase approach consisting of an analysis of the usefulness of the materials from a pedagogical standpoint as well as an analysis of the appropriateness of the materials from the standpoint of learner needs and teaching approaches, thus entailing the application of pedagogical beliefs about best practice. Similarly, Littlejohn's (2011, p. 185–97) textbook analysis at three levels is a widely cited method and focuses on: What is there in terms of the type of tasks and components included? What is required of users in terms of the learning activities and operations required to use the materials? What is implied in terms of the pedagogical beliefs embodied in the textbook's approach? Any evaluation of materials in terms of Global Englishes for language teaching is clearly aimed at Littlejohn's third question. We have articulated throughout this book, and particularly in Chapter 2, that GELT is not a methodology, thus it has flexibility in terms of tasks, activities and operations. Hence, an evaluation of materials would need to centre on what is implied in terms of the pedagogical beliefs that underpin materials.

Tomlinson (2016), in recent years, has created a checklist for specific evaluation of materials for the purposes of teaching English as an international language. This checklist includes evaluating texts for the following features:

- authentic texts and tasks (written texts by non-native speakers)
- spoken interactions between non-native speakers
- learner unstructured interaction
- pragmatic awareness activities
- strategies to achieve successful communication in a lingua franca
- language items and features important for international communication
- intercultural competence.

This is a welcome attempt to respond to what Tomlinson (2016) terms criticisms of 'global coursebooks for not catering for the needs of learners of English as a global language' (p. 53) and, although we agree with the need for new materials to 'meet the needs of learners of English who will be communicating more with other non-native speakers than with native speakers of English' (p. 53), it is unclear what informed the creation of this checklist, and why many of the items on Tomlinson's (2010) previous general checklist for evaluating ELT materials are no longer relevant. As a result, the checklist seems somewhat ad hoc and theoretical, neither pinned down by previous work in materials evaluation nor by any external theory. Galloway (2018a) further critiques Tomlinson's (2016) EIL evaluation framework for its lack of connection to his previous frameworks, which included items she saw as still being pedagogically important. Based on this critique, she offers her own framework for evaluation of materials for use in globally orientated classrooms, which follows a three-step procedure.

Whilst textbook evaluations serve a pedagogical need, they lack the research rigour needed for content analysis. They do not connect with other theories of scholarly work in applied linguistics or TESOL and, as such, they cannot make contributions to larger bodies of knowledge. For this reason, the majority of the more scholarly work in materials research centres on analysis of the elements within the materials, while drawing on other epistemologies to make stronger theoretical links. Gray (2016, p. 99) states that:

> Materials research currently reveals a variety of disciplinary influences, which include cultural and media studies (Gray, 2010a; Harwood, 2014), sociology (Littlejohn, 2012) and theoretical perspectives derived from postmodernism (Kullman, 2003, 2013), Marxism (Gray and Block, 2014) and critical pedagogy (Thornbury, 2013; Chun, 2016).

These works seek to explore and analyse materials as cultural artefacts in order to uncover what is sometimes termed 'the hidden curriculum', which conveys meaning to students and teachers about what the textbooks depict as cultural and linguistic norms.

Using GELT as a Framework for Textbook Analysis

This chapter presents a study that investigates the global orientation of popular English textbooks, which are widely used within the ELT contexts around the world and, thus, underpin a wide range of ELT curricula. The study has two aims:

1. To investigate the extent to which English's global position was reflected in popular teaching materials.
2. To showcase how the GELT framework can be operationalised for research purposes – in this case, a content analysis.

Therefore, in order to evaluate the global orientation of textbooks, a framework was adapted from GELT. Syrbe (2017) has already carried out some groundwork in this regard, with her exploratory analysis of four major textbook series, which she analyses via an adapted GELT framework. An outcome of her study was a recommendation to measure five facets of textbooks on a five-point scale.

Table 6.1 *Adapted GELT framework for textbook evaluation*

ELT ⟵	⟶ GELT	
	What models/norms of English are discernible in the book and audio materials?	
1. Standard English only	⟵⟶	5. Diverse, flexible and multiple forms
	Who are the target interlocutors in the materials?	
1. L1 users	⟵⟶	5. All English users
	What linguistic orientation is promoted in the book?	
1. Monolingual	⟵⟶	5. Multilingual/translingual
	How is culture depicted in the materials?	
1. Static L1 English cultures	⟵⟶	5. Fluid, diverse cultures

We have developed this suggestion in order to emphasise that GELT is not a black-and-white dichotomous paradigm (see the previous chapter for discussion), and that teaching materials do not fall into an either/or category of adopting or rejecting a Global Englishes ideology (see Table 6.1).

Our adapted framework examines elements in the curriculum, such as target interlocutors, models of English, target cultures and ownership of English. The textbooks were evaluated within four major dimensions:

1. What models of English are used in the book and audio materials?
2. Who are the target interlocutors in the materials?
3. How is ownership depicted in the materials?
4. What linguistic orientation is promoted in the book?

Two methods are utilised in this chapter to illustrate how GELT can be used for materials research at a practitioner level, as well as at a scholarly level. The first evaluation follows a similar method to that used in Masuhara and Tomlinson (2008) in their analysis of nine textbooks in the United Kingdom, which resembles a close-look evaluation described by McGrath (2016). It trades objectivity for speed and breadth of application by holistically evaluating the materials and assigning a score on a five-point scale, with a score of one representing a traditional orientation and a score of five representing a GELT orientation. We use this as it shows how the GELT framework can be used to evaluate textbooks at a practical level. It is intended for practitioner, rather than research, purposes, where the assigned score can be used for ranking purposes, rather than an objective measure. This is an initial evaluation method and should not be used in place of a more rigorous method for practitioners, such as the three-step evaluation recommended by Galloway (2018a).

Our second procedure is in-depth analysis, which uses specific and countable features of the textbook as proxy measures for a larger construct, in order to show how GELT can be used to elicit other types of data within textbooks. It follows methodological epistemologies of content analysis. This is similar to analyses conducted by Syrbe (2017) and Syrbe and Rose (2018) that aim at making a contribution to theoretical knowledge of textbook research – the results of which are aimed at researchers or curriculum planners. Due to a lack of word space in this chapter to present an in-depth analysis of all textbook features (and a lack of time resources to conduct an in-depth analysis for all research questions), a narrow sample of data is sometimes chosen for analysis. This analysis serves an illustrative purpose for applying the GELT framework, rather than being a comprehensive analysis of all possible features in the textbooks.

Textbook Samples

For the close-look evaluation, six textbooks were selected to offer a wide representation of the commercial textbooks in use in ELT around the world. Where series were used, we elected to evaluate upper-intermediate textbooks aimed at an adolescent/adult reader, as we assume the target learner is more likely to become a global user of English in the future, rather than just a formal language learner. The inclusion criteria were:

1. The textbook had to explicitly target learners outside Inner-Circle contexts in promotion materials.
2. The textbook had to be aimed at learners at the post-beginner, adolescent/adult level.

In order to identify appropriate textbooks, we formed an expert panel of twenty experienced teachers recruited within an in-service Masters' programme. These teachers were working in nineteen different nations, hence offering a global perspective on textbook use. We asked them to nominate the most influential textbooks used in their teaching context within two set categories of markets: general English and business English. Business English textbooks were chosen, due to their specific focus on a global English-using market. The top two textbooks within each category were selected for analysis. We further added two comparison textbooks that were marketed to be global in their approach to teaching English to assess textbooks that claimed to 'dare to be different' (McGrath, 2013, p. 198). The following were chosen:

- *New Headway: Upper-Intermediate. The New Edition* (Soars & Soars, 2008), as an example of a general textbook;
- *Interchange* 3 (Richards et al., 2005), as an example of a general textbook;
- *Market Leader: Upper Intermediate* (Cotton & Lansford, 2011), as an example of a business textbook;

- *International Express: Upper Intermediate* (Wallwork & Sheard, 2001), as an example of a business textbook;
- *Global: Upper Intermediate* (Clandfield et al., 2011), as an example of a marketed global textbook;
- *English Unlimited: Upper Intermediate* (Tilbury, 2011), as an example of a marketed global textbook.

Within this sample of textbook series, we settled on analysing the upper-intermediate textbook within each series. Our decision to do so was based on the assumption that learners at the higher level of the textbook series were more likely to need English for use in global contexts.

In our close-look evaluation, we holistically examined the textbooks, which required the researchers to read through the entire book, making qualitative notes on features related to the research questions. In our in-depth analysis, we collected quantitative data via proxy measures on each research question construct to ensure more subjective comparability across the six textbooks. This included:

1. The first twenty-five named characters as proxy representations of target interlocutors (which were systematically coded as L1 or L2 speakers).
2. The first twelve communications as proxy representations of type of communication (L1–L1; L2–L1; L2–L2).
3. The first twenty-five named geographic places as a proxy measure of ownership and cultural representativeness of English use.
4. Coded varieties of English in the first hour of recorded audio as measures of phonological variation.

While each of these constrained samples has limitations, due to the proxy used, the combination of close-look evaluation of the holistic sample and in-depth analysis of a specific sample has allowed us to make inferences based on a range of interpretive and objective data through a wide and narrow lens.

Findings

All textbooks were included in the close-up evaluation. The results are presented according to each criterion and are then discussed case by case, in order to present some of the evidence reviewed in making our evaluations. There are limitations to the results that must be acknowledged:

1. There is a subjectivity in the coding and interpreting elements due to what the researchers view as representative of each criterion;
2. There is a lack of data from the producers of the textbook creators, which may help to explain why specific content is included or omitted;
3. There is a lack of data from teachers and learners, which may explain how the textbook is used, including how it is adapted or supplemented in the classroom. As Littlejohn (2011, p. 181) states, we can investigate the materials 'as they are' but not the 'materials-in-action'.

Table 6.2 *Evaluation of English-language norms in textbook samples*

Textbook	Rating	Example Comments from Close-Look Evaluation
Market Leader	2	Glossary marks varieties as British or American only, portraying these as standard.
International Express	3	Promotes Inner Circle norms in terms of standard English grammar; challenges some pronunciation norms.
Interchange	2	Promotes Inner Circle norms in terms of standard English grammar; no discernible preference for vocabulary.
New Headway	1	Many references to British English norms; communicatively acceptable language forms labelled as incorrect.
English Unlimited	2	British-centred in vocabulary; a grammar-focused task avoids using the word 'mistake' in favour of the 'best option'.
Global	2	Global focus contrasts with sections on 'Typical errors', including the intelligible forms of English labelled as error.

To mitigate some of these limitations, we have provided a trail of evidence of examples so the reader can better understand how the scores were derived.

English-Language Norms: Close-Look Evaluation

Models of English were analysed in terms of the diversity of English-language norms depicted in the textbooks, and given a score agreed by two independent raters, which are summarised in Table 6.2. A score of one indicates that the textbooks were entirely representative of a 'traditional ELT' orientation as described in the GELT framework, with no display of flexibility. A score of two indicates a traditional orientation, with a few examples of flexibility in norms. A score of three indicates a traditional orientation, with acceptance of some flexibility in global use norms. A score of four indicates that the textbooks had a global orientation to norms, but still adhered to some traditional language norms. A score of five indicates that the textbooks were entirely representative of a 'global ELT' orientation as described in the GELT framework.

New Headway was the lowest rating textbook for the promotion of global norms of English use. The textbook contained many references to British English norms, perhaps best illustrated by British-centred vocabulary (e.g. my 'mate' Norman, p. 36; what 'rubbish', p. 25; I 'reckon', p. 111). Phonological norms were in standard British English (e.g. 'Phonetic Symbols', p. 159). Communicatively acceptable language forms, such as 'I was born in <u>one</u> town in Mexico' or 'I'*ve* learnt English' (p. 16), were labelled as incorrect forms of language use. There was also a reference to learners' future goals of speaking 'perfect English' (p. 47). Errors were also a feature in *Global*, despite it being promoted as being global in coverage. This positioning contrasted with sections on 'Typical errors', including the intelligible 'Well, I 'ope you'll be very 'appy in the new 'ouse' for most English users and a further example where we would challenge an 'error' to exist: 'Next week I will have a party at my house. Would you like to come?' (p. 27). *Market Leader* and *Interchange* tended to avoid the explicit labelling of correctness and standards. However, in *Market Leader's* glossary, the textbook marked varieties as British or American only, portraying these as benchmarks of language norms.

Interchange also promoted standards in its grammar-focused activities, but there was no explicit discernible preference for vocabulary standards.

English Unlimited offered more globally orientated messages than its counterparts in its grammar-focused activities, which avoided using the word 'mistake' in favour of asking students to choose the 'best option'. Despite this, the vocabulary was very British-centred (e.g. flats and flatmates throughout). Phonological depictions were British-centred with examples such as teach<u>er</u> (p. 159) representative of the schwa /ə/. Although this is representative of most non-rhotic accents, the absence of other alternative pronunciations was noted.

The highest rated textbook in this category was *International Express*, which, despite adhering to similar standard English in its examples throughout, contained a 'hidden gem' in section 6.2 where two people in the transcribed audio materials discuss fluency of speech. One speaker says (albeit using native speakers as benchmarks) that it isn't important to understand everything, nor to mimic some pronunciation norms, stating that many British English speakers do not pronounce th as /θ/, but are, nevertheless, understood. This was one of the few examples across the six textbooks where students were taught that adherence to standards was not always necessary to be understood (and also pointed out that norms were not adhered to in so-called norm-providing communities).

English-Language Norms: An In-Depth Analysis

Models of English were analysed in more depth in terms of the diversity of English used in the audio materials that accompanied the student textbook. This analysis involved using accents represented in the audio materials of the text as a proxy measure of representativeness. Recorded samples (excluding instructional phrases) within each text were used, and the accents of each recorded conversation or monologue in terms of its speech-community origin. If more than one type of accent was present in a dialogue, a raw time score was calculated for each speaker based on the length of the conversation divided by the number of speakers.

Full samples of *Interchange, Market Leader* and *New Headway* were used, as the audio either came with the student textbooks or was made available

Table 6.3 *An analysis of norms in supplied audio materials*

	Interchange		*Market Leader*		*New Headway*	
Accents	Seconds	Percentage (%)	Seconds	Percentage (%)	Seconds	Percentage (%)
RP[a]	574	15.94	1654.4	44.63	2487	68.97
AmE	2954	82.06	805.7	21.73	369	10.23
Other	72	2.0	308.7	8.33	644	17.85
TOTAL L1	**3600**	**100**	**2768.8**	**74.69**	**3500**	**97.06**
Undefined/other	-	-	193.5	5.22	88	2.44
NNES						
European	-	-	575.7	15.53	18	0.50
East Asian	-	-	169	4.56	-	-
TOTAL L2	-	-	**938.2**	**25.31**	**106**	**2.94**

[a] Includes British accents which were deemed to be similar to RP.

online to students. The in-depth analysis of the first approximately 3,600 seconds of the recordings is displayed in Table 6.3. For many of the textbooks in our sample, sufficient audio materials could not be obtained and, thus, a small sample of materials available online were used. For *International Express* and *Global*, this equated to just one unit of study, which was insufficient for a full in-depth analysis. Nevertheless, our analysis of this audio is discussed in comparison with our full analysis of *Market Leader, New Headway* and *Interchange* (see Table 6.3).

Table 6.4 displays the analysis of audio from the books where a full sample was not obtained. *Global* provided one unit of audio on their companion website for the pre-intermediate-level book, and thus, this was used for comparison. This sample was comprised of 65% of RP accents and 35% of other UK-based accents (i.e. West Country English/northern English/Scottish), resulting in a 100% coverage of L1 accents in the sample, all of which were from the United Kingdom. *English Unlimited* also had one unit available online. This sample included a 41.5% coverage of RP accents, an 8% coverage of General American English and 6.5% of other L1 accents, which included Scottish and Irish only; thus, 56% of the audio represented L1 speakers. Half of the audio sample was UK-based (49.5%) in accent. However, 44% of the audio comprised of L2 English accents, the vast majority of which were non-defined L2 accents (30%) and the remainder comprised of Venezuelan, Japanese and broadly European. The audio in *International Express* comprised of over 51% RP, 24% General American English and a further 8% of other L1 (Scottish English) accents, totalling over 83% of L1 English accent representation. The remaining 16.7% comprised of mainland European (possibly Latin American) and Japanese speakers of English.

Table 6.4 *An analysis of norms in a sample of audio materials*

	English Unlimited[a]		*Global*		*International Express*[a]	
Accents	Seconds	Percentage (%)	Seconds	Percentage (%)	Seconds	Percentage (%)
RP	281	41.45	385	65.03	460	51.22
AmE	55	8.11	-	-	213	23.72
Other	44	6.49	207	34.97	75	8.35
TOTAL L1	**380**	**56.05**	**592**	**100**	**748**	**83.3**
Undefined NNES	203	29.94	-	-	-	-
European	25	3.69	-	-	120	13.36
Latin American	55	8.11	-	-	-	-
East Asian	15	2.21	-	-	30	3.34
TOTAL L2	**298**	**43.95**	-	-	**150**	**16.7**

[a] Due to a lack of availability of upper-intermediate audio, a sample of pre-intermediate audio materials available online was reviewed.

English Unlimited appeared to be most inclusive of L2 English speakers in its audio, despite standard English accents (RP and General American) making up 49.66% of the sample analysed. *New Headway* was most representative of standard English, with 79.2% of its sample being categorised as RP or General American. Moreover, when deviations from standard English were present, the majority of these showcased other UK-based accents, with less than 3% of the audio including L2 English accents. The L2 English learner and user, therefore, were essentially absent from the *New Headway* audio.

Global contained no audio that included L2 users, ranking it lower than *New Headway. Global* was marketed as providing a wide variety of accents around the world (24 accents, p. 2), so it is possible that the available audio for our limited analysis failed to capture this representativeness. Indeed, this may be true for all of the textbooks for which we were only able to conduct a limited analysis (*Global, English Unlimited, International Express*). Compared to the 3,600+ seconds of audio analysed in the full textbook samples, *Global's* sample was just 592 and, thus, should not be considered as being representative of the entire book. Hence, a follow-up study should aim to conduct a full analysis across textbooks' audio materials.

Target Interlocutors: Close-Look Evaluation

The target interlocutors were analysed in terms of who were depicted as being users of English throughout the written textbook materials. The scores were agreed by two independent raters, on a five-point scale. A score of one indicates that the textbooks were entirely representative of a 'traditional ELT' orientation

Table 6.5 *Evaluation of target interlocutors in textbooks*

Textbook	Rating	Comment
Market Leader: Upper Intermediate	4	The target interlocutors are global; no single discernible target for English use throughout the book apart from global business; 'Language work' and 'Writing file' tasks predominantly UK-centric.
International Express: Upper Intermediate	3	The target interlocutors are global but in a slightly less labelled way than *Market Leader*. Global offices in London and Melbourne of the fictional company IntEx centred many tasks in the Inner Circle.
Interchange	3	English is mostly used with interlocutors who are not fixed to a particular country.
New Headway: Upper-Intermediate	1	English is almost exclusively used between learners and Inner Circle speakers, including Inner Circle expats in Expanding Circle countries, and communications between Expanding Circle and Inner Circle users.
English Unlimited: Upper Intermediate	3	The book mostly avoids references to geographical locations for target interlocutors. English is used as a tool to discuss a wide variety of people around the globe, but not necessarily providing them with an English-using voice. While there are many Anglo-Saxon names used in example communications, these are not explicitly tied to countries.
Global: Upper Intermediate	3	The target interlocutors are mostly not defined by geographic regions, and users of English in the book are often depicted as a global community. The book opens with a quote stating the 'English language is nobody's special property' (p. 2), but embodies a traditional orientation in other parts.

as described in the GELT framework, with the target interlocutors being positioned as L1 users only. A score of five indicates that the textbooks were entirely representative of a 'global ELT' orientation as described in the GELT framework, with the target interlocutors being representative of a diverse range of all global English users. These results are summarised in Table 6.5, including descriptions of how these scores were derived.

The most globally orientated textbook in this evaluation was *Market Leader*. There was no single discernible target for English use throughout the book apart from global business. The target interlocutors and users of the language in the textbook were global, from professors of marketing in Denmark to hotel managers in the Middle East and to Chinese business graduates from Parisian universities. These characters were often engaged in ELF communications. Moreover, these interlocutors of the language were depicted most often as being language users, rather than language learners. The textbook fell short in its 'Language work' and 'Writing file' tasks, which were predominantly UK-centred. Most of the letters and emails presented in the text involved correspondence between the UK-based companies and those based in Expanding Circle countries, thus portraying a message that English was still predominantly used for communication with the Inner Circle. The lowest rated textbook was *New Headway*, in which the English was almost exclusively portrayed as being between language learners and Inner Circle speakers. This included Inner Circle expats in Expanding Circle countries (e.g. English in Chile, pp. 10–11, Canadians in Korea, p. 12), and a letter from Brazilian-based 'Fernando' to 'James' and Tokyo-based 'Keiko' to 'Ms Jones' (p. 121).

Other textbooks received similar middle-range scores. Contrary to our hypothesis that the business and globally marketed textbooks would be more GELT-orientated than the general textbooks, *Interchange, International Express, English Unlimited* and *Global* were all given the same score in our evaluation, although this score was derived in different ways. For *International Express* the target interlocutors were global, but in a slightly less labelled way than *Market Leader.* The fictional company of the textbooks, within which the characters worked, had global offices in London and Melbourne, which caused much correspondence to be within and from these Inner Circle locations. Thus, while international in its positioning, the textbook often used these two contexts as anchors for global communication, thus embodying both traditional and global depictions.

Interchange and *English Unlimited* cleverly avoided Anglo-dominant content by depicting English as being mostly used between interlocutors who were not fixed to any particular country. In *Interchange* the interlocutors were mostly depicted as being the learners themselves – the users of the textbooks, for example, by adopting a *Student A* and *Student B* task construction. A similar trend was seen in *English Unlimited*, which more explicitly labelled speakers in their tasks and excerpts, but often avoided situating them within labelled speech communities. While there were many Anglo-Saxon names used in the example communications, these were not explicitly tied to countries. In the rare times when they were situated within a national context, the book seemed inclusive of ELF communication, even if it was not the dominant form. For example, a section on cross-cultural misunderstandings (p. 63) highlighted two native speaker communication examples, but also one example of a Korean–Italian ELF exchange.

Global provided mixed messages, by promoting ideals that the 'English language is nobody's special property' (p. 2) in its ethos while embodying a traditional orientation to learners mostly communicating with Inner Circle speakers in other parts of the book. This push-and-pull of traditional and global uses of the language provided it with a middle score, despite much promise in its opening pages.

Table 6.6 *Analysis of assumed target interlocutors*

Interlocutor	*New Headway*	*Inter-change*	*Market Leader*	*International Express*	*Global*	*English Unlimited*	TOTAL
L1 English	24	21	18	10	N/A	11	84
L2 English	1	4	7	15	N/A	14	41
Per cent L2 (%)	4	16	28	60	N/A	56	32

Target Interlocutors: In-Depth Analysis

In order to address the issue of the target interlocutor in a more in-depth way, additional analysis was conducted on displays of English-language communication within the books. We took a sample of the first twenty-six interlocutors within the book and placed them within an L1 or L2 speech community. Often this speaker background information was explicitly referred to in the textbooks, and at other times we had to infer this information based on the characters' given names. While we acknowledge that characters' names are not a clear indication of one's identity as an L1 or L2 user, they are, nevertheless, a way in which some readers of the textbook might infer identity. Seeing as the characters were fictional, we can also assume that names are the predominant way most readers would infer the characters' linguistic background. Thus, due to a lack of other alternatives, this formed the basis of our categorisation where nationally unmarked characters were represented. For all regionally unmarked names, we consulted a name frequency database and assigned speakers to the country where their name occurred most frequently, thus basing our assumptions on probability, rather than subjective judgement. While flawed in its assumptions (i.e. given names do not truly represent a language-using identity), the consistency with which we applied this as a proxy measure of target interlocutor identity nevertheless revealed some interesting results.

First, we examined the countries of the target interlocutors, and further tallied these into assumed L1, mixed L1/L2 and L2 communities. Table 6.6 shows the first twenty-five named interlocutors who engaged in communication within each of the texts. *International Express* and *English Unlimited* revealed the highest percentage of interlocutors of an assumed L2 English-speaking identity at 60% and 56%, respectively. *International Express*'s high score was derived in part due to two main characters (*Pei Lin* and *Diego*) who engaged in repeated ELF communications throughout the book. Despite high scores in our close-look evaluation of *Market Leader*, only 28% of the interlocutors in our sample from this book were from an assumed L2-using identity. Thus, while the book displayed a wide range of positive depictions of

Table 6.7 *Analysis of ELF interactions in textbooks*

	New Headway	*Inter-change*	*Market Leader*	*International Express*	*Global*	*English Unlimited*	Total
L1–L2	1	3	4	6	N/A	8	22
L2–L2	0	1	2	4	N/A	2	9
L1–L1	11	8	6	2	N/A	2	29
Per cent ELF (%)	8	33	50	83	N/A	83	52

English-using people and contexts, when actual examples of communication were presented to the reader, the L1 users of the language dominated.

Interchange, which had avoided marked examples of people using English in our close-look evaluation, scored poorly in our in-depth analysis, which revealed only 16% representativeness of assumed L2 English-using interlocutors. This was only moderately higher than *New Headway*, which included only one speaker of the first twenty-five interlocutors in the book, who was assumed to be an L2 English user. Upon inspection of *New Headway*, we were surprised to find that depictions of L2 English learners were notably absent in the book. That is, the book focused on an English-using context, which was almost exclusive in representation of communication between L1 English speakers. We were unable to analyse the interlocutors from the textbook *Global*, due to a lack of named characters in the depicted communications.

Next, we explored the nature of communication in terms of whether the communications were L1–L1, L1–L2 or L2–L2 when the interlocutors engaged with language use. Table 6.7 illustrates the assumed nature of communication between these interlocutors. Depictions of L2–L2 ELF communication were scarce, except for *International Express*, which contained four ELF communications of a sample of twelve, where no discernible native speaker was present. Both *Market Leader* and *English Unlimited* contained two such instances in each of their samples of twelve. If we take a broad definition of ELF communication, which includes L1 English users, *International Express* and *English Unlimited* contained 83% of such representations. Half of *Market Leader*'s communications were considered ELF, and *Interchange* was a third, at 33%. *New Headway* included just one depiction of an L1–L2 speaker interaction of its sample of twelve. This result was most shocking, as not only were L2 users of English mostly absent, but learners of English communicating with L2 users were, for all purposes, absent throughout the textbook – quite shocking for a textbook aimed at learners. We believe, due to this absence, that learners would have a difficult time imagining themselves in the English-using communities depicted in the textbook, which centred on L1 users speaking English with other L1 users.

English Ownership via Nation-Based Cultural Representations: Close-Look Evaluation

This section examined the references to people and places that formed the content of the textbooks. This was different to the communications explored in the previous section, as the evaluation examined static texts, national cultural references, pictures and historical figures, around which the content of the textbooks was often organised. This cast a wide net over *who* and *what* were being associated with English-language use. With this evaluation, we aimed to make an inference regarding portrayed ownership of the language in terms of the nations and cultures connected to it (see Table 6.8 for evaluations).

Market Leader and *English Unlimited* received the highest scores in our evaluations. *Market Leader*, in keeping with its international target market, showcased numerous non-English-speaking cultures, although these were often presented in somewhat static ways (e.g. 'Business culture in Kazakhstan', p. 61). This was quite different to *English Unlimited*, which, despite receiving the same score as *Market Leader*, seemed to adopt a strategy

Table 6.8 *Evaluation of English ownership in textbooks*

Textbook	Rating	Comment
Market Leader: Upper Intermediate	4	Many non-English-speaking cultures were present but often presented in somewhat static ways.
International Express: Upper Intermediate	3	Cultural depictions are worldwide; however, pop-cultural and news references are over-represented by the United Kingdom. Some across Expanding Circle cultural references, but some stereotypical. Some specialised UK-based cultural references.
New Headway: Upper-Intermediate	1	Predominantly English cultural references with few non-Anglophone cultural references; clear preference for British- and US-centred content; some tasks require shared knowledge of British culture.
Interchange	3	Mixed cultural references. Some sensitivity to using English across cultural borders. Examples drawn from non-English-dominant cultures such as Bollywood. Some activities indicate the Inner Circle as reference point.
English Unlimited: Upper Intermediate	4	Cultural depictions are worldwide. Literary cultural references to people are included from a number of countries. Across cultures, sections depict a static view of culture in various countries.
Global: Upper Intermediate	3	Global cultures, people and places are presented. Literary cultural references to people are included from a number of countries, but the UK and the US culture dominates in this domain, with an Anglo-centric display of authentic materials.

that being global meant to not reference too many countries and locations in their examples, for example, 'Making a complaint to an *international* airline', or 'Applying for a job in *Antarctica'* or 'Researching *exciting locations* for a theatre company'. While these were not explicitly tied to a country, many of the examples appeared very American/British (e.g. there was an American flag flying in the picture of a *'city river boat'*, and pound and dollar amounts were used throughout the book). They also appeared to equate their global outlook as being met by providing numerous non-Anglo historical and political references. In many cases this just did not make sense from a language point of view (e.g. there was a section on the historical leaders of Japan with no clear connection to learning English), and so it seemed that many of these examples were purely used to be 'international' in content coverage, and somewhat tokenistic in their inclusion.

International Express, Global and *Interchange* all received a mid-range score. In *International Express*, cultural depictions were worldwide; however, pop-cultural and news references were over-represented by the United Kingdom. The book's reference to the Expanding Circle cultures was aided by a business project that was referred to throughout the book called 'Latin goes East', which explored business opportunities between East Asia and Latin America. Nevertheless, this contrasted with some UK-based cultural references (e.g. to Monty Python, p. 22), which could be alienating to readers unfamiliar with this content. Some other cultural discussions (e.g. the dialogue in 7.4) displayed stereotypical depictions of foreign cultures. Thus, *International Express* offered uneven and, at times, conflicting cultural messages.

Interchange also included reference to a number of mixed cultural references, such as those located in Taipei, Shanghai, Indonesia and the Philippines. There were also some activities that showed sensitivity to using English across cultural borders (e.g. 'The wrong stuff', p. 83). Some examples existed entirely within the Outer Circle, such as drawing cultural references from Bollywood. However, other activities positioned the Inner Circle as a cultural reference point. For example, in 'It's against the law' (p. 100) the textbook compared the United States and Canada to 'other countries', which were all from the Outer and Expanding Circles. Similarly, 'Comparing cultures' (p. 118) used US culture as its reference point.

In *Global* numerous cultures, people and places were represented, including literary cultural references to people within a global sphere. Nevertheless, the UK and the US cultures dominated in this domain, with a prominently Anglocentric display of authentic materials. Although many texts were included representing global cultures, a closer evaluation revealed that 'authentic texts' (thereby representing the norms of reference to the language) were very Inner Circle-skewed, including excerpts from Jane Austin, H. G. Wells,

Ernest Hemmingway, Edgar Allan Poe, Arthur Conan Doyle, Tom Wolfe and Dr Spock. The emphasis on Inner Circle literary figures dwarfed mentions of other figures, such as Chinua Achebe or Vikram Seth, who was noted as an 'Indian Poet' 'who has lived in England, the US and China' (p. 79). When other cultures were discussed in authentic texts, such as Japanese and Chinese cooking (p. 130), these were taken from Inner Circle sources (e.g. *New Scientist*).

However, this was not done as unashamedly as *New Headway*, which seemed to use England as a cultural selling point for its learners. *New Headway* included many English cultural references, such as to 'Henry VIII' and 'Charles Dickens' (p. 18) and 'Princess Diana' (p. 39). While there were some cultural references where the Anglophone culture was absent, such as German tourists in Spain and global tourists in the Caribbean, Vietnam and Italy (pp. 20–1), there was clear reference to British- and US-centred content. For example, in Chapters 3 and 4, the news stories were predominantly UK- and US-based. Some tasks inferred a shared knowledge of British culture, such as knowledge of educational culture to understand the meaning of 'grammar school' and 'A-levels' (p. 110).

English Ownership via Nation-Based Cultural Representations: In-Depth Analysis

As with our analysis of the target interlocutors, we have conducted our in-depth analysis of cultural representations using a simplified proxy measure, which includes a count of the first named countries in the textbooks. While this is a narrow and static way to explore culture representativeness, and not in keeping with GELT's assertions to break down state-based depictions of culture, these textbooks are artefacts of such cultural views. If we were to analyse the texts through a transnational lens, for example, there would be very little relevant content to use. Thus, returning to static views of national cultures is one way, at least, to objectively (and simply) evaluate which national cultures are represented to learners as being connected to an English-using world. It is also a method that has been used in previous Global Englishes textbook evaluations (Syrbe, 2017) and is one way that we can obtain both quantitative and qualitative evidence.

One limitation of this analysis was that our sample of twenty-five first country mentions per book was rather small. Our adoption of this technique was to ensure consistency across the books, and the lack of mention of nations in some texts meant that the sample remained quite low. The negative effect of this was that our sample was reached within a few chapters in textbooks such as *New Headway*, while in others, such as *Interchange*, this sample included most of the book. Because in *New Headway* many earlier chapters centre on topics

Table 6.9 *Evaluation of global cultures in textbooks*

Nation	*New Headway*	*Inter-change*	*Market Leader*	*International Express*	*Global*	*English Unlimited*	TOTAL
Inner (%)	9	8	5	12	7	5	46
Outer (%)	2	2	4	1	6	4	19
Expanding (%)	14	15	16	12	12	16	85
Most frequent nation	USA (4)	USA (5)	USA (4)	UK (5) USA (5)	USA (4)	India (4)	USA (22)

such as travel, we feel this sample is not entirely representative of the entire book, as our close-look evaluation showed to be very UK-centric in its latter half. Nevertheless, in order to compare the books subjectively, we adopted this approach. This analysis is presented in Table 6.9, which outlines the national cultures within Kachru's three circles, which we have argued previously in this book to be a poor way to categorise linguistic variation, but a useful way to categorise English via nation-based socio-historical factors.

An oft-cited statistic on the global users of English is Crystal's division according to native, second and foreign users of the language, which roughly maps on to Kachru's Three Circle model. Crystal (2003, p. 61) estimates that there are: 320–80 million people who speak English as a first language; 300–500 million people who speak English as a second language; and nearly one billion people who speak English as a foreign language (or lingua franca). Taking Crystal's upper range of estimates, this would equate to 20% of users being within the Inner Circle, 27% in the Outer Circle and 53% in the Expanding Circle, or within a sample of twenty-five a 5:6.75:13.25 ratio of Inner-, Outer- and Expanding Circle representation. Of our sampled textbooks, *Global* came closest to this mark in its ratio of 7:6:12. *English Unlimited* (5:4:16) and *Market Leader* (5:4:16) were also somewhat representative of this ratio, although both texts favoured Expanding Circle contexts over Outer Circle ones in representation. *International Express, Interchange* and *New Headway* were all over-representative of the Inner Circle and underrepresentative of the Outer Circle.

Linguistic Orientation: Close-Look Evaluation

This section examined references to monolingual versus multilingual orientations. Scores were given on the five-point scale, based on interpretations of evidence that pointed to either a traditional or global orientation within the GELT framework (see Table 6.10). A score of one indicated an absolute

Table 6.10 *Linguistic orientation of textbooks*

Textbook	Rating	Comment
Market Leader: Upper Intermediate	3	Inclusion of non-English-language translated quotes at start of some chapters promoted importance of other languages. The use of other languages alongside English was notably absent despite opportunities to highlight this business practice.
International Express	2	The use of other languages alongside English was notably absent despite opportunities to highlight this business practice in the numerous global contexts; one example of a translanguaging strategy.
New Headway: Upper-Intermediate	1	Little reference to languages other than English; some examples showcase the learning of foreign languages other than English as a negative experience.
Interchange	3	Some content placed value on knowing other languages and respected multilingual speakers.
English Unlimited	2	Little reference made to other languages, despite opportunities to highlight multilingual historical figures in excerpts.
Global	2	Multilingualism was rarely discussed in the text; some evidence of a monolingual standpoint, with students' L1 depicted as source of interference and error in L2.

monolingual orientation, and a score of five indicated an absolute multilingual orientation.

The textbooks bunched in scores towards the monolingual orientation with little positive mention in the textbooks regarding multilingual users. In *New Headway* there was reference to languages other than English, except in the first chapter that discusses expat lives. In one case, a Canadian bemoans the fact that learning Chinese characters 'stinks'. In another case, an Englishman complains that, despite living in Chile for four years, he 'cannot make himself understood at a deeper level', and feels he 'doesn't belong', unlike English culture that 'fits him like a glove'. *New Headway,* therefore, had quite negative depictions of learning or using languages other than English.

International Express, English Unlimited and *Global* rarely discussed multilingualism. In *Global* multilingualism was rarely discussed in the text, and when it was the book took a monolingual standpoint. The listening exercises in unit 1 were particularly egregious, where four students discussed their errors in English as being caused by interference in the L1, such as a Spanish speaker mixing his and her, a Bosnian student mapping English on to the syntax of her L1 and a German student mistaking German vocabulary for English vocabulary, a French student not pronouncing /h/ in 'aitch' (p. 151) and an Italian student not spelling out acronyms due to transference from her L1. Learners were shown to be purveyors of mistakes and error. In *English Unlimited*, the use of other languages alongside English was notably absent, despite opportunities to highlight multilingual historical figures, who featured in excerpts.

In *International Express* the use of other languages alongside English was notably absent, despite opportunities to highlight this business practice in the numerous global contexts highlighted throughout the book. However, *International Express* was one of the few books that highlighted a translanguaging strategy (activity 10.2), which encouraged speakers to make use of their full linguistic repertoire in offering advice for note-taking. In one audio James asks Nicola 'Should notes be taken in English rather than the student's own language?' Nicola replies that the best strategy is to do what suits the students, and that clarity in note-taking should not be sacrificed because a student is worried about English-language abbreviations. The subtext in this advice is that other languages could be used to enhance note-taking clarity.

Market Leader included some non-English-language translated quotes at the start of each chapter (e.g. Swahili proverb, p. 22), which promoted the importance of other language users, placing them in a prestige position. However, the use of other languages alongside English was notably absent, despite opportunities to highlight this business practice in the numerous global contexts highlighted throughout the book. Some content in *Interchange* placed value on knowing other languages (e.g. asking what two foreign languages students would like to learn, p. 122; discussing the importance of choosing brand names that translate well into other languages, p. 83; and celebrating a speaker of nineteen languages as being 'gifted', p. 111).

Summary of Findings

New Headway received the lowest evaluations in our analysis. The textbook was unabashedly Inner Circle-focused. The promotion of Inner Circle cultures, such as the United States and the United Kingdom, seemed to be specific marketing ploys, which positioned learners as studying English to participate in these specific cultures. Of all the books *New Headway* appeared to be the least aware of English as a global language and, accordingly, made minimal attempts to prepare students to use it as such.

Interchange was evaluated as being a superior general textbook, as it made more explicit attempts to be more globally orientated than *New Headway*. While there were still numerous references to Inner Circle cultures, it was clearly more sensitive to its global learners who were not all learning English to participate in Inner Circle cultural contexts. The interchange was also helped by a few references that placed value on multilingualism, and on using the English language across linguistic and cultural communities. Some of our in-depth analyses revealed that the interchange was, nonetheless, heavily focused on L1 users as being the predominant target interlocutor for English use, and American English was the predominant language norm presented throughout.

International Express was one of the few books that highlighted a translanguaging strategy, which encouraged speakers to make use of their full linguistic repertoire in note-taking. Likewise, in a further discussion of listening, the book gave advice on strategies for negotiation of meaning. It offered contrasting advice, such as that students mimic sounds from audio cassettes, but also that some sounds like 'th' are understood even if they are not pronounced in the standard way.

Market Leader proved itself to the juggernaut of textbooks in terms of its global focus, achieving comparatively high evaluations in most areas. While it included references to American and English pronunciation norms, the audio samples were diverse, exposing students to a range of accents (even if some were inauthentic). It was culturally inclusive, albeit at times static in its depictions. While there still seemed to be an Anglo-cultural dominance in many tasks, text samples and the audio, it certainly was explicitly aware of English as a global language, and how business English students might likely need to use the language in the future.

English Unlimited, despite its promise of a global focus, was often evaluated as comparable with the long-running general textbook *Interchange*, and the business textbook of *International Express*. The textbook seemed to adopt a strategy that being global meant to not reference too many countries and locations in their examples, although many of the examples appeared very American/British-centred, despite not being explicitly defined as such. They also appeared to equate their global outlook as being met by providing numerous non-Anglo historical and political references. While this made the book seem much more global compared to the other texts, one might argue that this was at a tokenistic level. The book was improved by its strong depictions of ELF exchanges among its main characters.

Global was very promising during the first-glance evaluation, but once we conducted a close-look evaluation we realised that many of the global depictions were at a superficial level. This investigation led it to not outperforming (and indeed underperforming) many of the general and business textbooks within many of the GELT criteria. While it should be commended for adopting an openness to including a variety of speakers, this content clashed with other decisions in the book, which focused on 'error'. Our analysis revealed similar contradictions with the depictions of culture in the texts.

Conclusion: What Do Good GELT Materials Look Like?

Our textbook analysis can be used as a departure point from which to draw conclusions on what good GELT materials should look like. One of the first issues raised in the analysis is the importance of needs analysis in creating good materials. *Market Leader* proved itself to be more globally focused than the texts that specifically promoted themselves as being aimed at teaching EIL. *Market Leader* probably made its content decisions based on learners' business use needs, highlighting the important role of needs analysis in developing appropriate materials for a curriculum, a topic we discussed in Chapter 2. In Chapter 5 we further discussed GELT as English for a specific purpose, thus parallels between the material created for the specific purpose of using English as a business lingua franca somewhat align with elements within the GELT curriculum. Good GELT materials could build on this model and use needs analysis to inform the content of their textbooks, rather than making decisions at the ideological level, as we suspect was the case for the two global textbooks in our sample.

Our analysis has found that there was over-reliance on UK and American models of English, and an over-representation of L1 speakers. We conclude that this is not representative of how English will be used by most students who learn via these textbooks. Nevertheless, some texts showed positive signs of change. *Market Leader* and *English Unlimited* used a fairly high proportion of non-standard English in their audio, which showcases to learners that English norms (albeit only phonological ones) are flexibly used in global contexts. Eighty-three per cent of the interactions in some of the textbooks could be broadly defined as ELF (L1–L2 or L2–L2), and L2–L2 interactions accounted for one-third of the audio sample from *International Express*. This is a positive starting point for further commercial materials development in this area. It also indicates that some textbooks are beginning to become more inclusive, at least in the constrained context of accompanying audio materials. Good GELT materials could further this progress by including examples of not only phonologically varied English but also morphosyntactically varied English. ELF corpora may be key in this area. We reiterate Galloway's (2018a) call for 'more dialogue between ELF researchers, ELT practitioners and ELT materials writers and publishers' to 'facilitate the movement away from the focus on accuracy and native English towards a more realistic and representative view of how English functions as an international lingua franca' (p. 478).

Movement is also needed in the static depictions of English-speaking cultures in the textbooks. Indeed, culture was so nation-centric in its portrayals that we needed to resort to a static analytical framework within which to interpret them. Such treatment of culture is entirely incompatible with GELT. Good GELT materials would draw on work in ELF, such as that by Baker (see Chapter 1) to encourage students to see culture as fluid, and co-constructed. Good GELT materials should portray culture as being created in communities of practice and not depict learners as *joining* an English-using culture but *co-creating* it. As Galloway (2018a) notes:

> Materials writers are encouraged to draw on such opportunities and to encourage learners to reflect on their encounters . . . also reflecting on how communication between those from diverse lingua-cultural backgrounds differs to static predetermined NES norms. (p. 477)

Cultures should also not be defined by traditional state-based or ethnic-based borders. They can include any number of flexible English-using cultures in the workplace, social circles, or even virtual ones, where English is used to fill a communicative need within that culture. Louhiala-Salminen et al. (2005) note that 'learners should be trained to see themselves as communicators, with real jobs to perform and needs to fulfill; it is these jobs and needs that should be emphasised, not the language they use to carry them out' (p. 419).

Good materials should further equip learners with the strategies needed to use language in fluid and diverse contexts. In our analysis, we only recorded a handful of examples where learners were taught strategies to negotiate meaning or draw on their other linguistic resources when using English. These findings concur with recent evaluations of communication strategies in ELT materials, such as Vettorel (2018), who notes that the relevance of communication strategies in ELF has not yet been acknowledged in materials. This is despite the fact that:

> Communication strategies have been shown to have a particularly significant role in English as a Lingua Franca communication, that is characterized by negotiation and co-construction of meaning; in these encounters, where different linguacultures meet, ELF speakers employ a range of pragmatic strategies to solve, or pre-empt, (potential) non-understandings often drawing on their plurilingual repertoires, too. (Vettorel, 2018, p. 1)

Good GELT materials should go further than teaching language, by, instead, training students to use the language in flexible ways in order to achieve successful communication in a range of contexts. Thus, strategy training to be able to adapt, to clarify, to repair and to draw on other linguistic resources is an essential component for modern-day, global textbook content.

Due to the fact that commercial materials tend to drag behind learner needs, it may take some time for suitable commercial materials for GELT to begin to emerge. This is because global publishing houses tend to focus on the 'late majority' of an innovation as they are driven by profitability. As was discussed in Chapter 4, Global Englishes innovations are still in the early stages of the innovation process and, thus, it will take time for innovation to achieve a critical mass. In the interim, curriculum developers and materials writers may need to adapt existing materials or create their own for their local contexts. The flip side of this is that home-grown materials may be better catered to local learners' needs, as writers will be more attuned to their own language learners' needs. In fact, as Chapter 4 has shown many innovations in English language teaching, especially those driven by demands to teach English as a global language, are occurring despite the barrier of a lack of materials. Thus, rather than being driven by large publishing houses, changes are occurring at a grassroots level in teachers' own classrooms. The emergence of materials, however, would greatly speed up the innovation process and, thus, research into their current lacks can help inform the creation of new materials. As new materials emerge, especially those that are promoted as global in orientation, evaluation and analysis is essential, in order to investigate whether their claims ring true.

7 Global Englishes and Teacher Education

It is clear from this book thus far that the global spread of the English language and its use as a lingua franca raises questions about conventional modes of thinking in TESOL. As discussed in Chapter 4, teacher beliefs, education, support and training have been identified as key 'barriers' to consider in GELT curriculum innovation. Our innovation model (Figure 4.2) also places attitudes as key factors that affect innovation uptake. This chapter responds to the call for more research on the attitudes of these important stakeholders and also on how GELT can be incorporated into pre-and in-service TESOL practitioner training. We review key research and present an original empirical study to explore how familiarising pre-service and in-service teachers with Global Englishes subject matter can help them become part of this paradigm shift. The study also sheds light on incorporating a GELT perspective in varied teaching contexts.

GELT and TESOL Practitioner Education

The importance of teachers' beliefs was highlighted in Chapter 4 as being a key factor to ensure successful and sustained curriculum innovation. Chapter 4 also highlighted the fact that many ELF scholars have noted the need to raise teachers' awareness of ELF research. Many postgraduate TESOL and applied linguistics programmes now offer Global Englishes components and recent publications showcase such programmes in contexts around the globe (Matsuda, 2017). Some recent publications also offer lesson plans and activities (Galloway, 2017a; Galloway and Rose, 2015; Matsuda, 2017). Matsuda's (2009) examination of the content of teacher education programmes in Kachru's Expanding Circle, for example, found that, although the majority focus on American and British English, more than half offer courses that cover topics on the spread of English, World Englishes, and social and regional dialects of English. The lack of research-led practical suggestions for teachers to implement change was noted, however. Dewey (2014) makes a similar point, noting that MA TESOL modules that cover this subject tend to concentrate on

ELF research and theory, with relatively little consideration of the practical aspects of incorporating ELF in the classroom.

Challenges to the Hegemony of Western TESOL

By advocating the inclusion of GELT in TESOL practitioner education courses, we are not suggesting abolishing current content, but wish to encourage a critical examination of this through a Global Englishes lens. We want to position pre- and in-service TESOL practitioners, who are 'experts' in their contexts, not as passive receivers of an education, but as important agents of change in the curriculum innovation process. It has been two decades since Pennycook (1998) criticised TESOL programmes for reproducing images of 'the superior Self' over 'the inferior Other', and more than a decade since Holliday (2005) critiqued the dominance of native speakerism in Western TESOL, and characterised the 'English-speaking West as the source of dominant TESOL thinking' (p. 2). It is unfortunate that this may still be the case in some contexts.

Ilieva and Waterstone's (2013) curriculum examination found that the discourses and practices circulating in Western TESOL programmes are still informed by Western superiority. Dewey and Patsko (2017) also note that despite the incorporation of 'ELF and/or Global Englishes' in the syllabus of two initial English language teaching awards (the Certificate in English Language Teaching to Adults (CELTA) and Trinity Certificate in Teaching English to Speakers of Other Languages (CertTESOL)), the guidelines lack guidance about the associated pedagogical implications. The reference to 'variation' and 'variety' more or less interchangeably leads to a concern that ELF and varieties of English may become conflated in the minds of the teachers. Thus, it is uncertain 'whether the syllabus writers or trainers on CertTESOL courses will approach the topic of ELF in a way that is compatible with an ELF perspective' (p. 445), resonating with our call for research on classroom-based research (see Chapter 5). Such superficial coverage and native bias is unfortunate given the numerous studies reporting dissatisfaction with pre- and in-service teacher training courses and the relevance for diverse contexts, discussed next.

Challenges to the Relevance of TESOL Practitioner Education

Much has been written on the barriers that novice teachers may face (see Farrell, 2012) and the gap between what is taught on teacher education programmes and what happens in the classroom (Baecher, 2012; Faez & Valeo, 2012; Tarone & Allwright, 2005). Research has also been conducted within the field of TESOL on the relevance of preparation programmes (Barnawi & Le

Ha, 2014; Chowdhury & Phan, 2014; Hobbs, 2013; Holliday, 2005; Inoue & Stracke, 2013; Li & Edwards, 2013; Phan, 2007; Swan, 2015). Some of these examine the views of those enrolled on these programmes. Inoue and Stracke's (2013) interviews with eight English L2 students taking a postgraduate TESOL course in Australia revealed that they were aware of the privileged position of Inner Circle English(es) and of native English-speaking teachers, and valued their Australian qualification to differentiate themselves from other teachers in their home countries. However, six of the participants in this study questioned the current situation, having realised the importance of introducing World Englishes in their own teaching.

The importance of practitioners' own contexts was also highlighted in Hobbs's (2013) study with nine trainees and six experienced teachers who had completed a similar certificate course earlier in their career. Using field notes, questionnaires, interviews, course documents and emails, the tips and techniques introduced were found to be the most valuable compared to the language awareness input, which was seen as more 'theoretical' and less valuable. The study called for the inclusion of different teaching contexts, longer supervised teaching practice and for TESOL practitioner education to 'adjust to meet the shifting needs of English-language learners' (ibid., p. 173), due to the fact that bilingual proficiency is taking central stage among other things.

Others have examined the attitudes of practitioners after they return to their home contexts. Swann's (2015) interviews with fifteen teachers of English from seven countries revealed that CLT was a major issue, highlighting a 'mismatch between what the student teachers have been taught, and what they have to face in their teaching environments' (p. 65). In Saudi Arabia, Barnawi and Le Ha (2015) investigated the extent to which North American, British and Australian TESOL programmes have prepared teachers to teach in their home contexts. Their study used questionnaires, observations and interviews with two Western-trained Saudi TESOL language teachers over six months. The study found that they did not uncritically adopt assumptions of Western pedagogies and one used more context-sensitive methods and the students' mother tongue.

In China, Li and Edwards (2013) assessed the impact of a UK-based professional development programme on curriculum innovation and change using the diffusion of innovation theory. Interviews, focus group discussions and observations with forty-eight TESOL practitioners who had taken part in this training, nine who had not, and ten interviews with English managers revealed that there was evidence of innovation on return to China, although reinvention was common to ensure it fitted with local needs. These studies, as with those outlined in Chapter 4, highlight the importance of understanding the context within which practitioners are working. The few studies that have been conducted in relation to GELT are discussed next.

Practitioners' Attitudes Towards Global Englishes and ELT

Some studies have looked at practitioners' attitudes towards Global Englishes and some of these have also looked at their attitudes towards ELT (for an overview, see Galloway, 2017a; Galloway & Rose, 2015; Jenkins, 2007). While only one of these used mixed methods, we did note in Chapter 4 that several of these provided insights on the possible factors that influence these attitudes, including preconceived stereotypes (Jenkins, 2007), and others highlighted a theory–practice divide and the complexity of attitudes (Jenkins, 2007; Sasaki, 2004, cited in Yoshikawa, 2005; Seidlhofer & Widdowson, 2003; Sifakis & Sougari, 2005).

Some studies discuss their results in relation to the implications for teacher education. Blair (2015), for example, who uses the term 'ELF-aware teacher education' (p. 100), conducted interviews with twelve teachers and utilised discussion forums, emails and a joint interview with two teachers. The European L2 users from the Expanding Circle had received some, or part, of their teacher education in the United Kingdom. The teachers were found to display what Dewey (2012, p. 167) calls teachers' 'fundamental ambivalence about ELF' and proposes that teacher education programmes can integrate a 'post-native' sociolinguistic and ELF position by giving more prominence to sociolinguistic and sociocultural perspectives on SLA modules, including ELF use as a goal for learners, more focus on pragmatics inclusion of ELF/Global Englishes elements in pedagogy modules, and provide opportunities to explore diversity and challenge key constructs such as 'nativeness', among others things.

Doan's (2014) interviews with eleven lecturers taking a teacher education option in Vietnam to examine culture teaching from an EIL perspective concluded that a pluricentric perspective should be adopted that moves beyond the native speaker culture model. The author calls for an inclusive EIL paradigm that endorses the diversity of English and validates speakers of non-native English as authentic users of the language. Dilek and Özdemir's (2015) questionnaires with 300 pre- and in-service teachers in Turkey revealed that the former was more open towards ELF, more likely to question the normative perspective of English language teaching, and more critical of native speaker superiority. ELF instruction and familiarity with ELF were also found to have a positive effect on attitudes and they concluded with a call for the inclusion of an ELF-aware approach in teacher education to help the movement towards an ELF-aware approach in ELT.

Some studies provide accounts of practitioners' experiences introducing a GELT perspective into their classrooms. Manara's (2014) critical reflection of her experience of teaching EIL in an Australian context using narrative inquiry found resistance to ideas. Learners questioned its usefulness in contexts where tests adhered to standard norms. Similarly, Giri and Foo's (2014) study in Japan also highlights resistance. Using a critical reflective narrative approach with one non-native English speaker in TESOL (NNEST), the study examines the dilemma of being an EIL advocate in a society that values native English-speaking norms. Indeed, as discussed in Chapter 4, 'challenges to normative beliefs' may create the 'most resistance' (Ullucci, 2007, p. 1). However, beliefs are not static constructs and are subject to change as has been highlighted by the recent body of research on the influence of Global Englishes instruction on students' attitudes (Derwing et al., 2002; Galloway, 2011, 2013, 2017a; Galloway & Rose, 2013; Shim, 2002; Sung, 2015).

Influence of GELT Practitioner Education on Attitudes

As outlined in Chapter 4, research is varied on whether teacher education influences beliefs. In Japan, Suzuki's (2011) mixed methods study (questionnaire, individual in-depth interview, classroom observation, analysis of teaching materials, and analysis of students' writing) with three student teachers found that instruction in the diversity of English can affect student teachers' views of English. Suzuki also found the influence to vary depending on their past exploration, and knowledge, of non-native English. She concluded, however, that 'single-shot instruction in the diversity of English' is not enough due to their 'deeply ingrained beliefs that there is a single useful form of English for international communication, and this is standard English' (p. 151).

Hall et al. (2013) developed an online course for English language teachers to raise their awareness of the pluricentricity of English, including World Englishes and ELF, and the pedagogical implications. The course design was based on the conviction that beliefs must change within the profession before macro-level change can occur. It was piloted with seventeen pre- and in-service teachers and a teacher trainer from the Inner, Outer, and Expanding Circles. The majority showed recognition of the problems associated with a monolithic ontology of English. Overall, the course was found to have the potential to trigger change in their beliefs and practices, and in some cases to encourage them to seek to promote change in others. However, many teachers have a firm attachment to a monolithic ontology of English and other languages. This 'bottom-up' approach to applied linguistic research emphasises the need to listen to and interact with teachers and explore how their educational and professional experiences influence their beliefs. The trial feedback was encouraging, albeit revealing the expected 'magnitude of the challenge' (Hall et al., 2013, p. 16)

Vettorel (2016), who prefers the term 'WE and ELF-informed teacher education', found similar results in her examination of pre-service teacher beliefs. The participants were undertaking a university course in Italy, which included a module on the pedagogical implications of World Englishes and ELF. Pre-course and post-course questionnaires, interviews, class reflections and materials developed by the trainees revealed that it raised their awareness of the issues and there was evidence of a 'readiness to move towards a WE- and ELF-informed approach', also visible in the teaching ideas, which included several of Galloway and Rose's (2015) proposals for change. It modified their perspective and prompted them to reflect on the *barriers* to incorporating this perspective in their classroom. Barriers included its potential difficultness and complexity compared to only focusing on one variety, which may cause students' confusion (a concern raised by students themselves in Galloway, 2011, 2013, 2017a), a lack of time, a scarcity of materials and an attachment to standard English. They remained attached to the role of grammar and error correction and the need to provide learners with a standard 'reference model'. There was also a degree of uncertainty as to what model/standards they should follow. Forum discussions did highlight, however, that the course encouraged them to critically reflect and question the non-monolithic perspective of TESOL.

Lopriore (2016) investigated the attitudes of 250 native (15% of the sample) and non-native pre- and in-service teachers in Italy taking a teacher education courses that introduced ELF and the implications for pedagogy. Pre-course questionnaires, four focus group interviews, written narratives and lesson plans revealed that the participants were keen to explore new ways of teaching English, which were inclusive of World Englishes and ELF. The course enabled them to reflect on their own ELT contexts, critically examine materials in a 'new light' and plan locally relevant activities within a World Englishes, EIL and ELF-informed viewpoint. However, there was a lack of ways to improve learners' negotiating strategies and most trainees lacked a capability for observing and using interactive strategies. The study concludes with a call for more exposure to samples of meaning negotiation and for noticing activities through the VOICE corpus. Participants also referred to other tasks and duties, and difficulties were not found to be related to teachers' resistance to changes or in their attitudes, but due to the limited time for introducing innovations and selecting and adjusting materials. The study calls for action research in teacher education courses to trigger observations of their classroom practice.

Sifakis and Bayyurt's (2015, 2018) teacher education project (ELF-Ted project), focused on putting their transformative ELF-aware teacher education (ELFATE) framework into practice to raise TESOL practitioners' awareness of 'ELF teaching matters' (Sifakis, 2007, p. 355) and to encourage them to critically reflect on, and challenge, their own beliefs about language and teaching. Twelve teachers (eleven from Turkey and one from Greece) completed all three phases of the project. Evaluations were collected and two focus groups with Turkish participants during and after the pilot phase were conducted (Sifakis & Bayyurt, 2015). The framework raised participants' awareness of their deep-rooted convictions and helped them explore new perspectives, conduct action research and try out activities and lessons 'that deviate (sometimes significantly) from established or expected practices' (Sifakis & Bayyurt, 2016, p. 148). They found ELF a straightforward notion and viewed ELF-aware training as a means to become aware of new developments in ELT. The framework enabled them to pinpoint concrete examples of where native English norms are promoted. Reflections on their pedagogical practice led to self-confidence as non-native English speakers and teachers.

They reported learners' positive and enthusiastic reactions to the ELF-aware lessons, which the authors note is evidence of the need for locally designed materials and activities by those who intimately know their own context, resonating with our conclusion in Chapter 6 that materials be adapted to local needs. Participants felt that learners could become ELF-aware, without this necessarily influencing the way English is taught in Turkey, even in contexts where stakeholder perceptions strongly favour standard English.

However, the project did not result in a radical transformation; many were enthusiastic but continued to resort to 'traditional' methods when teaching. Three types of participants were identified: supporters, risk-takers, and sceptics. The study concludes that it is early days for 'ELF-aware pedagogy' due to the diversity in teaching contexts, teacher beliefs and learner needs, suggesting that 'only micro-innovation is possible' (Sifakis & Bayyurt, 2016, p. 150), referring to localised pedagogical interventions by individual teachers. They also highlight the importance of engaging with the possible barriers to curriculum innovation on TESOL practitioner programmes to help them manage innovation in their own contexts, calling for more action research data.

The Study

The study presented in this chapter was conducted with pre- and in-service TESOL practitioners taking a Global Englishes for Language Teaching course on a one-year Master's in TESOL programme at a university in the United Kingdom. The course was designed and delivered by one of the authors. In order to inform GELT practitioner education and provide insights into implementing GELT in diverse contexts around the globe, the following research questions were generated:

1. What are pre-service and in-service TESOL practitioners' attitudes towards the GELT course and its relevance for their own teaching practice?
2. What are their attitudes towards the proposals and barriers for GELT put forward in the literature?
3. To what extent did the GELT course influence their attitudes?

The study also aimed to address concerns that the pedagogical implications of Global Englishes research continue to be theorised in the literature without empirical data on implementing proposals for change. Further, the study provides practical suggestions on how to implement GELT.

The Setting

The Global Englishes for Language Teaching option course (for an overview, see Galloway, 2017b) was introduced in 2013. The MSc TESOL programme attracts both in-service and pre-service teachers, with the majority being from China. In the first semester, students take compulsory courses on TESOL methodology, curriculum, second language acquisition and research methods. In the second semester, they take two further research methods courses and two option courses. The GELT course runs for eight weeks; students participate in a one-hour pre-lecture workshop, a one-hour lecture and a two-hour workshop each week. Topics include the history of English, language variation, World Englishes, EIL, ELF and translanguaging research, the role of English in different contexts, language attitudes, identity, English language teaching, GELT, the internationalisation of higher education and the future of English. Core texts are Galloway & Rose (2015) and Jenkins (2015). The GELT framework aids reflective practice, encouraging reflection on readings and lectures in relation to their own beliefs, familiar curricula and learning and teaching contexts. They also reflect on key TESOL concepts and theories introduced in semester one and critically examine relevant research studies, prompting discussion on 'standard' English and, for some, their 'normative mindset' (Seidlhofer, 2008, pp. 3–4).

Research Design

Data was collected via an online questionnaire ($n = 41$) at the start and end of the course. Interviews ($n = 21$) were also conducted before and after the course, followed by six post-course focus groups ($n = 27$). A pilot study was conducted in 2015 to test the instruments, which were adjusted accordingly. Data was collected between 2016 and 2017 with two cohorts of students, who studied the same content and were taught in the same way. The questionnaire elicited background information and all instruments elicited views on GELT, the course and the proposals and barriers (Galloway and Rose, 2015). Interviews, conducted in English, began by allowing participants a chance to talk freely about their teaching and language-learning experience and familiar ELT context, followed by semi-structured prompts based on Kvale's (1996) question types. Focus groups prompts, based on Krueger's (1998) five category framework, were conducted last and aimed to provide an opportunity to reflect on attitudes and experiences in comparison to their peers (Krueger & Casey, 2015) and to create an interactive environment to discuss these attitudes and exchange ideas (Rossman & Rallis, 2016).

Data Analysis

Quantitative data analysis was conducted using the IBM® SPSS v.22 statistical software. Descriptive statistics were utilised to summarise the data. Non-parametric statistical tests, including Mann–Whitney U tests and Kruskal–Wallis analysis of variance tests, were used with the ordinal data. Qualitative analysis was conducted in NVivo 11. Qualitative data sets were treated as separate 'cases' and analysed separately. The focus group data was analysed as the joint product of the group discussion, rather than the reflection of individual views (Smithson, 2000) and the main focus was on group dynamics, how participants established common ground (Överlien et al., 2005) and the ways in which this influenced expressed opinions. The pre-course and post-course data were compared to address research question 3.

Limitations

One of the limitations relates to the fact that research data were collected in one of the researcher's own classrooms (for an overview of the complexities of doing such research, see Galloway, 2017c). However, participation was voluntary, did not affect course grades and anonymity has been protected. The single setting of the study and relatively small quantitative sample pose further limitations. However, the mixed methods study aimed to give participants a voice and address any possible relationships of unequal power caused by the dual role of the researcher/course instructor. Additional steps to ensure the credibility of the findings included member checking of the transcripts, thick description of the setting and cross-coder analysis.

Questionnaire Results

Participant Overview

Fifty-seven participants completed a pre-course questionnaire, and 38 completed a post-course questionnaire. Demographic information of the participants was taken from the pre-course questionnaire. As noted in Galloway et al. (under submission), the majority of the respondents were female (n = 41), under the age of thirty (n = 42) and from China (n = 35). Other countries included Indonesia (n = 3), the United Kingdom (n = 3), Hong Kong (n = 2), the United States (n = 1), Malaysia (n = 1), Japan (n = 1) and Thailand (n = 1).

About a quarter (n = 12) did not have any teaching experience, but some had either less than 1 month (n = 8), 1–3 months (n = 8), 4–12 months (n = 10), 1–4 years (n = 5) or more than 5 years (n = 3).

Attitudes Towards the GELT Optional Course and Barriers for Implementation

Students responded on a four-point Likert scale (*1 = strongly disagree* to *4 = strongly agree*). In the pre-course questionnaire, 40 of the 41 agreed or strongly agreed that *the Global Englishes option course will be useful for my future English teaching career* (M = 3.22, SD = 0.48) and 38 agreed or strongly agreed that *Global Englishes should be a topic on all MSc TESOL/English language teacher education programmes* (M = 3.10, SD = 0.49).

Students were introduced to Galloway and Rose's (2015) six GELT proposals for change to ELT, and the barriers to implementing change, in an introductory lecture on Global Englishes in semester one. In the pre-course questionnaire, attitudes towards all of these were very positive with all mean scores over 3.00 (Table 7.1). They all also thought all six proposals would be possible to achieve in their teaching contexts, although they were least confident about changing English teacher-hiring practices (Table 7.1).

With regard to the barriers, they strongly believed that *language assessment* (M = 3.38, SD = 0.54) was a barrier, with 22 agreeing and 16 strongly agreeing. Twenty-three agreed and 16 strongly agreed that *attachment to 'standard' English* (M = 3.38, SD = 0.54) was a barrier; 25 agreed and 14 strongly agreed with *teacher education* (M = 3.33, SD = 0.53); 30 agreed and 9 strongly agreed with *lack of Global Englishes ELT materials* (M = 3.20, SD = 0.46); and 29 agreed and 8 strongly agreed with *teacher-hiring practices* (M = 3.13, SD = 0.52) (see Table 7.2).

Influence of GELT Course on Attitudes

To investigate whether there were significant differences between the pre- and post-course questionnaire, a Mann–Whitney U test was performed (Table 7.3). There were some significant differences, although since nearly all either agreed or strongly agreed that the *GELT course will be useful for their future teaching career* (40 out of 41 in the pre-course survey and 31 out of 35 in the post-course survey) and that *Global Englishes should be a topic on all MSc TESOL/English language teacher education programmes* (38 out of 41 in pre and 33 out of 36 in post), the course did not significantly influence attitudes to these prompts.

However, at the end of the semester, students put less importance on the need for English teachers to have a *knowledge of English grammar* (M = 3.48

Table 7.1 *Frequencies and percentages of participants' attitudes towards the relevance of GELT proposals for their future teaching context*

Item	Description	Mean	SD
Relevance to their future teaching context	*Raise awareness of Global Englishes*	3.46	0.51
	Emphasise respect for diverse culture and identity	3.41	0.55
	Raise awareness of ELF strategies	3.28	0.51
	Emphasise respect for multilingualism	3.21	0.41
	Change English teacher-hiring practices	3.21	0.62
	Increase Global Englishes exposure	3.18	0.51
Positive to achieve in future teaching context	*Raise awareness of Global Englishes*	3.36	0.54
	Emphasise respect for diverse culture and identity	3.28	0.51
	Emphasise respect for multilingualism	3.23	0.49
	Raise awareness of ELF strategies	3.15	0.54
	Increase Global Englishes exposure	3.10	0.45
	Change English teacher-hiring practices	2.95	0.61

Table 7.2 *Frequencies and percentages of students' attitudes towards the relevance of the barriers to their teaching context*

GELT	Mean	SD
The future of English	3.48	0.51
Language assessment	3.38	0.54
Attachment to 'standard' English	3.38	0.54
Teacher education	3.33	0.53
Lack of Global Englishes ELT material	3.20	0.46
Teacher-hiring practices	3.13	0.52

in the pre-course versus M = 3.16 in the post-course questionnaire, U = 586.0, p = 0.013, r = −0.28) and *good pronunciation* (M = 3.41 versus M = 3.19, U = 613.0, p = 0.021, r = −0.26). They were also significantly more positive about the need for English teachers to have experience using *English as a Lingua Franca* (M = 3.45 in the pre-course versus M = 3.67 in the post-course, U = 548.0, p = 0.037, r = −0.24). However, positive attitudes towards the importance of considering some GELT proposals in their future teaching contexts

Table 7.3 *Comparison of pre- and post-course attitudes*

Item Description	Group	N[a]	Mean Rank	U	p	r
The Global Englishes option course will be useful for my future English teaching career.	Pre	41	38.51	717.0	0.995	0.00
	Post	35	38.49			
Global Englishes should be a topic on all MSc TESOL/English language teacher education programmes.	Pre	41	36.01	615.5	0.133	-0.17
	Post	36	42.40			
The following skills are important for an English teacher in this context:						
Knowledge of English grammar	Pre	44	46.18	586.0	0.013	-0.28
	Post	37	34.84			
Good pronunciation	Pre	44	45.57	613.0	0.021	-0.26
	Post	37	35.57			
The following topics covered on the course will be useful:						
English as a Lingua Franca	Pre	40	34.20	548.0	0.037	-0.24
	Post	36	43.28			
The following GELT proposals introduced briefly in semester one are important to consider in my future teaching context:						
Raise awareness of ELF strategies	Pre	39	32.54	489.0	0.026	-0.25
	Post	34	42.12			
Emphasise respect for multilingualism	Pre	39	32.88	502.5	0.031	-0.26
	Post	34	41.72			
The following barriers to introducing a Global Englishes perspective into the ELT classroom briefly introduced in the 'Language and the Learner' lecture are relevant to my context:						
Language assessment	Pre	39	32.82	500.0	0.038	-0.24
	Post	34	41.79			
Attachment to 'standard' English	Pre	40	32.95	498.0	0.039	-0.24
	Post	33	41.91			
Lack of Global Englishes ELT material	Pre	40	33.00	500.0	0.021	-0.27
	Post	34	42.79			

[a] N: Number

Scores ranged from 1 (Strongly disagree) to 4 (Strongly agree) lessened, such as the need to *raise awareness of ELF strategies* (M = 3.56 versus M = 3.28, U = 489.0, p = 0.026, r = −0.25) and *emphasise respect for multilingualism* (M = 3.44 versus M = 3.21, U = 502.5, p = 0.031, r = −0.26).

When asked about the possibility of implementing these proposals in their context, students did report higher mean scores after the course, but the difference was not significant. This is related to the fact that both before and after the course, students had higher mean scores (>3.0) for all five barriers to introducing GELT in their contexts. Almost all either agreed or strongly agreed before and after the course, but at the end of the semester, there were significantly higher levels of agreement that *language assessment* (M = 3.65 versus M = 3.38, U = 500.0, p = 0.038, r = −0.24), *attachment to 'standard' English* (M = 3.64 versus M = 3.38, U = 498.0, p = 0.039, r = −0.24) and *lack of Global Englishes ELT materials* (M = 3.47 versus M = 3.20, U = 500.0, p = 0.021, r = −0.27) represented barriers to GELT in their contexts.

Open-Ended Questionnaire Results on Attitudes

Forty-seven participants provided responses in the pre-course questionnaire and a number of themes were identified (Table 7.4). Seventy-one comments (pre- and post-course combined) related to *reasons for choosing the course*, with a general *interest in Global Englishes* being the most popular response (*n* = 35). They are 'interested in English as a lingua franca both as a phenomenon and a research paradigm', 'want to understand more about it and consider its relevance to my context', 'interested in the concept about Global Englishes, and how English is perceived and accepted in different contexts and speakers' and because they 'have been wondering why we need to follow American English norms when in reality nowadays our communications in English are mostly with non-native speakers'. Many referred to its perceived *relevance for ELT and/or own career* (*n* = 16) because Global Englishes is 'a growing field that will affect most of [them] in [their] future careers' and 'English teachers need to know to be able to deal with the most recent knowledge of English teaching'. Eleven want *clear GELT guidelines* to aid curricular innovation because they are 'interested in learning how to use ELF in a classroom of an EFL country' and 'would like to know if it can be taught'.

References to *relevance to career* were made throughout, not only with regard to why they chose the course. Nineteen felt GELT was relevant to their future, fifteen wanted to apply GELT theory in their classrooms, two believed it was relevant to their dissertation and two planned to undertake a PhD or other research related to GELT. However, when asked about the relevance and feasibility of Galloway and Rose's (2015) proposals for change for their future teaching contexts, only eleven commented. Only one was critical, noting that they are 'too general and related to policy' and others were positive because they are 'important with regard to Global Englishes' and that 'Global Englishes should be an important part of English teaching'

Table 7.4 *Thematic comparison for pre- and post-course open-ended questionnaire responses*

Themes	Pre	Post
Relevance to career	**19**	**16**
Incorporate GELT	15	11
Dissertation	2	2
PhD or other future research	2	3
Raise awareness of GE	**27**	**19**
Students' awareness	13	7
Teachers' awareness	9	4
Others' awareness (e.g. parents, 'people', policymakers)	5	8
Proposals	**11**	**16**
Barriers	**11**	**16**
Attachment to SE and/or lack of awareness of GE	4	16
Assessment	4	4
Lack of materials	2	3
Teacher-hiring practices	1	3
Guidelines	X	1
Teacher training	X	3
Lack of time	X	1
Parents	X	1
Policy	X	1

because it 'is important for the development of current English and English teachers'. However, one proposal, the need to *raise awareness of GE* emerged as a major theme throughout the data (*n* = 27).

On the other hand, five of Galloway and Rose's (2015) barriers were noted, including *assessment* (*n* = 4), *attachment to standard English and/or lack of awareness of Global Englishes* (*n* = 4), *lack of materials* (*n* = 2) and *teacher-hiring practices* (*n* = 1). Comments included 'I think the hardest part for language teaching related to Global Englishes should be that it is hard for teachers to choose a possible assessment. There is no right or wrong in this aspect' and 'The attachment to "standard" English is quite hard to remove, which leads to the barrier of recruitment practices'.

Some post-course comments (*n* = 22) were categorised as providing *GELT course evaluations* and eighteen expressed positive attitudes. The course provided them with 'a new insight on English teaching', enabling them to 'make students aware of the Global Englishes and encourage them to be themselves rather than crazy for native English'. It 'changed my view of English teaching which I never thought it on a global context before'. Many found it relevant to their own contexts and for ELT in general, they would consider incorporating it into their classrooms. The course provided 'broader and deeper understanding of the implications of the global spread of English' and they now feel 'better equipped with helping students to be free from their strong belief that they have to sound like a native speaker if they want to be considered as a competent user of English'. However, four referred to their *confusion* 'about how to use these topics in ELT' and there was a concern over 'how to put it into real practice' and a desire for 'real examples to see what is GELT-like'.

Open-Ended Questionnaire Results on GELT Influence on Attitudes

Qualitative data from the questionnaire also indicated that the course influenced participants' attitudes (Table 7.4). As in the pre-course data, participants still plan to 'bring the theories [which they learned on the course] into practice', 'create actual teaching plans which involve ELF strategies and awareness raising activities in terms of such as respecting multilingualism' and 'to make a plan of teaching English which is useful for students' needs in the future'. However, fewer commented on the *relevance to career* and *future teaching*. They referred to more of the proposals, however, and referred more to their own contexts. Illustrative comments included:

> In my teaching context, sometimes students are from diverse cultures, and I think it is important that they learn how to appreciate various cultures'. And 'I believe it is important to raise the awareness by introducing these topics and mostly can be done. However, there are some practices like hiring which cannot be easily changed because it is related to the perspective of the policymakers.

Overall, there was an increased awareness of the barriers to GELT in their own teaching context (thirty-four comments in the post-course questionnaire compared to eleven comments in the pre-course questionnaire). Comments were also more detailed, and all barriers were referred to. There were four times as many references to *attachment to standard English and/or a lack of awareness of Global Englishes*. Further barriers identified included *policy, lack of guidelines, lack of time* and *parents*. However, some were optimistic about addressing these, noting it would be 'fun to try and expand [their] future classrooms beyond SE [standard English]' and that they were determined to 'try [their] best'. Others, however, were concerned that 'some practices cannot be easily changed', that the barriers 'will continue to be there for quite a long time' and that 'it is unlikely' to introduce GELT into their context 'anytime soon'.

Interview Results

Interviewee profiles (pseudonyms used) are shown in Table 7.5 and the themes that emerged in the pre-course interviews are displayed in Table 7.6. In the interviews, many discussed their *language ideologies* (coded fifty-eight times), which were often at odds with these *teaching and/or learning experiences*. For

Table 7.5 *Interviewee and focus group profiles*

Name	Int[a]	FG[b]	Country	ELT Context	Age	Gender	IELTS[c]	Education	English Teaching Experience
Ching	Y	FG2	China	China	23	F	7	BA (English)	No experience
Amir	Y	FG2	Indonesia	Indonesia	27	M	7.5	BA (English Teaching/ Education)	2 years (English teacher in a multinational company)
Sandy	Y	FG2	US	Japan	29	F	N/A	BA (Communication Studies – minors in German, Japanese and ESL) Teaching certification for K-12 ESL classes in the USA	8 years (4 years: English tutor for Japanese students in the US; 4 years: Assistant language teacher in Japan)
Lingyi	Y	FG2	China	China	26	F	7.5	BA (English)	3 months (Part-time summer English teacher)
Fei	Y	FG3	China	China	24	F	6.5	BA (Teaching Chinese as a Foreign Language)	No experience (Part-time Chinese tutor in a private language school)
Fan-ko	Y	FG3	China	China	25	F	7.5	BA (English)	2 months (Chinese tutor)
Jiaying	Y	FG3	China	China	25	F	7.5	BA (English Language and Literature)	No experience
Chengxin	Y	FG3	China	China	27	M	7	BA (English)	No experience
Yun	Y	FG4	China	China	23	F	7.5	BA (Civil Aviation)	2 months (Part-time assistant teacher of IELTS)
Yifan	Y	FG4	China	China	23	F	7.5	BA (English)	No experience

Table 7.5 (*cont.*)

Name	Int	FG	Country	ELT Context	Age	Gender	IELTS	Education	English Teaching Experience
Peng	Y	FG4	Taiwan	Taiwan	27	F	8	BA (Japanese Language and Literature plus English Language Teaching)	2 years (English teacher in Taiwanese senior high school)
Rob	Y	FG4	UK	South Korea	32	M	N/A	BA (English)	5 years (English tutor in South Korea)
Indah	Y	FG5	Indonesia	Indonesia	25	F	7.5	BA (English Teaching/ Education)	2 years (English tutor at a language institution and a high school in Indonesia)
Do	Y	FG5	Taiwan	Taiwan	27	M	7.5	BA	3 years (English teacher in Taiwan)
Nobuko	Y	FG5	Japan	Japan	48	F	8	BA (Japanese Literature)	18 years (Private tutoring and language schools in Japan)
Jingshu	N	FG5	China						
Yang	Y	FG6	China	China	22	F	7.5	BA (Teaching Chinese as a Foreign Language)	1 year (English tutor for middle school students and internship as a Chinese tutor)
Wanrong	Y	FG6	China	China	27	F	7	BA (English)	4 years (Junior high school English teacher in Taiwan)
Ruiqin	Y	FG6	China	China	22	F	6.5	BA (English language Teaching/ Education)	3 months (Internship as a teaching assistant)
Sam	Y	FG6	UK	Japan	27	M	N/A	MA (Japanese)	2 years (English teacher in Japan)

Zhu	N	FG6	China	China					
Yating	N	FG6	China	China					
Sihan	Y		China	China	23	F	7	BA (Finance/Translating and Interpreting)	No experience
Xiaojing	N	FG1	China	China	24	F	7.5	BA (English)	No experience
Wenyan	N	FG1	China	China	27	F	7.5	BA (Translation and Interpretation between English and Chinese)	No experience
Ting	N	FG1	China	China	25	F	7	BA (English)	3 years (English teacher in middle school)
Yijun	N	FG1	China	China	26	F	7.5	BA (Teaching Chinese to Speakers of Other Languages)	No experience
Hui	N	FG1	China	China					

[a] Int: interviewee;
[b] FG: focus group;
[c] IELTS: International English Language Testing System

Table 7.6 *Thematic framework for the pre-course interviews*

Theme	Interviewees	References
Language ideologies	**16**	**58**
Reasons for choosing the course:	**21**	**111**
Relevance to ELT and/or own career	21	69
Interest in GE	16	22
Clear GELT guidelines	12	13
Dissertation	2	4
Other (e.g. course structure, assignment)	3	3
Expectations	**20**	**39**
Relevance to career:	**21**	**50**
Incorporate GELT	12	19
Questionable relevance of GELT	11	31
Proposals	**21**	**52**
Barriers:	**21**	**93**
Attachment to SE and/or lack of awareness of GE	15	30
Assessment	14	19
Teacher-hiring practices	10	14
Parents	8	15
Lack of materials	8	10
Teacher training	3	5

example, in Indah's context, the 'native' English-speaker model is used, yet she is aware that, 'although people from different parts of the world speak different Englishes, they still get their meaning across' and because of this, students 'don't have to speak like an American . . . as long as the person you're talking to understands what you're saying' (Indah, Indonesia). Before coming to the United Kingdom, Fei 'thought we should know American English or British English, and especially about the culture or accents' because of her ELT context, yet 'after I came here I found that many teachers, they're not native speakers and they can speak English perfectly and they can teach us the knowledge about English' (Fei, China).

Students' reasons for choosing the course were similar to the questionnaire data; the majority had a general *interest in GE* (coded 22 times in 16 interviews). Several felt it had *relevance to ELT and/or own career* (coded 69 times in all interviews) and wanted *clear GELT guidelines* to aid curricular innovation (coded 13 times in 12 interviews). When discussing their *expectations*, they also expressed their interest in 'how to apply GE in the classroom' (Sandy, USA), 'further [their] understanding of GE, and also to really apply some theories into teaching' (Fan-ko, China). Yifan (China) wanted to 'learn how to incorporate the ELF in the ELT', making specific reference to how to assess students. Amir (Indonesia) wanted to learn about 'implementing this Global Englishes concept in classroom practices'.

Comments on the *relevance of Global Englishes to career* (coded 50 times in 21 interviews) were made throughout the interviews. Twelve participants wanted to *incorporate GELT* (coded 19 times), although 11 referred to the *questionable relevance of GELT* (coded 31 times). As Rob (UK) summed up, many 'feel conflictive'; they supported GELT in principle but were unsure how to implement it and of its feasibility in their context. They were concerned that, 'if there is no standard, (. . .) what shall we teach?' (Yun, China).

Attitudes towards the proposals for change were predominantly positive. They are seen to be 'very relevant' (Chengxin, China) and 'very useful' (Ching, China), and many noted that they are 'needed' (Fei, China) in their contexts. The most frequently discussed proposal was the need to increase Global Englishes exposure, and emphasise respect for multilingualism and for diverse cultures and identity. However, with regard to the feasibility of implementing these in their contexts, few felt that 'all these changes are possible' (Yifan, China) and a majority raised concerns as to whether they could be implemented, making reference to possible barriers.

Once again, discussions on proposals were followed with discussions surrounding the *barriers* (coded 59 times). All of Galloway and Rose's (2015) barriers were discussed, including *attachment to standard English and/or lack of awareness of Global Englishes* (coded 30 times across 15 interviews), *assessment* (coded 19 times across 14 interviews), *teacher-hiring practices* (coded 14 times across 10 interviews), *lack of materials* (coded 10 times across 8 interviews) and *teacher training* (coded 5 times across 3 interviews).

Parents were also identified as a further barrier (15 times across 8 interviews) and their attachment to standard English and lack of awareness of Global Englishes was seen to be important. As Rob (a UK national with a teaching context in South Korea) noted, 'parents want their children to be taught by Western teachers, they want that exposure. They want that perfect pronunciation. I don't believe it's possible, but I don't think you can convince those parents'. He spoke about this extensively in the South Korean context, noting that while 'people like the idea of Global Englishes . . . it doesn't get students a better grade necessarily', adding that 'parents don't want to pay for their students unless they see pay-off, better exam results', which influences policymakers and curriculum developers.

This is also a concern in the Chinese context, where Yun noted that, while it was fine to let teachers know the concept of Global Englishes, when deciding on the syllabus, teachers 'need to get the acceptance of the parents and the students of the new concept of ELF' (Yun, China). Another suggested that, 'Maybe you can train the teachers to accept the Global Englishes perspective and the students as well, but how can you persuade the parents to accept it'

Table 7.7 *Thematic framework for the pre- and post-course comparison*

Theme	Pre		Post	
	Interviewees	References	Interviewees	References
GELT course evaluation	x	x	20	169
Overall impression			20	80
Expectations	x	x	19	20
	x	x	18	48
Influence on attitude	20	39	18	21
Teacher education	x	x		
Critical reflections on GE-related topics	x	x	19	101
Relevance to career	21	50	21	42
Incorporate GELT	12	19	19	38
Questionable relevance of GELT	11	31	2	4
Proposals	21	52	19	35
Barriers	21	93	21	80
Attachment to SE and/or lack of awareness of GE	15	30	10	13
Assessment	14	19	11	13
Teacher-hiring practices	10	14	4	6
Parents	8	15	7	11
Lack of materials	8	10	12	13
Teacher training	3	5	6	6
Policy	x	x	5	6

(Lingyi, China). This resonated with another interviewee from China, who noted that parents

> only care about the result of the learning and not the process. So I think it's hard for the parents to change this kind of concept. Although we have implemented such a kind of Global English education in primary and middle schools, but for the parents, how can the parents accept such kind of change and how do we persuade them to do that, I think it's hard. (Fan-ko, China)

Thus, the barrier of parents' expectations of an education in standard English seemed to be a recurring theme in the China educational context.

In the post-course interviews, 169 comments were generally coded as referring to *GELT course evaluations* and 80 of these referred to their *overall impressions on the GELT course* (across 20 interviews), which were mostly positive (See Table 7.7). Comments included 'I really enjoyed Global Englishes [course]', I am 'really happy with it' and 'I found it really useful'.

It met their *expectations* and was believed to have had a positive *influence on their attitude* towards English and ELT, raising their awareness of alternative approaches and generating an interest in the topic. One participant commented, 'I was shocked at times during the class, I think it was just bringing things to my attention that I would not have even thought about as being an issue' (Sandy, USA). It also led to a desire for some to explore the field further, illustrated by the following comment: 'I'm not familiar with this concept; however, after this course, I became interested in it and I wanted to investigate our opinions about it' (Jialin Lu, China). Eighteen interviewees referred to the importance of GELT for *teacher education* (coded 21 times) and the influence of the course was also evident in their *critical reflections on GE-related topics* (coded 101 times across 19 interviews).

The interviews also provided evidence of an increased desire to incorporate GELT, as illustrated by the following comment: 'It is really useful, it changed some of my attitudes and I hope I can incorporate it in my future teaching' (Ruiqin, China). It also encouraged some to reconceptualise English, as another student noted: 'I think the most important thing I learned from this course is to think critically about the language I have been learning for so long' (Peng, Taiwan). After the course, more interviewees expressed a desire to incorporate GELT into their future teaching than in the pre-course interview, with most planning to incorporate GELT into their teaching (coded 38 times across 19 interviews) and 'use the knowledge [they] have learned into [their] future career as potential teacher[s]' (Chengxin, China). Wanrong (China) felt that it 'made me focus on what I will introduce in pedagogy about Global Englishes' and Ruiqin (China) found it 'really useful, it changed some of my attitudes and I hope I can incorporate it in my future teaching'. Only two, as opposed to eleven in the pre-course interview, referred to a *questionable relevance of GELT.*

Once again, proposals were discussed in relation to barriers, but comments in the post-course interview were observed to be more critical and more closely related to their own teaching contexts. With regard to the proposals, Indah (Indonesia) 'totally agree[s] with everything, with everything', but feels there is a need to 'change the system for assessment' and thinks the 'teaching hiring system in Indonesia' is problematic because 'some of the native English teachers, they just come without any qualification degree because they speak the language from birth, they can teach the language in Indonesia'. Others were aware that change was necessary 'but it won't be easy' (Fan-ko, China) and innovation was 'possible but it needs a long time' (Fan-ko, China). A few interviewees noted an increased awareness of the difficulties of change. Before the course, Ching (China) thought the GELT innovations were 'very useful [and] important' and was optimistic about implementing them. After the course, however, she commented that the 'course has raised awareness but

I think there is a long way to go to do this in China, because we lack materials, we lack tests, we lack models'. Similarly, before the course, Yifan (China) thought that 'basically all these changes are possible in the Chinese context', but after the course noted that, 'I think these barriers cannot be addressed'.

Focus Group Results

Of the 27 focus group participants, 19 were previously interviewed (see Table 7.5). They came from China (17), the United Kingdom (2), the United States (1), Taiwan (4), Japan (1) and Indonesia (2) and were all familiar with the East Asian context, helping them establish rapport as both MSc TESOL students, and pre-service and in-service TESOL practitioners. They all shared knowledge of GELT via the course, and knowledge of the same context. Table 7.8 shows the list of themes generated.

Discussions on *reasons for choosing the course* were short and were not discussed by every group, and comments were not as detailed as the interviews. Only three reasons were discussed in four groups; *interest in GE* (6 references), *relevance to ELT and/or own career* (5) and *other (course structure, assignment)* (1). With regard to the relevance for career, in Focus Group 4, Yun (China) noted that she wanted to know 'how to actually teach the Global English'.

Discussions on *relevance to career* were made throughout all of the focus groups (40 times across 6 focus groups) with regard to *GELT course evaluation*. It was the second most frequently discussed theme in the entire data set, discussed at length and often returned to when discussing other topics. Fourteen expressed doubts about the *questionable relevance of GELT*. However, *overall impressions* were mostly positive, and centred on the fact that it should be part of *teacher education* (coded 17 times across 6 focus groups) and had a positive *influence on attitudes* (coded 16 times across 6 focus groups). Overall, data suggested that they were 'really happy that [they] have taken this course' (Wenyan, China, Focus Group 1), as it 'really helped' (Lingyi, China, Focus Group 2) them to understand the topic, and they 'really liked' (Ching, China, Focus Group 2) what they had learned. Wenyan (China, Focus Group 1) 'really think[s] that Global Englishes is the most important course during the whole year' and having GELT on teacher education courses would 'really be able to help them [the trainee teachers] to change' (Nobuko, Japan, Focus Group 5), because in the future they 'really need to tell' (Indah, Indonesia, Focus Group 5) their students about GELT.

Barriers were a dominant theme (161 times across all focus groups by 26 out of 27 participants), concurring with the findings in the other data. The one participant who did not mention barriers was mostly silent in the discussion. On the other hand, in her focus group, her peers each commented on the barriers

Table 7.8 *Thematic framework for focus group discussions*

Code	Overall	No. of Students	Focus Group 1					Focus Group 2				Focus Group 3				Focus Group 4				Focus Group 5				Focus Group 6					
			Hui	Yijun	Xiaojing	Wenyan	Ting	Sandy	Amir	Lingyi	Ching	Pei	Chengxin	Jiaying	Fan-ko	Rob	Yifan	Yun	Peng	Indah	Do	Jingshu	Nobuko	Sam	Yang	Wanrong	Zhu	Ruiqin	Yating
Language ideologies	18	16		x	x		x	x	x			x	x	x		x	x	x	x	x	x	x	x						
Reasons for choosing the course	12	9	x					x	x		x						x	x									x	x	x
Interest in GE	6	6	x					x	x		x																	x	x
Relevance for ELT and/or own career	5	5						x	x								x	x										x	
Other (e.g. course structure, assignment)	1	1																									x		
GELT course evaluation	120	26	x		x	x	x	x	x	x	x	x	x	x	x	x	x	x	x	x	x	x	x	x	x	x	x	x	x
Relevance to career	40	25	x			x	x	x	x	x	x	x	x	x	x	x	x	x	x	x	x	x	x	x	x	x	x	x	x
Questionable relevance	14	10							x	x	x	x		x	x	x		x	x	x									
Overall impression	39	17			x	x	x	x	x	x	x	x	x	x	x	x	x	x	x	x			x						
Teacher education	17	19	x		x		x	x	x	x	x		x		x	x	x	x	x	x	x	x	x	x				x	
Influence on attitude	16	12				x	x		x			x	x	x			x			x			x		x			x	x
Barriers	161	26	x	x	x	x	x	x	x	x	x	x	x	x	x	x	x	x	x	x	x	x	x	x	x		x	x	x
Attachment to SE and/or lack of awareness of GE	49	24	x	x	x	x	x	x	x	x	x	x	x	x	x	x	x		x	x	x	x	x	x	x		x	x	
Lack of materials	40	18	x	x	x	x	x	x	x					x		x	x	x	x	x			x	x	x			x	x
Assessment	22	15		x	x			x	x		x	x		x		x	x			x	x	x	x		x		x		
Teacher-hiring practices	19	13		x	x	x		x	x	x		x	x	x	x	x								x				x	
Parents	13	9		x	x					x	x		x		x	x			x			x							
Policy	8	6			x			x													x	x			x				x
Students' motivation	5	5			x							x			x					x				x					
Teacher training	5	5								x	x	x			x						x								
Proposals	27	20	x	x	x	x	x	x	x	x	x	x	x		x	x		x	x	x				x	x		x	x	

six times on average; some as many as twelve times. These barriers also prompted longer discussions and, as noted above, were often raised when discussing other topics, such as the reasons why they chose the course (see Extract One).

EXTRACT ONE (Focus Group 6)

YATING: I think Global Englishes is a very young concept, and the reason I chose this course is I think the syllabus is very interesting, so I chose this course and, uhm, to be honest I think I cannot use something in this course in my future teaching, because first we have no material about Global Englishes, and next I think policies in China do not support our idea. I think we can introduce this idea in China and, you know, examination is the most important thing. If we have some examinations about Global Englishes maybe parents and students would be more likely to accept this new concept.

This was also the case in Extract Two, which also demonstrates how discussions on the proposals for change led to discussions on barriers.

EXTRACT TWO (Focus Group 1)

XIAOJING: I think it's a good thing but it doesn't mean that we can make it right now, because you know the teacher-hiring practices is not just about what universities want or what schools want, but like what China wants. It's a policy thing, usually, because I've done research and people all say that, especially those teachers from India, they say, you know, many, like my friends, they want to teach in China, they are as proficient as me but they cannot, because they cannot have that kind of visa to teach in China. So it is really hard for them to change, although I know it is in progress, but still not there yet, so. I don't know when it is going to change.

As in the interviews, only very short statements were made about the proposals and there was a sense that they are 'a good thing but it doesn't mean that we can make it right now' (Xiaojing, China, Focus Group 1). There were some short exchanges about various proposals (Extract Three), but these were not extensive.

EXTRACT THREE (Focus Group 6)

SAM: I think this one is definitely possible – emphasise respect for diverse culture and identity. I think you can do that in the classroom quite easily.

RUIQIN: Yes.

SAM: And hopefully that would encourage learners to consider going abroad for themselves. And I guess that in itself increases Global Englishes exposure.

RUIQIN: Just trying to spread the ideas first and then maybe changes will emerge slowly.

As in the interviews, *attachment to SE and/or lack of awareness of Global Englishes* was the most commonly discussed barrier (49 times across all focus groups by 24 participants), followed by *lack of materials* (40 references), *assessment* (22 references), *teacher-hiring practices* (19), *parents* (13), *policy* (8) and *teacher training* (5). A new barrier, *students' motivation* (5), was also discussed, referring to a feeling that students 'don't care' (Fan-ko, China, Focus Group 3) about learning English in general, let alone Global Englishes. Focus group participants positioned themselves as 'experts' in their context, encouraging lengthy discussions on the barriers. Most centred on China, but in those groups where contexts differed, there was still an attempt to establish common ground by highlighting similarities (Extract Four).

EXTRACT FOUR (Focus Group 2)

SANDY (Japanese context): There's people from South Africa, there's people from Singapore, there's people from like the UK, and there's people from Australia and America, the majority of the people that are hired on this particular programme are Americans, so it's like, when I went my year was like 800, compared to like maybe 300.

PENG (Taiwanese context): I think the situation is similar in Taiwan. In Taiwan, they also prefer the native American norms and . . .

Those who were interviewed also discussed these much more frequently and in more depth. Yang (China, Focus Group 6), for example, made twelve references to *barriers,* yet only a single comment in the interview. They were also more confident in the focus groups, presenting their opinions as fact. In Focus Group 1, for example, Ching (China) noted that, 'It still happens in China, that's a fact, probably because they know nothing about Global Englishes'.

Summary and Discussion of Findings

In addition to exploring pre-service and in-service TESOL practitioners' attitudes, this study also aimed to explore the contexts in which they are working and investigate the potential influence of a GELT course. In the questionnaire, 85% of the participants were female and 73% were from China. In the interviews and focus groups, the majority were also from China, although all (except one student from Indonesia) had experience as either a learner or a practitioner in the East Asian context (Table 7.5). Such familiarity with a specific context also enabled lengthier and more in-depth discussions regarding this region. In the questionnaire, only 12% had more than three years' teaching experience, but the qualitative data sets included a range of both pre- and in-service practitioners.

The interview and focus group proved a useful way of gaining insights into these contexts and the study revealed that their language ideologies were often at odds with this ELT context. As expected, native English-speaker norms dominated and the questionnaire highlighted that English teachers are mostly recruited from the United States and the United Kingdom, the two contexts that are also most dominant in ELT materials.

Attitudes Towards the GELT Course and Its Relevance

There was strong agreement that the course would be useful for their future teaching career and also that it should be a topic included on all postgraduate TESOL programmes. The qualitative data provided insights into their reasons for choosing the course, although this did not generate lengthy discussions in the focus groups. In all data sets, a general interest in Global Englishes was the most popular response, followed by relevance of GELT for their own teaching career. Some took the course to learn more about implementing GELT or how to 'solve that problem' of 'how to actually teach the Global English' (Yun, China, Focus Group 4). In their discussions of their expectations of the course, interviewees noted a desire to learn how to apply theory to practice and similar discussions featured in the focus groups when discussing their expectations. The relevance for future teaching was a major theme in all of the data sets, and discussed in every focus group, at length and often returned to when discussing other topics. However, the open-ended questionnaires revealed some confusion over how to do this and some interviewees also discussed the questionable relevance of GELT for their contexts, a concern also raised in the focus groups. Rob's comment that many practitioners 'feel conflictive' supports previous research, in that many accept innovation in principle but have problems with practice. As in Giri and Foo (2014), there appears to be a dilemma: teachers advocate for GELT, but also recognise the problems in doing this in contexts that value native English-speaking norms. Such comments relate to concerns in Vettorel (2016), where there was a degree of uncertainty as to what model/standards they should follow.

Attitudes Towards the Proposals and Barriers for GELT

Prior to taking the course, attitudes towards all of Galloway and Rose's (2015) GELT proposals were very positive regarding their achievability in their own contexts, although they were least confident about changing English teacher-hiring practices. Support for the need to raise awareness of Global Englishes emerged as a major theme throughout the data. There was an acknowledgement that headway has been made in this area with regard to raising teachers' and students' awareness, but this study reveals that one of the central concerns was how to deal with other stakeholders, including parents and policymakers. This was identified as a major potential barrier to curriculum innovation in the East Asian context. In the interviews, many students raised concerns about how to implement change and comments on the proposals mostly related to the barriers.

It is clear that the attachment to standard English norms and the dominance of native English norms in assessment were of particular concern. As in Manara's (2014) study, there is a concern over the usefulness of GELT in contexts where standard language ideology is strong. Parents, and their attachment to 'standard' English, were added to the list of barriers. One participant (Rob, UK) feared that it was not possible to convince parents in the South Korean context, and this was also stated to be a concern in the Chinese context. Thus, raising parents' awareness of Global Englishes may be an essential step to dismantling this barrier. However, as noted in Chapter 4, with more research and awareness of the relative advantage (Rogers, 2003) of GELT, such attitudes may change. It may be challenging to persuade the parents, but many once thought this of students and teachers and beliefs are not static constructs and are subject to change, as demonstrated in this study and others. Unlike in Lopriore's (2016) study, nobody mentioned a lack of time for introducing innovations and selecting and adjusting materials, which is promising.

The Influence of the GELT Course

Attitudes towards TESOL practitioners' desirable skills changed. After the course, teachers put less importance on the need for knowledge of English grammar and good pronunciation and were more positive about the need for experience using ELF. While this was not commented on in the qualitative data, this indicates an increased awareness of the use, and importance, of ELF. Indeed, recent studies on students' attitudes have highlighted the importance of ELF familiarity and experience on attitudes (e.g. Galloway, 2011, 2017a; Wang, 2015). It has been previously noted that 'the lack of experience of ELF communication creates a myth of intelligibility, whereas linguistic experience helps to resolve the myth' (Wang, 2015, p. 103). Such observations were supported in our data, such as Fei (China) noting in her interview that, before coming to the United Kingdom and using ELF with her teachers, she felt more strongly about the need to learn native English.

Course evaluations in all data sets were mostly positive. It met the interviewees' expectations and had a positive influence on their attitude towards

English and ELT, raising their awareness of alternative approaches and generating an interest in the topic. In both data sets, it was said to have raised their awareness of alternatives, was thought to be relevant to their contexts, and there is an overall desire to incorporate GELT into their classrooms. Participants also reported that the course was useful to help them incorporate GELT in the future and, as in Sifakis and Bayyurt's (2015, 2018) study, the course raised their awareness of their own orientations and helped them explore new perspectives. The study reveals that the course met its aims of encouraging reflection on English itself and ELT practice. After the course, the participants were more critical in their accounts, highlighting the importance of such courses to encourage critical reflection on normative assumptions about both language and language learning, assumptions that ultimately influence how policies are enacted and students' learning experiences. The course provided the opportunity to reflect not only on their own contexts, pedagogical experiences and practices but also on a non-monolithic perspective of TESOL, which resonates with the findings of Vettorel (2016).

We cannot expect practitioners to incorporate GELT without adequate guidance and training and the importance of including GELT courses in teacher education programmes was noted in all of the focus groups. Wenyan (China, Focus Group 1) thought that 'Global Englishes is the most important course during the whole year' and Nobuko (Japan, Focus Group 5) commented that GELT courses could 'help them [the teachers] to change' (Nobuko, Japan, Focus Group 5). Such findings indicate an awareness of the critical role teacher education programmes play, and also of the importance of Global Englishes courses within such programmes.

There were also differences in attitudes before and after taking the course. More interviewees expressed a desire to incorporate GELT into their future teaching after the course and only two teachers, compared to eleven before the course, questioned the relevance of GELT for their context. It should be acknowledged, however, that some teachers did express doubts. Such complexity in attitudes is also evident in the fact that fewer references were made to the proposals for change in the open-ended data, yet comments were more critical and related more to their own educational contexts.

Proposals for change were almost always discussed alongside the barriers to innovation. Increased awareness of the barriers to GELT was evident in all data sets. As in Vettorel (2016), the course prompted reflection on these, and after the course, they were discussed more frequently, in more depth, and additional barriers were also put forward, including policy, lack of guidelines, lack of time and parents' and students' motivation. This increased awareness highlights the need to incorporate GELT into teacher education programmes from the outset, which 'would provide the time necessary to reflect on the implications of ELF for their teaching practice and would give space to explore materials and tasks from an ELF perspective' (Dewey & Patsko, 2017, p. 449).

Overall, as in previous studies (Dilek & Özdemir, 2015; Hall et al., 2013; Sifakis & Bayyurt, 2015, 2018; Suzuki, 2011; Vettorel, 2016), the course influenced attitudes, yet there is a clear conflict; they accept GELT in theory, but recognise the complexities associated with implementing it in practice. It is promising that the course made some interviewees optimistic about overcoming these barriers and it is hoped that more research and more coverage of GELT on teacher education programmes will allow further contextualised reflection. However, this study reveals that there is a clear need for research with other key stakeholders such as policymakers, and thus this concurs with the view that '[m]acro-innovation usually comes from "above," it is usually the result of centralised policy-making' (Sifakis & Bayyurt, 2016, p. 150). The 'bottom-up' approach advocated for by others (e.g. Hall et al., 2013) is desirable, but it is not only practitioners that we need to listen to and interact with, but also other stakeholders, including parents and policymakers. This study has revealed more contextualised challenges, particularly in the East Asian educational context, yet it has also identified that those taking the teacher education course are 'supporters' of change (Sifakis & Bayyurt, 2015, 2018) and time will tell if they will become 'early adopters' when they return to their home contexts. A degree of scepticism about change is unsurprising.

Conclusion

Norm-bound attitudes are clearly problematic for GELT and this study has revealed that, despite positive orientations towards GELT, there are concerns over incorporating this perspective at the practical level. However, while attitudes may be slow to change, and indeed while 'macro-level' change will take time, this study revealed that even a semester-long course can influence attitudes and allow pre-service and in-service teachers to ruminate over potential pedagogical innovation. The course in this study provided an opportunity to reflect on current practice and traditional TESOL concepts and theories and problematise GELT-related change. This study provides more insights into the possible barriers to GELT and it is hoped that more research, particularly research on how innovation is implemented in practice, will help. Future research should collect data from the 'innovators' and 'early adopters', including interview transcripts, extracts from diaries or the lessons they design. These research artefacts can then be fed back into teacher education programmes for further reflection on how others have diverged from the traditional ELT curriculum. We call for more research to help inform this movement and research that can bring real-life practice into the classroom. This study was one step in this direction, asking teachers what they thought about the proposals for change that have been put forward at the theoretical level, but we need to see how they interpret and operationalise them in the classroom. We also call for research with other key stakeholders.

8 Global Englishes and English Medium Instruction

Introduction

An oft-cited definition of internationalisation of higher education is 'the process of integrating an international, intercultural or global dimension into the purpose, functions or delivery of post-secondary education' (Knight, 2003, p. 2). Rose & McKinley (2018) note, 'internationalization is viewed at its worst as an economic ploy to drum up student numbers and tuition, and at its best as a way to positively influence the universities' global outlook' (p. 113). Internationalisation in its worst form, as an enterprise to bring in student money, has been heavily criticised, especially in the approaches taken by English-speaking nations like the United Kingdom and Australia, which adopt a highly commercial approach to international students (Forbes-Mewett & Nyland, 2012, p. 191). These universities tend to view internationalisation as a source of income, cashing in on their Anglophone status, rather than seeing internationalisation as an opportunity to diversify their student body to develop their global human resources. Nevertheless, for many universities internationalisation is pursued for its non-fiscal benefits, which include positive effects on a university's reputation, research quality, teaching quality and graduate employability (Delgado-Márquez et al., 2013). Thus, many universities pursue internationalisation policies to leverage such benefits without due attention to the challenges that relate to the growing language of instruction in 'international' programmes, which is predominantly English.

Internationalisation and English as a medium instruction in the twenty-first century are inextricably intertwined, as universities turn to Englishisation in order to internationalise (Kirkpatrick, 2011). A side effect of internationalisation is the rapid emergence of EMI in higher education around the world. Wilkinson (2013, p. 3) notes that EMI programmes have become 'commonplace in many institutes of higher education where English is not the native language'. Galloway et al. (2017) identify eight driving forces behind the EMI trend:

- gaining access to cutting-edge knowledge and increasing global competitiveness to raise the international profile

- increasing income (and compensating for shortages at the domestic level)
- enhancing student and lecturer mobility
- enhancing the employability of graduates/international competencies
- improving English proficiency
- reflecting developments in English language teaching (ELT)
- using English as a neutral language
- offering EMI for altruistic motives.

Some scholars see EMI programmes as a powerful means of rectifying a competitive disadvantage that non-Anglophone countries have in the market for international students (Earls, 2016). Others see EMI as having a detrimental effect on access to education by positioning the English language in a gatekeeping role for admission.

EMI has boomed in recent decades in higher education in order to prepare students for the linguistic demands of an English-speaking global market and to increase the international profile of the university (Wächter & Maiworm, 2014). Englishisation and internationalisation have occurred so rapidly that it is estimated that half of the world's international students are learning through English (Ball & Lindsay, 2013). Europe is a prime example of these two forces at play, where policies emerging from the Bologna Process and the ERASMUS programmes have seen a need for a lingua franca of education to ensure mobility, cementing the importance of English for facilitating a movement of students from across national and linguistic borders. Because English has already established itself as the lingua franca of academia and publishing, many universities also turn to English as a natural choice for the lingua franca of higher education classrooms.

The boom of EMI in Europe has been widely documented with oft-reported statistics (Brenn-White & Faethe, 2013; Wächter & Maiworm, 2014); however, this movement is happening worldwide (Llurda, 2013) and, certainly, we can see an EMI boom emerging in many East Asian nations with the expansion of 'internationalization at home' programmes (Galloway & Rose, 2015, p. 232), especially in Japan and China (Galloway et al., 2017). The trend to offer an 'international education' in a 'domestic' context has also been observed in Taiwan, as it strives to remain competitive with its larger neighbour (Song & Tai, 2007). The internationalisation and Englishisation of Japanese higher education has been recently stimulated by a string of highly funded policies that aim to increase its universities' global presence and to attract international students (Rose & McKinley, 2018). One survey on the EMI provisions in fifty-five countries concluded that 'the general trend is towards a rapid expansion' (Dearden, 2014, p. 2). This expansion of EMI has led to a growth in research on the EMI phenomena in places such as Turkey, the Middle East and throughout South-East Asia, marking a spread of EMI from the traditional EMI hot spots of the Netherlands and Northern Europe (see

Wächter & Maiworm, 2014). In short, EMI is becoming pervasive throughout the Expanding Circle and is becoming particularly pronounced in the Asia-Pacific (see Walkinshaw et al., 2017).

This boom in EMI in recent years goes largely unmonitored in terms of the language used in these courses. Importantly, while a switch in the medium of instruction has been widely undertaken, the question of 'what English?' has not been widely explored, indicating an urgent need to examine the 'E' in EMI (Galloway, 2017a). This chapter fills this gap by exploring the role of English in EMI, including how it is used alongside other languages as an academic lingua franca. This chapter draws upon data from a published British Council report (Galloway et al., 2017) and incorporates additional data and analyses, in order to explore students' and teachers' perceptions of EMI in the East Asian context.

Englishes in English Medium Instruction

English Medium Instruction is a term widely used, but difficult to define. Macaro et al. (2018) offer the following definition: 'the use of the English language to teach academic subjects (other than English itself) in countries or jurisdictions in which the majority of the population's first language is not English' (p. 36). This definition is not uncontroversial, specifically as many educational contexts are fiercely multilingual, and, thus, it is difficult to define what the majority language is in a truly international university. Nevertheless, the main defining criteria is that EMI occurs in national contexts where English is not the predominant language of communication outside of the classroom. By this definition then, EMI programmes could be considered to operate in Thailand, but not in Singapore, and in Germany, but not in Ireland. They could also arguably operate in countries such as Hong Kong and Malaysia, which, despite a historical tie to the United Kingdom, exist in a predominantly non-English-using society.

It is important to note that a language development objective is not openly declared in definitions of EMI, which makes it distinct from other forms of content-related language teaching models, such as content and language integrated learning (CLIL) approaches, bilingual education models and content-based instruction models of language teaching. Nevertheless, universities often make reference to the language-learning benefits of EMI, which indicate an expectation that English-language proficiency will develop in tandem with subject discipline knowledge. Some institutions purport that EMI 'is a relatively simple and cheap solution to both the problems of internationalisation and upgraded local language proficiency' (Hamid et al., 2013, p. 11). However, the relationship between EMI and language development is tenuous, with many EMI programmes providing little institutional support for the language-related needs of their students, assuming that language entry requirements for these courses act in a suitable gatekeeping capacity to ensure students are able to study through the medium of English. Other universities, however, build language support into programme structures, operating more similarly to a CLIL curriculum in higher education.

Models of EMI and GELT Compatibility

A recent review of EMI research has revealed a lack of consensus over the role of English in EMI and has identified a number of models of EMI currently being developed (Macaro et al., 2018). These models include the preparatory year model, the institutional support model and the pre-institutional selection model.

The preparatory year model appears around the world but is very common in Turkey and Middle Eastern countries, where EMI programmes are targeted at a mostly domestic student population. In this model, students will enter year-long intensive English for academic purposes and study skills courses to build up their English-language proficiency before entering their subject-specific degree course. This model tends to suit students of lower English proficiency, who have not yet reached the threshold of proficiency necessary to study content through English. A Global Englishes approach to language teaching within these preparatory year models would allow students to become better prepared to use English as an academic lingua franca, by making them more aware of the language used as the medium of instruction, and by increasing their confidence as multilingual users of English. A GELT curriculum would also, presumably, better prepare them for post-graduation, if English was needed for their future professional practice.

The institutional support model tends to occur in institutions where proficiency is higher, but many students still need language support in order to study the content effectively. This model will typically involve students taking modified content courses in their early years with a large amount of support from EAP or ESP courses. The language support is generally reduced over time in favour of unsupported content courses in the later years of study. However, the reduction in support varies from institution to institution. The internal structures of the institutional support model vary considerably. In some undergraduate courses, where English development is deemed as being as important as content development, there may be as many credits of language classes as there are of content classes. This model is seen worldwide but is quite common in East Asian contexts. Again, a GELT curriculum for language support classes would resonate well with parallel content classes. As Chapter 2 outlined, GELT is a type of ESP, thus much of the curricular ideology that underpins ESP also underpins GELT. Chapter 2 on syllabus design also outlined how a multilayered syllabus can cater to the teaching of both academic skills and Global Englishes content.

The pre-institutional selection model runs most similarly to universities in Anglophone countries. There is usually minimal language support provided in favour of language proficiency benchmarks (e.g. IELTS or Test of English as a Foreign Language (TOEFL)) that are used as selection criteria for entry into the courses. This model is quite common in mature EMI contexts, such as those in the Netherlands and Northern European universities. GELT is incompatible with EMI programmes that neither cater for the language development of its learners nor put emphasis on language proficiency as defined by standardised tests pegged to 'native speaker' norms.

'What English?' in EMI

A number of scholars (e.g. Galloway et al., 2017; Kirkpatrick, 2017) have recently argued that English should never be the sole language of education, even in EMI settings. Kirkpatrick (2017) vehemently lobbies against the political ideology that EMI should be English only, and questions the type of English that is most suitable in EMI settings:

> The 'E' in EMI is often understood to refer to a native speaker variety of English. This insistence on a native speaker variety as the benchmark needs to be reconsidered, and the use of English as a lingua franca should be supported. After all, a major role of English in today's world is as a lingua franca. The majority of today's speakers of English are multilinguals for whom English is an additional language rather than native speakers. This actual practice should inform language policy. (p. 9)

Despite an increasing body of research that challenges native speaker hegemony, English-only ideologies remain strong in language education, including EMI. Such challenges to native speaker hegemony resonate with GELT, which also sees learners' linguistic repertoire as a resource for learning. Thus, research that investigates English-only policies and native speaker centrality is at the nexus of EMI and Global Englishes. There is a clear need to understand how languages operate in this emerging lingua franca setting.

A pertinent point in terms of language use in EMI is the use of the L1 alongside English in the classroom. This is a debate that has emerged in recent years in the field of language teaching:

> the question of whether the first language (L1) should be used in the oral interaction or the written materials of second or foreign language (L2) classrooms is probably the most fundamental question facing second language acquisition (SLA) researchers, language teachers and policymakers in this second decade of the 21st century.
>
> (Macaro, 2014, p. 10)

However, EMI should ideologically be different. If English is merely the instructional language, and the goal of EMI is content learning, then it would make sense that stakeholders of EMI should not be opposed to other languages in the classroom. After all, if the use of other languages, such as learners' L1, facilitates content learning, then ideologically one might assume it should be used freely. The reality, however, is quite different. To the contrary, the use of L1 in EMI contexts is surrounded by debates similar to those in the use of the L1 in English language teaching.

This is perhaps the reason code switching has emerged as a topic of research interest in EMI settings (see, e.g., Barnard & McLellan, 2014), and within, more recently, debates on multilingualism in higher education (see, e.g., Earls, 2016) and translanguaging in EMI (see, e.g., Paulsrud, 2016). Many view that code switching is a natural behaviour where speakers make use of their multilingual repertoire, but it is seen as problematic by top-down monolingual policies that ignore the possibility of multilingual use (Wei & Martin, 2009). Others see code switching as being invaluable for pupils who struggle to understand difficult subject matter whilst concurrently using a foreign language as the medium of instruction (Ferguson, 2009). Ferguson (2003, 2009) further suggests that code switching is useful to teachers in facilitating the transmission of knowledge, managing the classroom environment and establishing rapport with their learners. This claim is also supported by some empirical research (see Tarnopolsky & Goodman, 2014). The findings of Lo & Macaro (2015) suggest that an L2 medium of instruction results in less interaction between the teacher and students, as the teacher talk increases and the student talk decreases. Such findings seem to suggest that rigid English-only policies in EMI settings may result in less dynamic classrooms and a return to teacher-centred pedagogy.

Under the umbrella of code switching, Macaro (Lee & Macaro, 2013; Macaro & Lee, 2013; Tian & Macaro, 2012) has been involved in important work on the use of the L1 in the L2 classroom, a research area he has described as having increased in academic attention in L2 language-learning contexts (Macaro, 2014). This work has now extended to EMI contexts, as researchers struggle with understanding how other languages are best used in a diverse array of EMI environments, some of which are predominantly bilingual, while others are intensely multilingual. Recent years have witnessed the emergence of an entire edited volume (Barnard & McLellan, 2014) on code switching in EMI contexts in East Asia, marking a growing interest in this phenomenon outside European higher education, which has predominantly featured in much code-switching research in educational settings.

While code switching has received attention in EMI, other forms of fluid language use have received less attention, such as practices that could be broadly defined as being translanguaging, although there has been a boost in translanguaging research recently, including an entire edited volume on *Translanguaging in Higher Education* edited by Mazak & Carroll (2017). As shown in Chapter 1, translanguaging is less concerned with an examination of the functions of each language in education, but is, rather, an examination of how both languages intersect in classroom practices. Translanguaging allows students and lecturers to move freely between languages without this process being explicitly linguistically signposted.

Practices in some EMI contexts in Europe could be broadly categorised as being examples of translanguaging. It has been observed that language mixing in exams, for example, is permitted in Swedish EMI higher education programmes (Söderlundh, 2012), although the extent to which both languages can be used in a single exam is unclear. This study also observed that lecturers were willing to accommodate and adapt to linguistic diversity in the classroom, particularly in terms of local language use in the EMI classroom. Also in the Swedish context, there has been a description of parallel language use, which represents a fluid acceptance of using languages that best meet student needs and contexts. For example, the course material may be in English but lectures can be delivered in Swedish, unless international students are present when the lecturer makes the switch (Airey, 2011). Such practices show a fluidity of language that is different to code switching. As many EMI programmes have English-language-learning support programmes associated with them, GELT would seem highly relevant to these contexts, as both GELT and these open EMI contexts view language use as being fluid and challenge the boundaries between the languages themselves, encouraging flexibility and creativity.

EMI in East Asia

There seems to be a fundamental difference between the L1 use in mature EMI contexts in Northern and Western Europe and the emerging EMI contexts in East Asia, where the role of language development seems to be built within the model of EMI. Galloway et al. (2017) have suggested that one of the major driving forces of EMI in China and Japan is to raise language proficiency. Thus, language learning is, perhaps, more inextricably linked to EMI programmes in this context when compared to Western and Northern European ones. Such contexts may be more resistant to other languages being used in EMI contexts, and could more closely resemble practices in EFL teaching, which have tended to adopt teaching approaches that adhere to monolingual ideologies.

Much EMI research 'has been conducted in European contexts, and there is a paucity of research on EMI in Asian countries, especially China' (Hu & Lei, 2014, p. 552), and this undoubtedly reflects the historical roots of EMI within a mobile and integrated Europe, which was further boosted by the *Bologna Declaration* of 1999 and through the ERASMUS and ERASMUS+ programmes. China is of further interest, due to ongoing pushes for EMI in the region, despite the relatively low proficiency levels compared to more mature EMI markets, such as Hong Kong and Western Europe. In 2001 the Ministry of Education in China stipulated that 5–10% of all undergraduate courses at Chinese universities should be in a foreign language, and since then top-down directives for EMI have further intensified (Hu & Lei, 2014).

Japan is in a similar situation, and a number of aggressive internationalisation policies in the post-2000 era have pushed for increased numbers of international students, staff and research via EMI programmes (for discussion, see Rose & McKinley, 2018). Brown (2014) notes that the push for EMI is also coming from language educators themselves, who are 'turning to EMI pedagogies for authenticity and validity in language learning, and to strengthen their own professional identities' (p. 50). Studies in the Asian context are on the rise, with a number of studies in Japan (Bradford, 2016; Brown, 2014; Burgess et al., 2010) and China (Hu, 2009; Huang, 2006). However, compared to Europe, there is yet to be a thorough investigation of attitudes towards language use in EMI. The governments of China and Japan have been noted to actively promote 'the use of EMI in both private and public (state-funded) universities' (Macaro et al., 2018, p. 49). Thus, this context served as a natural setting for our own investigation of language use in emerging EMI contexts in a variety of state and privately funded settings.

Methodology

This chapter reports on data collected in a larger study of EMI conducted in China and Japan, led by Galloway. Some of the data from this project has been reported elsewhere (e.g. Galloway et al., 2017). In this chapter we take some data from this study to explore just one construct in the GELT paradigm, that is the positioning of the first language in the EMI classroom. Our study was not concerned with analysing code switching vis-à-vis previous research on EMI (Tarnopolsky & Goodman, 2014), which would involve an analysis of the language recorded in classrooms according to function in a similar vein to Lo and Macaro (2014). Code switching, while serving a clear pedagogical function, does not sit comfortably within the ideology of Global Englishes, which seeks to explore more fluid understandings of how English is used across multilingual communities that speak a number of shared and unshared languages in their speakers' linguistic repertoires. As outlined in Chapter 1, GELT is more than just code switching, since translanguaging goes beyond this language-segmented depiction of communication. The data for the study aimed to measure the underlying beliefs and positions of main EMI stakeholders on the use of English, the L1 and other languages in the EMI classroom.

Research Questions

Our main research questions were:

1. What are the norms of language use in EMI classrooms in China and Japan in terms of proportion of English, L1 and other language used?
   a. Is there a difference between practices reported by students and teachers?
2. What are the stakeholder (students' and teachers') beliefs on the use of other languages, including the L1, in these EMI contexts?
   a. If multiple languages are used, what functions do they serve in these settings?

Data Collection and Setting

The data to answer these questions was extracted from a much larger British Council project (Galloway et al., 2017), which explored the EMI phenomenon in higher education in Japan and China. Questionnaires, interviews and focus groups with staff and students were used to collect data and provided insights into the differing approaches to, driving forces behind, and attitudes towards EMI. It responds to Dearden's (2014, p. 2) call for a 'research-driven approach which consults key stakeholders at a national and international level' by providing insights on staff and student perceptions. As Galloway et al. (2017) explain:

> The empirical and critical examination of the rapid expansion of EMI in Japan and China provides initial insights to act as a platform for further research and also staff training. The study also raises questions as to whether approaching EMI monolingually is the best way forward. (p. 3)

This allowed for a contextualised understanding of EMI, as the researcher visited each of the institutions to collect data. As Shohamy (2012, p. 197) notes: 'the teaching of EMI at universities cannot be detached from broader settings where medium of instruction approaches are implemented'.

The data collection for the main study (Galloway et al., 2017) took place at twelve universities in the form of student focus groups, teacher focus groups, interviews and staff and student questionnaires. Questionnaires were conducted with 579 students at all of the participating universities in Japan and China and, due to access limitations, with twenty-eight members of staff at eight universities in Japan and China. Some results of an additional 123 international students (not used in the Galloway et al. study), who were studying in Japan were added to the data set when a comparison group was needed for certain research questions. The questionnaire was administered online and elicited anonymous responses. Interviews were conducted with 18 students and 28 staff members (10 EAP and 18 content teachers) at 6 of the universities. Also four focus groups with students

Table 8.1 *Qualitative data from participant universities (adapted from Galloway et al., 2017)*

University	Student Interviews	Content Staff Interviews	EAP Staff Interviews	Student Focus Groups	Staff Focus Groups
Japan					
University A	2	1	5	–	–
University B	–	–	2	–	–
University C	3	2	2	–	–
University D	2	3	4	1 (*n*=5)	1 (*n*=3)
University E	2	–	4	–	–
China					
University W	7	4	–	1 (*n*=4)	1 (*n*=5)
University X	2	–	1	–	–
University Y	–	–	–	1 (*n*=5)	1 (*n*=4)
University Z	–	–	–	1 (*n*=8)	1 (*n*=4)

and four focus groups with content staff were conducted. The instruments were piloted with a small set of Japanese university students in January 2016 and adjustments were made accordingly. Table 8.1 provides details of the universities included in the qualitative part of the study.

Analysing the Data

Quantitative data analysis was conducted using *PASW 18.0.* Firstly, the data was summarised using descriptive statistics. Next, the data from the main study was reanalysed according to the research question. Non-parametric tests, including Mann–Whitney U tests and Kruskal–Wallis H tests, were used to compare the differences in means between variables of interest, such as Japanese and Chinese students, local and international students, proficiency and experience using English in non-local contexts. Non-parametric tests were used due to unevenly distributed data.

All of the qualitative data sets were reanalysed in *NVivo 10* building on the thematic analysis used in the larger EMI study by Galloway et al. (2017). The coding followed the methodology of typical qualitative content analysis (e.g. Mayring, 2000), in that:

1. A thematic framework for staff and students' focus group data and interview data were created in separate data sets.
2. The focus group data was thematically analysed; however, the key focus remained on the nature of the social interaction within each group (Halkier, 2010).

3. When analysing emergent themes in the focus group data, the attention remained on groups as a whole, as opposed to the individuals within them (Krueger, 1994), marking a different approach to coding from the interviews, which were treated as individual data.
4. The coding acknowledged that the data emerging from the focus groups was a joint product, rather than being merely a reflection of individual perspectives (Smithson, 2000).
5. When analysing the interaction within the focus groups, particular attention was paid to how, and whether, the groups established common ground, and how individual participants contributed to this common ground (Överlien et al., 2005).

Thus, the analysis of the focus group data concentrated on the content of the discussions, on the dynamics of the interactions and on the consensus and commonality when reached within the groups. The analysis of the individual interviews, although coded according to the same emergent thematic framework, was seen as individual expressions of attitudes and beliefs.

Language Use in EMI Settings: Initial Findings

First, the study sought to investigate the level at which English was used in each participant university. The students were asked to report on the use of English in lectures, course materials, classes and exams. The results of the English use at the universities were reported in Galloway et al. (2017), but in an abridged format. Thus, we present the data here, alongside an additional 123 responses, in a more detailed manner to delineate further differences between the students' and teachers' reported English use.

The findings indicate that English was used more predominantly in the Japanese EMI contexts, compared to the Chinese EMI contexts. As Galloway et al. (2017) observe:

> The Japanese students noted that the language of instruction, materials and exams were mostly only English, while less frequent use of English was reported by the Chinese students. (p. 15)

This point is evidenced by data from the staff questionnaire, which is displayed beside the student responses in Table 8.2. As reported in the main study (Galloway et al., 2017), the results show a discrepancy between the levels of English used in EMI contexts as reported by staff, compared with the students in their programmes. The difference is more pronounced in China than in Japan. For example, while all the Chinese staff report the use of English in lectures, materials, classes and exams as 'very often' or 'always' the students report is quite different, ranging from 55.5% (very often or always) in classes to 65% (very often or

Table 8.2 *English used in EMI as reported by students and teachers*

		Students				Staff	
		Japan		China		Japan	China
Description	Label	N	%	N	%	N	N
My lectures are in English	Never	2	0.5	8	4.4	1	0
	Rarely	5	1.2	25	13.7	0	0
	Sometimes	22	5.5	53	29.1	0	0
	Very often	85	21.1	52	28.6	2	1
	Always	289	71.7	44	24.2	13	6
My course materials are in English	Never	2	0.5	5	2.7	1	0
	Rarely	2	0.5	16	8.8	0	0
	Sometimes	21	5.2	41	22.5	0	0
	Very often	82	20.3	55	30.2	2	2
	Always	296	73.4	65	35.7	13	5
My classes are in English	Never	1	0.2	4	2.2	1	0
	Rarely	2	0.5	16	8.8	0	0
	Sometimes	26	6.5	61	33.5	0	0
	Very often	85	21.1	50	27.5	2	1
	Always	289	71.7	51	28.0	13	6
My exams are in English	Never	3	0.7	6	3.3	1	0
	Rarely	2	0.5	23	12.6	0	0
	Sometimes	27	6.7	37	20.3	0	0
	Very often	54	13.4	39	21.4	1	1
	Always	317	78.7	77	42.3	14	6

always) in course materials. The discrepancy in the Japanese context between staff and student reporting is less pronounced and, thus, there is considerable evidence that EMI in Japan adheres more to an English-only or English-dominant EMI environment than is seen in the Chinese university cases.

A reanalysis of the interview data according to our research questions confirmed the main report's findings that the divisions between languages in class were not as clearly defined as the teachers suggested (see Galloway et al., 2017). Many of the participants in the Chinese universities suggesting practices drew on both English and the dominant local L1 during classes. A student at a Chinese university explains:

> The teacher may speak in Chinese in class so we can understand more, but the PowerPoint and the textbook and our test is in English and this can maybe increase our ability of English, because my listening and speaking is so poor. I am good at reading and writing but my listening and speaking is poor. (Student interview, China data set)

Another student, who was a biotechnology student, noted a similar difference, with English being the formal language of content input in the sources used, but Chinese being the predominate language of spoken discourse. She stated that the 'teacher uses English mostly to teach us but they speak Chinese as well', but in her classes 'our textbook is in English but the teachers speak Chinese' (Student Interview, China data set). In a further example, of a liberal arts major at a Japanese university, the languages used were clearly defined by the context of use:

> Class materials, textbooks, and lectures are all in English. Some professors do explain things in Japanese, as most of the students are Japanese and that's a faster way to teach sometimes. (Student interview, Japan data set)

Interviews with learners confirmed that many of the Japanese contexts in the data set appeared to use English more widely, as evidenced by the following quote: 'Apart from our [out-of-class] activities, everything is in English, the textbooks are in English, the workshops for TOEFL and TOEIC [Test of English for International Communication] are in Japanese, but everything is in English' (Student Interview, Japan data set). Thus, everything, except exam preparation classes, was conducted in English. At another university, the rules of English were more malleable, as one postgraduate research student explains:

> I wrote my proposal in Japanese, which is acceptable. My Masters thesis was written in English. For the Masters, the rules for the course state that English is recommended, but is not compulsory. (Student interview, Japan data set)

This flexibility at the same university also extended to classroom discussions, as one student explains:

> There's a group of exchange students talking in English, then there's another group of only Japanese students who are talking in Japanese. It's two languages going on at the same time, but, because the professor gives lessons in English, when he calls on me I have to talk in English, so it's pretty complicated. (Student Interview, Japan data set)

Such descriptions reflect a translanguaging ideology of language use, where students are allowed to draw upon their linguistic repertoires and to choose the language most appropriate to the task or to the people with whom they are communicating. However, this university policy of openness with language use appeared to be an anomaly, rather than the norm, and was not a dominant theme.

Monolingual Orientation in the Classroom: Quantitative Findings

A secondary focus of the study aimed to reanalyse questionnaire data from Galloway et al. (2017) to investigate the intensity of the monolingual

Table 8.3 *Responses to 'I believe that EMI programmes should only permit the use of English in lectures and classes'*

	Students				Staff	
	Japan		China		Japan	China
Label	N	%	N	%	N	N
Strongly disagree	14	3.5	2	8.2	1	0
Disagree	78	19.4	39	42.3	1	2
Agree	228	56.6	147	42.9	11	3
Strongly agree	83	20.6	57	6.6	3	2

orientation within the EMI programmes of the participants. In the questionnaire, the students and staff were asked to directly respond to the statement 'I believe that EMI programmes should only permit the use of English in lectures and classes.' The student and staff respondents in Japan and China are detailed in Table 8.3. The students at the Japanese universities (n = 387) reported a higher level of agreement with this statement (M = 2.94, SD = 0.78) than the students at the Chinese universities (n = 193, M = 2.48, SD = 0.71). The results of a Mann–Whitney U test found this difference to be significant (U = 32876, p = 0.010).

Not wanting to only investigate nation-based variation in the data, we also sought to investigate whether other differences were found according to other variables. As other applied linguistics research has suggested that motivation is an important factor in the uptake of CLIL and EMI (see Lasagabaster & Doiz, 2017), we investigated whether students' motivation for enrolling in an EMI programme was a predictor of their English-only beliefs. In order to make this comparison, the students were divided into two groups according to how they answered a question regarding their reasons for applying to an EMI programme, with the students who positively responded to the question of whether they enrolled in EMI programmes to learn/improve English (n = 387) in one group, and those who negatively responded to the question in the other (n = 193). Although this is a crude measure of language motivation, it effectively isolated the students who were linguistically motivated to study in an EMI environment from those who were motivated by non-linguistic drivers.

A Mann–Whitney U test revealed a significantly higher level (U = 32876, p = 0.01) of agreement with the English-only statement in the linguistically motivated group (M = 2.91, SD = 0.78) than in the group who were not linguistically motivated (M = 2.75, SD = 0.71). These results are unsurprising, considering that students who aim to use EMI as a vehicle for English improvement may be more focused on learning the language than content, so may be willing to sacrifice the acquisition of content, which could be facilitated via use of the L1, in favour of English-language development opportunities they believed to be facilitated by a strict English-only environment. Likewise, students who enrol in EMI programmes for non-language-related reasons may value the facilitative effects of the L1 on their content learning.

Use of the L1 in the Classroom: Quantitative Findings

A second question asked for opinions about the use of the L1 in the classroom, asking students and staff to respond to the question: 'I believe that EMI programmes should permit staff and students to use English and their mother tongue.' The question aimed to investigate whether stakeholders believed use of the L1 should be permitted for any purpose (pedagogical or otherwise) in the classroom. This was in response to the positive function of L1 use noted in the literature, such as facilitating the transmission of knowledge, managing the classroom and establishing rapport with learners (Ferguson, 2003, 2009). Responses to the item are shown in Table 8.4. The results of a Mann–Whitney U test revealed no significant differences in this statement between the students in Japan and China. Further tests also revealed no significant differences according to other group variables, such as motivations for undertaking EMI.

We were also interested in exploring the L1 status of the participants and how this might impact on their views of English. For this analysis, we added in data from the 123 international students in the Japanese context. (Note: there were insufficient international student participant numbers in the China study to warrant statistical analysis of this type, so the Chinese EMI programmes were removed for this analysis to eliminate the confounding variable of a national difference.) Three groups were created for the students enrolled in EMI in Japan: Japanese students, international students of a non-English L1

Table 8.4 *Responses to 'I believe that EMI programmes should permit staff and students to use English and their mother tongue'*

	Students				Staff	
	Japan		China		Japan	China
Label	N	%	N	%	N	N
Strongly disagree	22	5.5	13	7.1	1	1
Disagree	119	29.5	41	22.5	6	1
Agree	216	53.6	105	57.7	9	3
Strongly agree	46	11.4	23	12.6	0	2

Table 8.5 *Analysis of items 16 and 17 comparing students of different L1 backgrounds*

Description	Group	Mean	SD	Chi-square	p	Significance
Q16. I believe that EMI programmes should only permit the use of English in lectures and classes.	Japanese L1	2.93	0.72	8.869	0.012	J < Other L1
	Other L1	3.20	0.77			
	English L1	2.79	0.69			
Q17. I believe that EMI programmes should permit staff and students to use English and their mother tongue.	Japanese L1	2.75	0.72	9.755	0.008	J > Other L1 Other L1< Eng L1

background, and international students of an English L1 background. A Kruskal–Wallis H test was applied to explore the difference between the three groups.

The results are presented in Table 8.5 for both items. The Japanese students reported a significantly lower level of agreement with the belief that EMI programmes should use only English in lectures and classes than the students of 'Other L1s'. The 'Other L1' group also showed a significantly higher level of agreement with the statement than the English L1 students. The same significance in relationship in inverse was found for the statement 'I believe that EMI programmes should permit staff and students to use English and their mother tongue '. The students of non-English and non-Japanese L1s were in significantly less agreement to the statement than the students of a Japanese L1 and English L1. Thus, the group that appeared to be most rigid about English-only use in EMI (and less open to the use of other languages) were the L2 English-speaking international students, followed by the L2 English-speaking Japanese students, and then the L1 English speakers. The L2 speakers, therefore, seemed more intent on the use of English than the L1 speakers, perhaps due to them perceiving EMI as an avenue for English-language use and practice. The results were unexpected and, thus, an exploration of qualitative data was necessary in order to better explain this difference in opinion.

Exploring the Use of Other Languages, Including the L1, in EMI Settings

The open-ended responses to the question of whether EMI classrooms should be English only helped to add a richer understanding of why certain opinions were held. In total 305 open-ended responses were coded. These are presented according to emergent themes in this section alongside relevant data from the student and staff focus groups.

Students Who Supported a Monolingual Orientation

A majority of students, who agreed with the questionnaire item that English should be used in classes and the mother tongue restricted, provided general answers that could be categorised under a theme that an English-only environment would help them to improve their English-language abilities. Illustrative statements from the learner questionnaire are provided in Table 8.6 and include sentiments such as 'It is helpful for studying English'. Other comments indicated that an English-only environment would create an immersion-like environment, which would habitualise their language use to be more 'English-speaking'. See Table 8.6 for a list of illustrative comments in support of an English-only policy taken from the open-ended response item on the questionnaire.

Table 8.6 *Sample open-ended comments regarding 'English only'*

Sample reasons given for supporting an English-only EMI classroom
• 'It is helpful for studying English' • 'Only by this [having an English-only classroom] can the mindset of English be taught' • 'Immersion in English atmosphere helps improve English' • 'I think that using English only can give the students a sense, an atmosphere, of speaking English so that they can make progress' • [Learning through English only will help students to] 'think in an English way' • 'We can't make progress in our English if we use first language after class' • 'English should be used not only in lectures but also in daily lives if you really want to improve your skills' • 'The use of English on campus helps students improve their level much more quickly' • 'If the lectures are in English, exams, assignments, and everything else should be too' • 'What do you mean? The EMI programme is an English instruction programme, so everyone is required to use English' • 'Because it's EMI' • 'If we don't use English, why call it an EMI programme? Only by using English can we have a better ability in using English' • 'Because this is an *English* programme' [student's own emphasis]

This sentiment was also observed in the interview data, illustrated by comments such as the following in one Japanese student's interview:

> I prefer it to be English only, because the reason why I wanted to come to [this university] was because I would be able to speak English on a regular basis, when I'm in school. I don't expect to speak English outside school, because I live in Japan and that's the way it should be, but at least when I'm in school I like to have as many opportunities to speak English. (Student interview, Japan data set)

For this student, it was essential to create an English-only environment so that language could be developed.

Furthermore, many students used the open-ended questionnaire items to make stronger claims. One student claimed that the English-only ideology should be more greatly enforced 'because force is sometimes necessary'. Another student echoed this sentiment, claiming that it was necessary to 'force students to use English, so their English improves'. Two students expressed the only reason they complied with the English-only policy was because it was enforced, stating that they 'will get marked absent if we speak Japanese in class'. Three further students reasoned that forcing the use of English in lectures and class was necessary 'Because [for] the majority of students, English is not their first language', and an 'English-only environment will be more helpful for English learning', and, thus, 'Students have to try to use English even when it's difficult'. One comment explicitly stated the purpose of EMI was to improve the language ability of students, in stating 'Because EMI classes are to improve English and study English, so using other language does not help the student'. This sentiment was echoed in much of the interview data, illustrated by the following excerpt from an interview with students at a Japanese university:

> My Japanese friends who are also enrolled in the FLA [first language acquisition] programme, they prefer talking in Japanese to English, because they're not really confident in English, so I tend to use Japanese in class discussions, which I'm kind of disappointed about. (Student interview, Japan data set)

Other students used the open-ended comments to suggest that the English-only policy was not only appropriate in lectures and classes but should be applied to other educational domains. One student stated that 'If you are to cultivate the student's integrated skills in English, then the range of EMI should not be limited in lectures and classes.' In another interview, one student elaborated on this ideology, stating:

> I think that EMI programmes should suggest strongly students to use English outside lectures. Native language is usually come up without thinking, but in English, you need to get myself accustomed. To improve students' English performance, they

should use them as much as they can; and that should be suggested by EMI programmes too. (Student interview, Japan data set)

Others suggested that programmes should not only encourage 'the use of English in lectures and classes', but also 'should use in the exams and practice in our daily life', a sentiment echoed in many other comments. Another claimed, 'If the lectures are in English, exams, assignments and everything else should be, too.' This extended beyond just educational domains, and into the students' social domains as well, as students recommended using English outside class as well.

For many students who supported an English-only policy, there was no mention of content learning. For these students, the purpose of EMI appeared to be development of second language proficiency, rather than the acquisition of content knowledge within their discipline of study, stating, 'if we don't use English, why call it an EMI programme?' For these students, the use of languages other than English in classes challenged the very purpose of enrolling in an EMI programme, because 'Mixing languages does not help students commit to an EMI programme', and it is 'much faster for students to learn English when no other languages are used in the classroom'. One student expressed resentment at the use of other languages in EMI classes, stating that 'Some students discuss in Japanese. It irritates me, because listening to English and Japanese discussion is confusing and it is not effective for students to study English.' Such comments clearly support the monolingual orientation that has underpinned much of ELT.

Other students provided more pragmatic reasons for English only in classrooms and lectures, drawing attention to the fact that English was the only shared language for classes that included international students, so the policy was necessary 'so students from other countries can understand'. One student stated that 'There are some students coming from other countries and if we use Japanese in English environment, it's not fair for the international students.' Some students saw English as egalitarian, stating 'I don't like speaking Japanese when some of the classmates do not understand it' and 'English is the only language everyone understands.' Another stated that he/she was studying at 'an international university, which means that the only language all students can understand is English, if students or professors use other languages they will exclude others from learning'.

Students Who Challenged a Monolingual Orientation

To the contrary, those who disagreed with the English-only policy underpinned their opinions with a rationale that using other languages was beneficial to

Table 8.7 *Sample open-ended comments supporting 'the use of other languages'*

Sample reasons given for supporting the use of other languages in EMI
• 'Using multiple languages is easier to understand' • 'Some terms might be explained in another language if necessary' • 'Sometimes we need other languages to explain something' • 'Sometimes it's necessary to explain difficult points in the mother tongue' • 'Students can't understand some exact meaning which can only be expressed explicitly in their mother tongue' • 'If we are taught only in English, we will have some trouble in understanding knowledge the teacher introduces to us. After all, English is not our mother tongue' • 'Because some students don't know English at all, they need an explanation in their mother tongue sometimes' • 'For some students who aren't good in English, like me, we need the Chinese to explain to us, to help us understand what it is we are learning' • 'Because sometimes the use of L1 could be more useful to understand the notion or concept in depth' • 'Because the main purpose of taking lecture is to understand the lecture, so if students didn't understand the contents, teachers should try to explain students in their native language or in an easy way' • 'When I cannot understand in English, I want the teacher to explain in Japanese' • 'When I want to learn specific topics, using Japanese is easier to understand the details of them than in English' • 'If using other languages other than English is necessary to understand some difficult contents of the lecture, using other languages should be allowed' • 'While English should be strongly encouraged, there may be instances in which the mother tongue may prove to be more effective/useful' • 'If an individual's mother tongue could be allowed, then so could other languages, to expand the range of communication' • 'If students are completely lost and can't follow the class, that is the time they [should] be allowed to use their mother tongue' • 'I somehow agree with this as stated above. In order to improve their speaking and writing skills, students should be permitted to use English when they talk to staff and peers. However, in order to have a depth of knowledge of a subject that students are interested in, being an expert of the subject both in English and their mother tongue is also important' • 'I think we should allow students to use other languages in class. The teacher has to use English, but some Japanese students think in Japanese and then use English to speak, but they can explain better in Japanese, and this causes them not to speak' • 'Sometimes it is still very hard to ask something in English and the question could end up unclear if we avoid asking just because we don't know how to say it'

understanding the content. Illustrative comments from the open-ended questionnaire item are included in Table 8.7.

Some students recognised the importance of English in classes but noted the benefit of using the students' L1 in certain situations. One student commented that

I believe a full English environment can be more effective to improve one's English skills and grow the linguistic sense. I am not strongly disagree because according to my experience sometimes we do need the mother tongue to explain some of the meanings so that we could understand them immediately and thoroughly.

(Student interview, Japan data set)

A similar student, torn between the perceived benefits of an English-only classroom, but acknowledging the facilitative benefits of L1 use, stated that the 'Mother tongue should only be used outside class or in specific situations', thus drawing functional and geographic domains around the language used. A further student commented that where English can be used, it should: 'It may be easier for some students to understand material if it is explained in their mother tongue, but it should not be used too often because students should challenge themselves to think and understand in English.'

In the interview data, it seemed that the class cohort was a factor that dictated language use:

If everyone is Japanese, then we speak Japanese. The university states everything is to be in English, but some professors do use Japanese, for example in Chinese lessons, there's a professor who is not good at English, but is good at Japanese. And sometime the grammar or expressions can be similar, so it's easier to explain them in Japanese, if all students are Japanese. But if there is an international student there, then it is in English. I took Mongolian classes, and the same thing happens there.

(Student interview, Japan data set)

This phenomenon is similar to findings of EMI research in Europe, where users switch between languages depending on the shared languages of the student cohort (Airey, 2011). A lecturer in Switzerland, for example, may begin a lecture in German if all students present can understand German, but then may switch to English when a non-German-speaking student enters the lecture theatre. Such sentiments were also revealed through the student interviews, where a more nuanced attitude towards L1 use could be found, acknowledging that the L1 had value for certain situations and to perform certain functions. Illustrative excerpts are provided below.

Some students saw the purpose of EMI as being to create an international programme that would be English-led, but not exclusively so. One student at a Japanese university with a long history of English-medium and bilingual programmes stated that 'Both Japanese and English teaching are vital to [my university's] ethos'. A further student commented that the language used should be adaptable to the background of the students communicating. He argued that during discussions 'with people who have the same nationality, using our mother tongue should be permitted in order to understand opinions precisely and quickly'. Another student challenged the concept that internationalisation equals Englishisation, in stating, 'I think that just because the programme aims for internationalism, doesn't necessarily mean they should only use English in the programme.'

Perhaps the most articulately written opinion of this type was seen in the open-ended response from a learner at a Japanese university, who stated,

> Since EMI not only allows us to speak and listen to English daily, it is another great factor that people from many different background gathers. It might be narrowing the potential of global interaction by simply forcing the students to only speak in English. For example, there are words and expressions which might be difficult to say in English. If students are allowed to use their own language, it might bring better results for all of us. (Student interview, Japan data set)

Comments such as this seem to connect with EMI's relationship with globalisation. EMI, as a product of internationalisation in higher education, is not intended for the sole purpose of language development, nor content acquisition in a second language, but for the development of global human resources through internationalised learning experiences.

The data also revealed opinions arguing against English only in the name of equality, and access to an effective education. These students expressed that English only was 'not reasonable for all students', or that 'everyone has the right' to use their native language, with one student noting that

> The more often we speak English the more we will improve. However, I think that we should be able to speak a little of our native language in order to make sure we don't leave anybody behind. (Student interview, China data set)

Another argued that 'If there are misunderstandings, they should be explained in the appropriate language'. These students explicitly stated a need for prioritising students' understanding, even if this meant other languages were used. Furthermore, other students claimed the enforcement of an English-only policy resulted in advantaging more proficient speakers, because an overemphasis on English 'will make students feel more anxiety' and would prevent 'students from speak[ing] their opinions because of the lack in confidence in their English'.

This sentiment was echoed in interview data where some students expressed negative effects of an English-only policy on classroom participation. Contrary to opinions that English only was more inclusive for international students, many non-Japanese-speaking international students were advocates of a multilingual classroom. One L1 English-speaking exchange student studying in an international programme in Japan stated in his interview:

> I am not a big fan of English only. Having the availability to [use another language] when you don't understand is a very convenient tool to have. The readings and textbooks should be in English, and they are here. Some teachers provide extra materials if you're interested or if you're not understanding. (Student interview, Japan data set)

Thus, the qualitative data revealed quite opposing positions on the use of other languages in EMI contexts, with some students exhibiting strong opinions that advocated for English only in all classroom (as at times, out-of-class) contexts, and others seeing the value in other languages for a variety of purposes and for a variety of specific situations and functions.

Beliefs about 'What English?' in EMI: Quantitative and Qualitative Data

A third question investigated student and staff attitudes towards the native speaker centrality, thus exploring Kirkpatrick's (2017) observation that native speaker hegemony exists in EMI, and needs to be challenged in order for EMI to be successful. Thus, one questionnaire item elicited opinions of the perceived importance of teachers to embody 'native-like', standard qualities in their English-language use. This item was included in order to explore issues surrounding native speakerism, a topic that we noted of being of research interest in Chapter 5. In one task students and teachers were asked to respond on a Likert scale to the importance of qualities of a teacher, including an evaluation of the importance of a 'native-like accent'. The results indicated a high preference for native-like accents, with 76.7% ($M = 2.98$) of the students in Japan and 76.3% ($M = 2.89$) of the students in China agreeing with the statement. The results of a Mann–Whitney U test confirmed no significant differences in this statement between the two groups. When the results were compared according to reasons for enrolling in EMI, a further Mann–Whitney U test revealed that students who enrolled in EMI programmes to learn/improve English reported a significantly higher level ($U = 25270.5$, $p = 0.005$) of agreement with this statement ($M = 3.07$, $SD = 0.61$) than students who did not ($M = 2.90$, $SD = 0.69$). This indicates that those students who are more motivated by learning language within EMI classes adhere more closely to native speaker norms (in terms of spoken accent) than students who choose EMI based on content learning or other goals.

We were interested in exploring the L1 status of the participants and how this might impact on their views of importance of native-like characteristics of their EMI teachers. Thus, for this analysis, we added in data from the international students in the Japanese context and removed the Chinese EMI data to eliminate some of the confounding variables. The three groups of students who reported on the importance of a native-like accent for their EMI teacher were Japanese students ($M = 3.08$, $SD = 0.71$), international students of a non-English L1 ($M = 2.81$, $SD = 0.73$) and international students of an English L1 national background ($M = 2.46$, $SD = 0.71$). The results of a Kruskal–Wallis H test revealed significant differences ($p < 0.001$) between the three groups. Importantly, the students of a Japanese L1 placed a significantly higher value on the native-like accent of their EMI teacher than the students of other (non-English/non-Japanese) L1s. Then, in turn, this 'Other L1' group placed a significantly higher value on the native-like accent of their teachers than the students of an English L1.

This finding warranted a further investigation using the qualitative data, however, few mentions were noted in the interview data. Only one student made an explicit comparison with 'native' English, arguing that, in her EMI programme, she wanted more opportunities to travel to native English-speaking countries to find opportunities to improve her English as the English used in her EMI course was insufficient:

> I think the most important support would be to give us more chances to go abroad, yes, to study in America or England. I think that the English spoken in these different countries, speaking and listening, is totally different, and it would improve my English level.
>
> (Student interview, China data set)

A further student concluded that 'Maybe accepting more native English-speaking professors is the best way forward' for the EMI programme. These students, however, seemed to be in the minority in terms of evidence yielded from the qualitative data. Most students were of the opinion that teachers needed to know English well enough to convey the subject knowledge effectively, and the nativeness of the teachers' English was not an issue.

Other students explicitly valued the importance of knowledge of content subject matter, and of the local educational context, as being more important than native-like fluency in English, as illustrated by the following comment:

> Not all teachers have a fluent grasp of English, but I don't feel you need to be really fluent. It's not always about what you know but how you communicate it. Every professor knows how to teach based on the standards of the country they come from. In America we write a lot of notes, the teachers here all have a different style and it's hard to say what's effective. The students are also diverse. Although it's supposed to be based on the American system, the teachers are not teaching that way. You need to know absolutely your subject matter, but you need to recognise when your students don't understand, especially when the students all have a different level of understanding.
>
> (Student interview, Japan data set)

In a similar vein, some students supported the idea that their EMI teacher should be multilingual. They saw value in a teacher being functional in not only the English language but also the students' L1, as illustrated by the following illustrative comment from the interview data:

> Staff should be multilingual. They should be able to speak the most popular language amongst the students other than English, so that students having trouble with vocabulary can be helped quickly. (Student interview, Japan data set)

This rhetoric was also found in the Chinese EMI context, with one student interviewee noting that 'I think it would be better if my EMI teacher was Chinese, because it is easier to understand each other.' International experience was also seen as being more important for many students than the type of English they used. The importance of teachers understanding not only students' L1 but also the cultural backgrounds of students was echoed by at least twelve students.

Discussion and Implications

One of the biggest differences we found in language use in EMI contexts in this region was that the Chinese context appeared to use much more of the L1 within the classroom when compared to the Japanese context, despite teachers reporting the contrary. This discrepancy was explained in the main study as follows:

> The study also revealed that EMI is delivered differently in Japan and China, with more English used in the former. Staff reported using the students' mother tongue as a pedagogical tool, showing an understanding of students' needs. They did appear, however, concerned as to how and when to use the students' mother tongue, and that students may end up depending on it too much. This is further complicated by the fact that student interviews revealed that such language use is seen as a sign of a lack of English proficiency. (Galloway et al. 2017, p. 32)

This finding should be seen as a positive one, and is one that resonates with a GELT ideology. Rather than use of the L1 being seen as a sign of language lack in English, it should be seen as a tool for education – especially when the outcomes of education revolve around the learning of content, rather than the language itself. 'It is imperative that we raise students' awareness that English does not have to be acquired monolingually, nor is it used monolingually' (Galloway et al., 2017, p. 32). If a GELT curriculum can accompany such EMI programmes, language courses can better educate learners of the important role of other languages in education, and thus raise awareness of their positive applications to EMI.

The Japanese adherence to English-only norms in this study may further be due to a strong monolingual ideology in the L1 in Japan, which has been reported elsewhere (e.g. Galloway and Rose, 2015; Seargeant, 2009). Japan is more than 98% ethnically Japanese, and the Japanese language is the only official language of the nation. China, on the other hand, is a deeply multilingual country. The use of *Putonghua* as the national lingua franca of China also provides a domestic context that is accustomed to lingua franca languages being used alongside others. While this is one explanation, another could be the lack of international students in the Chinese context compared to the Japanese context in the EMI programmes we explored. Because the students in most of the EMI programmes in China shared knowledge of *Putonghua* as well as English, this may have promoted its use. The interview data in Japan indicated that some Japanese students felt it was unfair to use the non-shared language of Japanese in the presence of international students within their programme, so this may have encouraged the use of English only.

However, when attitudes towards the use of English only were further explored in the qualitative and quantitative data, we discovered a strong preference for English-only use, particularly from the L2 English-speaking students. It became apparent that supporters of a monolingual orientation within EMI programmes did so based on the belief that it would help them to develop their English-language proficiency. Such findings in Japan are corroborated by previous research that has shown that Japanese students' predominant reason for taking EMI courses is to improve their English ability (Chapple, 2015).

If the driving forces behind monolingual ideology in EMI contexts does, indeed, stem from a belief that English only in EMI will benefit English-language development, as the data suggests, then it is necessary to problematise this largely untested and unsubstantiated relationship. There is a scarce amount of research that has measured language gain in EMI settings, and the evidence that does exist is not positive (Macaro et al., 2018). A study in the United Arab Emirates, for example, found that students only gained on average one-half of an IELTS proficiency band over four years of EMI study – something that can be achieved in 200 hours of study in a general English course (Rogier, 2012). A study by Hu et al. (2014) found that EMI students made the same proficiency gains on two different proficiency tests as a comparison group of students studying through the medium of Chinese while taking typical general English-language classes. While other studies have shown proficiency gains in EMI, particularly in receptive skills (e.g. Aguilar & Muñoz, 2014), the evidence is simply not strong enough to argue that EMI needs to be English only in order to leverage the benefits of this somewhat weak relationship. Thus, if language proficiency gains in EMI are a clear policy goal, then such programmes need to be accompanied by language classes. Due to the ideology underpinning Global Englishes matching the lingua franca functions of English within EMI, a GELT curriculum is ideally suited to support this dual-purposed EMI model.

Even in high-proficiency environments such as Norway, studies have shown that listening comprehension is worse through the medium of EMI than through the medium of the L1 (Hellekjaer, 2010). Use of the L1 and translanguaging of other language may be one strategy to help to alleviate the comprehension challenges associated with EMI. While some students in our sample disagreed with such practices, arguing that it would alienate speakers who did not share knowledge of languages other than English, the L1 English speakers in our data set were the most open linguistic group to embrace such practices. We concur with Galloway (2017a) in that monolingual ideologies still 'dominate university language policies (even unwritten ones) and tensions often occur between the everyday multilingual practices of students and university classrooms that can become artificially monolingual' (p. 7).

We need to consider what a Global Englishes orientation in an EMI setting should look like. It is easy to argue for the use of the L1 as a resource in ELT, but in EMI settings, particularly those in Japan populated with international students, can one do this when English is the only shared lingua franca language of the classroom? It is important to note, however, that the use of the L1 has been observed in other EMI contexts of mixed student populations (Costa, 2012) and, thus, might be considered normal practice for students when entering an EMI context within a country where they do not speak the L2. EMI need not mean English only or English always, or that all communication needs to happen in mutually intelligible languages, so long as everyone has access to the information needed to succeed. Perhaps the best example was seen within one participant university in Japan, where the students reported a practice where the teachers gave students the freedom to use whatever language best fitted the learning task. This resulted in translanguaging practices, such as conducting group work in a range of shared spoken languages based on the English-medium content, but then returning to English for functions such as reporting back to the class. In short, a Global Englishes orientation to EMI practice would argue that language does not need to be 'policed', especially if the goals of EMI in terms of content are being acquired via the student body's linguistic repertoire.

Conclusions and Further Research

The study reported here examines a single dimension of the GELT framework, related to views of the use of the L1 as a resource (GELT orientation) or a hindrance (traditional ELT orientation). Even within this single dimension, we find stark differences in reported L1 use in EMI settings, as well as beliefs that underpin *how much* and *in what circumstances* the L1 should be used, if at all. In presenting the results of our data according to one dimension of the GELT framework, we hope to have indicated further avenues that GELT can be used to explore English use in EMI, which is a booming ELF context. In drawing on other elements of the GELT framework, further research questions can be explored in EMI, including:

1. Who are the teachers of EMI? How does their L1 status affect stakeholder perceptions of them? What value do qualifications and competence have in comparison to L1 status?
2. What are the cultures of EMI? How do English users create an EMI culture conducive for communication in a diverse student population?

3. What English norms are prevalent in EMI? Are these norms diverse, flexible and multiple?
4. What materials are used in EMI contexts? Are they globally representative, or norm-driven?
5. What are the language needs of EMI students? Are these language needs globally or locally or norm defined?
6. What is the role of language in EMI assessment practices? Are EMI students assessed according to language accuracy or communicative competence?
7. What are the language-learning goals of EMI, if any? Are these appropriately benchmarked?
8. Does EMI embody a monolingual or multilingual/translingual orientation? How can translanguaging be best integrated into EMI practice?

In a recent systematic review of EMI research, the following research area was posited as being a key factor in need of examination:

> We need to arrive at some sort of a consensus about what kind of English will be/should be used in EMI HE. Again, this needs further unpacking: are we talking about a "native speaker English" or other nativised varieties of English, or indeed of English as a lingua franca (ELF) [Jenkins, 2015]? If it is ELF, then how does this affect international students from different geo-linguistic areas, including English-dominant ones?
>
> (Macaro et al., 2017, p. 38)

While our study has examined perceptions of the use of English alongside other languages in EMI contexts in Japan and China, we have failed to unpack the nuances and intricacies surrounding 'what English?' is used in such contexts, and perceptions surrounding lingua franca English use and variations in the Englishes used within EMI. EMI contexts – particularly those that have a diverse student body of a range of L1s – are a microcosm of effervescent ELF use in a context geographically removed from a native speaker-dominant environment. However, they remain a largely unexplored research environment within which to explore Global Englishes issues related to English-language use. In considering that many programmes in EMI emerging contexts such as China and Japan also offer language support classes, these contexts also offer vibrant opportunities for Global Englishes-orientated language teaching and GELT research.

Part II Conclusion

This concludes the second part of the book, which has explored research directions related to Global Englishes for language teaching. In addition to outlining appropriate research topics and methodological approaches, we have also showcased three self-contained studies to highlight diversity in Global Englishes research related to English-language-learning contexts.

Our investigation of English-language books showcased how the GELT framework can also be used as a framework for research. In its descriptions of the various dimensions of needed change in English language teaching, the framework can further be used to evaluate other facets of a curriculum. While we, alongside others (e.g. Syrbe, 2017), have applied the framework to evaluate materials (Chapter 6), other researchers have used it inform evaluations of whole programmes (see McKinley, 2018). Thus, the framework can be applied to other areas of teaching to help highlight areas of needed curriculum change. The framework can also be adapted to inform data collection instrument design, and to measure the effects of curriculum innovation in English-language classes.

Our investigation of the teacher education programme outlined in Chapter 7, further shows how GELT can be used to innovate pre-service and in-service TESOL programmes. In this programme, key concepts related to GELT were used to inform the content of a masters-level TESOL course, and to measure changes in students' perceptions of teaching English as an international language. In addition to constructs in the GELT framework, the GELT proposals and barriers (see Galloway & Rose, 2015) were particularly useful in providing our research participants with tangible issues to respond to in our questionnaires and focus groups. Recently, a good amount of literature is emerging from teacher education programmes that seek to better prepare teachers to teach English as an international language (see Matsuda, 2017). We need in-depth research to accompany such programmes to tangibly measure their effects on teachers' thoughts and actions, including potential longer term effects on pedagogical practice after teachers enter or return to the classroom.

While considerable work in teacher education is occurring under the umbrella of ELF-aware pedagogy, we believe GELT has an added advantage that many of the ideas we present have already been tried and tested in language classrooms (see Galloway 2011; 2013; 2017a; Galloway & Rose, 2014; 2018; Rose & Galloway, 2017). Thus, GELT pedagogical innovations are research-informed and teacher-led, rather than being applied as top-down constructs from research which extends beyond the language-learning domain. The GELT framework also deconstructs the multiple facets of pedagogical change into sizable and digestible dimensions, which can be easily transformed into teachable units in teacher educations programmes. Further, the curriculum perspective offered in Chapter 2 shows how a GELT perspective can map on to existing constructs which are typically taught in TESOL programmes (needs analysis, objectives, syllabus, methods, assessment and evaluation). As teacher education programmes continue to innovate, there will be increased opportunities to research the impact of these programmes on teachers' attitudes and their future practices.

Our investigation of the 'E' in EMI showcases how Global Englishes is further relevant to practices in the periphery of language teaching. As Briggs and Smith (2017) note:

> In EMI courses English is the conduit through which content subjects are delivered: students acquire knowledge of content material while, ideally, also improving their English language proficiency. Key to distinguishing EMI from other methods is the ancillary role of English language development—a side effect of instruction rather than an explicit pedagogical target. (p. 28)

Thus, even though English language teaching is not central to EMI, it is nonetheless implicitly connected. The same global forces that have caused a worldwide boom in EMI programmes are the same forces that have necessitated change in language teaching practices. Therefore, these changes are equally applicable to EMI in order to challenge native speaker centrality and monolingual hegemony. Most EMI contexts, with internationalisation and content learning at their core, need not promote a monolingual orientation to English use, nor an ideology that reinforces notions of native language norms. A GELT curriculum, whether part of an EMI preparatory programme or an EMI language support course, can help stakeholders to challenge standard notions of English.

While this book has outlined a number of areas of self-contained research, our example studies in the final three chapters of this book are nonetheless limited in scope and context. Rather than being exhaustive of research in each area, they are intended to provide visibility to the tip of a 'GELT research iceberg', which is indicative of the much larger body of research still yet to be explored. Chapter 5 has endeavoured to provide a roadmap for future research, but this roadmap will need to be adapted as new ideas emerge, and new contexts for language use emerge.

Future research should aim to connect the concepts in Part I of the book, which establishes the theoretical undercurrents and pedagogic applications of Global Englishes, with Part II of the book, which highlights a need to research innovations in practice. Global Englishes for language teaching occupies the very space between theory and practice, where many scholars have noted a considerable divide. From its very inception in Galloway's (2011) seminal study, the GELT framework has been proposed as a means to bridge this very gap. Since this time, we have occupied this space with a modest amount research on our own pedagogical practices, but far more is needed if a true 'paradigm shift' or 'turn' is to be realised. We hope this book will enable scholars and teachers alike to forge new pathways forward so that TESOL can continue its transformative journey as an adaptable profession that has grown and matured as the needs of our learners, and the very language we teach, has changed.

References

ACE. (2014). *The Asian Corpus of English*. Director: Andy Kirkpatrick; Researchers: Wang Lixun, John Patkin, Sophiann Subhan. Available at http://corpus.ied.edu.hk/ace/

Aguilar, M. & Muñoz, C. (2014). The effect of proficiency on CLIL benefits in engineering students in Spain. *International Journal of Applied Linguistics*, **24**(1), 1–18.

Airey, J. (2011). Talking about teaching in English: Swedish university lecturers' experiences of changing teaching language. *Ibérica*, **22**, 35–54.

Albl-Mikasa, M. (2013). Express-ability in ELF communication. *Journal of English as a Lingua Franca*, **2**(1), 101–22.

Albl-Mikasa, M. (2015). ELF speakers' restricted power of expression: implications for interpret-ers' processing. In M. Ehrensberger-Dow, B. Englund Dimitrova, S. Hubscher Davidson, & U. Norberg, eds., *Describing Cognitive Processes in Translation: Acts and Events*. Amsterdam: John Benjamins, pp. 43–62.

Albl-Mikasa, M. (2018). ELF and translation/interpreting. In J. Jenkins, W. Baker, & M. Dewey, eds., *The Routledge Handbook of English as a Lingua Franca*. Abingdon: Routledge, pp. 369–84.

Ali, S. (2009). Teaching English as an international language (EIL) in the Gulf Corporation Council (GCC) countries: the brown man's burden. In F. Sharifian, ed., *English as an International Language: Perspectives and Pedagogical Issues*. Bristol: Multilingual Matters, pp. 34–57.

Allwright, D. (1991). *The Death of the Method. CRILE Working Paper No. 10*. Lancaster: Lancaster University.

Alsagoff, L. (2012a). Another book on EIL? In L. Alsagoff, S. L. McKay, G. Hu, & W. A. Renandya, eds., *Principles and Practices for Teaching English as an International Language*. New York: Routledge, pp. 1–10.

Alsagoff, L. (2012b). Identity and the EIL learner. In L. Alsagoff, S. L. McKay, G. Hu, & W. A. Renandya, eds., *Principles and Practices for Teaching English as an International Language*. New York: Routledge, pp. 104–22.

Alsagoff, L., McKay, S. L., Hu, G., & Renandya, W. A., eds., (2012). *Principles and Practices of Teaching English as an International Language*. Bristol: Routledge.

Amin, N. (1999). Minority women teachers of ESL: negotiating white English. In G. Braine, ed., *Non-Native Educators in English Language Teaching*. Mahwah, New Jersey: Lawrence Erlbaum Associates, pp. 77–92.

Andon, N. & Eckerth, J. (2009). Chacun à son gout? Task-based L2 pedagogy from the teacher's point of view. *International Journal of Applied Linguistics*, **19**(3), 286–310.

Asher, J. (1977). *Learning Another Language Through Actions: The Complete Teacher's Guidebook*. California: Sky Oaks Productions.

Atkinson, D. (2011). *Alternative Approaches to Second Language Acquisition*. London: Routledge.

Baecher, L. (2012). Feedback from the field: what novice PreK-12 ESL teachers want to tell TESOL teacher educators. *TESOL Quarterly*, **46**(3), 578–88.

Baik, M. J. & Shim, R. J. (2002). Teaching World Englishes via the Internet. *World Englishes*, **21**(3), 427–30.

Baker, C. (2001). *Foundations of Bilingual Education and Bilingualism*, 3rd edn. *Bilingual Education and Bilingualism 27*. Bristol: Multilingual Matters.

Baker, W. (2009). The cultures of English as a lingua franca. *TESOL Quarterly*, **43**(4), 567–92.

Baker, W. (2011). Intercultural awareness: Modelling an understanding of cultures in intercultural communication through English as a lingua franca. *Language and Intercultural Communication*, 11(3), 197–214. doi:10.1080/14708477.2011.577779

Baker, W. (2012a). From cultural awareness to intercultural awareness: culture in ELT. *ELT Journal*, **66**(1), 62–70.

Baker, W. (2012b). *Using E-Learning to Develop Intercultural Awareness in ELT: A Critical Evaluation in a Thai Higher Education Setting. ELT Research Papers 12–03*. London: British Council.

Baker, W. (2015). Culture and complexity through English as a lingua franca: rethinking competences and pedagogy in ELT. *Journal of English as a Lingua Franca*, **4**(1), 9–30.

Ball, P. & Lindsay, D. (2013). Language demands and support for English-medium instruction in tertiary education. Learning from a specific context. In D. Doiz, D. Lasagabaster, & J. Sierra, eds., *English-Medium Instruction at Universities Worldwide: Global Challenges*. Bristol: Multilingual Matters, pp. 44–61.

Barnard, R. & McLellan, J. eds. (2014). *Codeswitching in University English-Medium Classes: Asian Perspectives*. Bristol: Multilingual Matters.

Barnawi, O. Z. & Le Ha, P. (2015). From Western TESOL classrooms to home practice: a case study with two "privileged" Saudi teachers. *Critical Studies in Education*, **56** (2), 259–76.

Basturkmen, H. & Wette, R. (2016). English for academic purposes. In G. Hall, ed., *The Routledge Handbook of English Language Teaching*. Abingdon: Routledge, pp. 164–76.

Bayyurt, Y. & Akcan, S. eds. (2015). *Current Perspectives on Pedagogy for English as a Lingua Franca*. Berlin, München, Boston: De Gruyter Mouton.

Bayyurt, Y. & Altınmakas, D. (2012). A World Englishes course at a foundation university in Turkey. In A. Matsuda, ed., *Principles and Practices of Teaching English as an International Language*. Bristol: Mulitlingual Matters, pp. 169–82.

Beebe, L. (1980). Sociolinguistic variation and style shifting in second language acquisition. *Language Learning*, **30**, 443–7.

Belcher, D. & Lukkarila, L. (2011). Identity in the ESP context: putting the learner front and center in needs analysis. In D. Belcher, A. M. Johns, & B. Paltridge, eds., *New Directions in English for Specific Purposes Research*. Ann Arbor: University of Michigan Press, pp. 73–93.

Benesch, S. (2001). *Critical English for Academic Purposes: Theory, Politics and Practice*. Mahwah, NJ: Lawrence Erlbaum.

Berns, M. (2015). Pedagogy and World Englishes: the legacy of Yamuna Kachru. *World Englishes*, **34**(1), 22–30.

Bilingual Business Program. (2010). *Learning Outcomes for BBL Courses*. Tokyo: Rikkyo University.

Blackledge, A. & Creese, A. (2010). *Multilingualism: A critical perspective*. London: Continuum.

Blackledge, A., Creese, A., & Kaur Takhi, J. (2014). Beyond multilingualism: heteroglossia in practice. In S. May, ed., *The Multilingual Turn: Implications for SLA, TESOL and Bilingual Education*. New York, NJ: Routledge, pp. 191–215.

Blair, A. (2015). Evolving a post-native, multilingual model for ELF-aware teacher education. In Y. Bayyurt & S. Akcan, eds., *Current Perspectives on Pedagogy for English as a Lingua Franca*. Berlin, München, Boston: De Gruyter Mouton, pp. 89–102.

Block, D. (1996). Not so fast! Some thoughts on theory culling, relativism, accepted findings and the heart and soul of SLA. *Applied Linguistics*, **17**, 65–83.

Block, D. (2003). *The Social Turn in Second Language Acquisition*. Edinburgh: Edinburgh University Press.

Block, D. (2014). Moving beyond 'lingualism': multilingual embodiment and multimodality in SLA. In S. May. ed., *The Multilingual Turn: Implications for SLA, TESOL, and Bilingual Education*. New York: Routledge, pp. 54–77.

Blommaert, J. (2010). *The Sociolinguistics of Globalization*. Cambridge: Cambridge University Press.

Bokhorst-Heng, W. D. (2005). Debating Singlish. *Multilingua*, **24**(3), 185–209.

Borg, S. (2003). Teacher cognition in language teaching: a review of research on what language teachers think, know, believe, and do. *Language Teaching*, **36**(2), 81–109.

Borg, S. (2009). Language teacher cognition. In A. Burns & J. Richards, eds., *The Cambridge Guide to Second Language Teacher Education*. Cambridge: Cambridge University Press, pp. 163–71.

Borg, S. (2015). *Teacher Cognition and Language Education: Research and Practice*. London: Continuum.

Bradford, A. (2016). Toward a typology of implementation challenges facing English-medium instruction in higher education: evidence from Japan. *Journal of Studies in International Education*, **20**(4), 339–56.

Breen, M. (1984). Process syllabus for the language classroom. In C. Brumfit, ed., *General English Syllabus Design*. ELT Documents 118, pp. 47–60.

Breen, M. (2001). Syllabus design. In R. Carter & D. Nunan, eds., *The Cambridge Guide to Teaching English to Speakers of Other Languages*. Cambridge: Cambridge University Press, p. 154.

Breen, M. P. & Candlin, C. N. (1987). Which materials? A consumer's and designer's guide. In L. Sheldon, ed., *ELT Textbooks and Materials: Problems in Evaluation and Development*. London: Modern English Publications.

Breen, M., Hird, B., Milton, O., & Thawaite, A. (2001). Making sense of language teaching: teachers' principles and classroom practices. *Applied Linguistics*, **22**(4), 470–501.

Brenn-White, P. M. & Faethe, E. (2013). *English-Taught Master's Programs in Europe: A 2013 Update*. New York: Institute of International Education.

Briggs, J. G. & Smith, S. A. (2017). English medium instruction and idiomaticity in English as a lingua franca. *Iranian Journal of Language Teaching Research*, 5(3), 27–44.

British Council. (2018). Regional English Training Centres Project (RETC Project). Thailand: British Council. Retrieved 24 January 24 2018, from www.britishcouncil.or.th/en/regional-english-training-centres-project-retc-project

Brookfield, S. (2003). Putting the critical back into critical pedagogy: a commentary on the path of dissent. *Journal of Transformative Education*, **1** (2): 141–9.

Brown, H. (2014). Contextual factors driving the growth of undergraduate English-medium instruction programmes at universities in Japan. *The Asian Journal of Applied Linguistics*, **1**(1), 50–63.

Brown, J. D. (1995). *The Elements of Language Curriculum: A Systematic Approach to Program Development*. Boston, MA: Heinle & Heinle.

Brumfit, C. J. & Johnson, K. (1979). *The Communicative Approach to Language Teaching*. Oxford: Oxford University Press.

Bruster, B. G. & Peterson, B. R. (2013). Using critical incidents in teaching to promote reflective practice. *Reflective Practice*, **14**(2), 170–82.

Bruthiaux, P. (2003). Squaring the circles: issues in modeling English worldwide. *International Journal of Applied Linguistics*, **13**(2), 159–78.

Brutt-Griffler, J. & Samimy, K. K. (1999). Revisiting the colonial in the postcolonial: critical praxis for nonnative-English-speaking teachers in a TESOL program. *TESOL Quarterly*, **33**(3), 413–31.

Buckingham, L. (2014). Attitudes to English teachers' accents in the Gulf. *International Journal of Applied Linguistics*, **24**(1), 50–73.

Burgess, C., Gibson, I., Klaphake, J., & Selzer, M. (2010). The "Global 30" Project and Japanese higher education reform: an example of a "closing in" or an "opening up"? *Globalisation, Societies and Education*, **8**(4), 461–75.

Burhan-Horasanlı, E. & Ortaçtepe, D. (2016). Reflective practice-oriented online discussions: a study on EFL teachers' reflection-on, in and for-action. *Teaching and Teacher Education*, **59**, 372–82.

Busch, D. (2010). Pre-service teacher beliefs about language learning: the second language acquisition course as an agent for change. *Language Teaching Research*, **14**(3), 318–37.

Byram, M. (1997). *Teaching and Assessing Intercultural Communicative Competence*. Bristol: Multilingual Matters.

Caleffi, P. (2016). ELF in the speaking and listening activities of recently published English language coursebooks. In L. Lopriore & E. Grazzi, eds., *Intercultural Communication: New Perspectives from ELF*. Rome: Roma Tre-Press.

Canagarajah, A. S. (1999). Interrogating the "native speaker fallacy": non-linguistics roots, non-pedagogical results. In G. Braine, ed., *Non-Native Educators in English Language Teaching*. Mahwah, N.J.: Lawrence Erlbaum Associates, pp. 77–92.

Canagarajah, A. S. (2005). Introduction. In A. S. Canagarajah, ed., *Reclaiming the Local in Language Policy and Practice*. Mahwah, NJ: Lawrence Erlbaum.

Canagarajah, A. S. (2007). Lingua franca English, multilingual communities, and language acquisition. *The Modern Language Journal*, 91, 923–39.

Canagarajah, S. (2011a). Codemeshing in academic writing: identifying teachable strategies of translanguaging. *The Modern Language Journal*, **95**(3), 401–17.

Canagarajah, S. (2011b). The plurilingual tradition and the English language in South Asia. *AILA Review*, **22**, 5–22.

Canagarajah, S. (2013). *Translingual practice: Global Englishes and cosmopolitan relations*. New York: Routledge.

Canagarajah, S. (2014). Theorizing a competence for translingual practice at the contact zone. In S. May, ed., *The Multilingual Turn: Implications for SLA, TESOL and Bilingual Education*. New York, NJ: Routledge, pp. 78–102.

Canagarajah, S. (2016). TESOL as a professional community: a half-century of pedagogy, research, and theory. *TESOL Quarterly*, 50(1), 7–41. https://doi.org/10.1002/tesq.275

Canale, M. (1983). From communicative competence to communicative language pedagogy. In J. Richards & R. Schmidt, eds., *Language and Communication*. London: Longman, pp. 2–27.

Canale, M. & Swain, M. (1980). Theoretical bases of communicative approaches to second language teaching and testing. *Applied Linguistics*, **1**, 1–47.

Carless, D. (2004). Issues in teachers' reinterpretation of a taskbased innovation in primary schools. *TESOL Quarterly*, **38**(4), 639.

Carless, D. (2007). The suitability of task-based approaches for secondary schools: perspectives from Hong Kong. *System*, **35**(4), 595–608.

Carless, D. (2009). Revisiting the TBLT versus P–P–P debate: voices from Hong Kong. *Asian Journal of English Language Teaching*, **19**(May), 49–66.

Carlson, R. O. (1968). Summary and critique of educational diffusion research. In Michigan State University & Michigan Vocational Educational Research Coordinating Unit, eds., *Research Implications for Educational Diffusion: Major Papers Presented at the National Conference on Diffusion of Educational Ideas*. Michigan: Michigan State University, pp. 4–23.

Carter, R. & Nunan, D. (2001). *The Cambridge Guide to Teaching English to Speakers of Other Languages*. Cambridge: Cambridge University Press.

Cavalheiro, L. (2013). Reflections on ELT pedagogy: functioning and communicating in English. *Sintagma Journal of Linguistics*, **25**, 7–18.

Chan, J. Y. H. (2014). An evaluation of the pronunciation target in Hong Kong's ELT curriculum and materials: influences from WE and ELF? *Journal of English as a Lingua Franca*, **3**(1), 145–70.

Chang, M. (2011). Factors affecting the implementation of communicative language teaching in Taiwanese college English classes. *English Language Teaching*, **4**(2), 3–12.

Chapple, J. (2015). Teaching in English is not necessarily the teaching of English. *International Education Studies*, **8**(3), 1–13.

Chomsky, N. (1965). *Aspects of the Theory of Syntax*. Cambridge, MA: MIT Press.

Chowdhury, R. & Phan, L. H. (2014). *Desiring TESOL and International Education: Market Abuse and Exploitation*. Bristol: Multilingual Matters.

Clandfield, L., Benne, R. R., & Jeffries, A. (2011). *Global. Upper Intermediate*. Oxford: Macmillan Education.

Clark, E. & Paran, A. (2007). The employability of non-native-speaker teachers of EFL: a UK survey. *System*, **35**(4), 407–30.

Cogo, A. (2012). English as a lingua franca: concepts, use, and implications. *ELT Journal*, **66**(1), 97–105.

Cogo, A. & Bowles, H. (2015). *International Perspectives on English as a Lingua Franca: Pedagogical Insights*. Basingstoke: Palgrave Macmillan.

Conteh, J. & Meier, G. S. (2014). *The Multilingual Turn in Languages Education: Opportunities and Challenges*. Bristol: Multilingual Matters.

Cook, G. (2003). *Applied Linguistics*. Oxford: Oxford University Press.

Cook, G. (2012). ELF and translation and interpreting: common ground, common interest, common cause. *Journal of English as a Lingua Franca* **1**(2), 241–62.

Cook, V. (1999). Going beyond the native speaker in language teaching. *TESOL Quarterly*, **33**(2), 185–209.

Cook, V. (2012). Multi-competence. In C. Chapelle, ed., *The Encyclopedia of Applied Linguistics*. Chichester: Wiley-Blackwell, pp. 3768–74.

Cook, V. (2016a). Premises of multicompetence. In V. Cook & L. Wei, eds., *The Cambridge Handbook of Linguistic Multicompetence*. Cambridge: Cambridge University Press.

Cook, V. (2016b). Where is the native speaker now? *TESOL Quarterly*, **50**(1), 186–9.

Cope, B. & Kalantzis, M. (2000). *Multiliteracies: Literacy Learning and the Design of Social Futures*. London: Routledge.

Corder, S. (1967). The significance of learners' errors. *International Review of Applied Linguistics in Language Teaching*, **5**, 161–70.

Costa, F. (2012). Focus on form in ICLHE lectures in Italy: evidence from English-medium science lectures by native speakers of Italian. *AILA Review*, **25**(1), 30–47.

Cotton, D. & Lansford, L. (2011). *Market Leader: Upper Intermediate*, 3rd edn. Harlow: Pearson Longman.

Council of Europe. (2001). *The Common European Framework of Reference for Languages: Learning, Teaching, Assessment*. Cambridge: Cambridge University Press.

Council of Europe. (2005). *Common European Framework of Reference for Languages: Learning, Teaching, Assessment (CEFR)*. Retrieved 8 February 2018, from www.coe.int/en/web/common-european-framework-reference-languages/

Creagh, S. (2017). Multiple ways of speaking back to the monolingual mindset. *Discourse: Studies in the Cultural Politics of Education*, **38**(1), 1–11.

Creese, A. & Blackledge, A. (2011). Separate and flexible bilingualism in complementary schools: Multiple language practices in interrelationship. *Journal of Pragmatics*, **43**(5), 1196–1208.

Crystal, D. (2003). *English as a Global Language*. Cambridge: Cambridge University Press.

Cummins, J. (1979). Linguistic interdependence and the educational development of bilingual children. *Review of Educational Research*, **49**(2), 222–51.

Curran, C. A. (1972). *Counseling-Learning: A Whole Person Approach for Education*. Apple River: Apple River Press.

D'Angelo, J. (2018). The status of ELF in Japan. In J. Jenkins, W. Baker, & M. Dewey, eds., *The Routledge Handbook of English as a Lingua Franca*. Abingdon &, New York: Routledge, pp. 165–75.

Davies, A. (1991). *The Native Speaker in Applied Linguistics. The Handbook of Applied Linguistics*. Edinburgh: Blackwell Publishing.

Davies, A. (2003). *The Native Speaker Myth and Reality*. Clevedon: Multilingual Matters.

Davies, A. (2013). *Native Speakers and Native Users: Loss and Gain*. Cambridge: Cambridge University Press.

Day, R. & Bamford, J. (1998). *Extensive Reading in the Second Language*. New York: Cambridge University Press.

Dearden, J. (2014). *English as a Medium of Instruction: A Growing Global Phenomenon*. London: British Council.

Delgado-Márquez, B. L., Escudero-Torres, M. Á. & Hurtado-Torres, N. E. (2013). Being highly internationalised strengthens your reputation: an empirical investigation of top higher education institutions. *Higher Education*, **66**(5), 619–33.

Deng, C. & Carless, D. (2009). The communicativeness of activities in a task-based innovation in Guangdong, China. *Asian Journal of English Language Teaching*, **18**, 113–34.

Derwing, T. M., Rossiter, M. J., & Munro, M. J. (2002). Teaching native speakers to listen to foreign-accented speech. *Journal of Multilingual and Multicultural Development*, **23**(4), 245–59.

Dewey, M. (2012). Towards a post-normative approach: learning the pedagogy of ELF. *Journal of English as a Lingua Franca*, **1**(1), 141–70.

Dewey, M. (2014). Pedagogic criticality and English as a lingua franca. *Atlantis Journal of the Spanish Association of Anglo-American Studies*, **36**(2), 11–30.

Dewey, M. (2015). ELF, teacher knowledge and professional development. In H. Bowles & A. Cogo, eds., *International Perspectives on English as a Lingua Franca. Pedagogical Insights*. Basingstoke: Palgrave Macmillan, pp. 176–93.

Dewey, M. & Patsko, L. (2018). ELF and teacher education. In J. Jenkins, W. Baker, & M. Dewey. eds., *The Routledge Handbook of English as a Lingua Franca*. Abingdon: Routledge.

Dick, B. & Greenwood, D. J. (2015). Theory and method: Why action research does not separate them. *Action Research*, **13**(2), 194–7.

Dilek, İ. & Özdemir, E. (2015). Re/considering the English language teacher education programs in Turkey from an ELF standpoint: what do academia, pre-service and in-service teachers think? In S. Ackan & Y. Bayyurt, eds., *Current Perspectives on Pedagogy for English as a Lingua Franca*. Berlin: Mouton de Gruyter, pp. 135–52.

Doan, N. B. (2014). Teaching the target culture in English teacher education programs: issues of EIL in Vietnam. In R. Marlina & R. A. Giri, eds., *The Pedagogy of English as an International Language: Perspectives from Scholars, Teachers, and Students*. New York: Springer, pp. 79–93.

Dogancay-Aktuna, S. & Hardman, J. (2012). Teachers education for EIL: working toward a situated meta-praxis. In A. Matsuda, ed., *Principles and Practices of Teaching English as an International Language*. Bristol: Multilingual Matters, pp. 103–18.

Donato, R. (2000). Sociocultural contributions to understanding the foreign and second language classroom. In J. Lantolf, ed., *Sociocultural Theory and Second Language Learning*. Oxford: Oxford University Press, pp. 27–50.

Dörnyei, Z. (2007). *Research Methods in Applied Linguistics: Quantitative, Qualitative, and Mixed Methodologies*. Oxford: Oxford University Press.

Dörnyei, Z. (2009). The L2 Motivational Self System. In Z. Dörnyei & E. Ushioda, eds., *Motivation, Language Identity and the L2 Self*. Bristol: Multilingual Matters, pp. 9–42.

Dörnyei, Z. & Csizér, K. (2002). Some dynamics of language attitudes and motivation: results of a longitudinal nationwide survey. *Applied Linguistics*, **23**(4), 423–62.

Dörnyei, Z., Csizér, K., & Németh, N. (2006). *Motivation, Language Attitudes and Globalisation: A Hungarian Perspective*. Clevedon: Multilingual Matters.

Dörnyei, Z. & Ryan, S. (2015). *The Psychology of the Language Learner Revisited*. New York: Routledge.

Doughty, C. & Pica, T. (1986). Information gap tasks: do they facilitate second language acquisition. *TESOL Quarterly*, **20**(2), 305–25.

Earls, C. W. (2016). When English just is not enough: "multilingualism with English" in contemporary European higher education. *International Journal of Applied Linguistics*, **26**(3), 329–47.

Ellis, N. (1993). Rules and instances in foreign language learning: interactions of explicit and implicit knowledge. *European Journal of Cognitive Psychology*, 5, 289–318.

Ellis, N. C. (1996). Sequencing in SLA: phonological memory, chunking, and points of order. *Studies in Second Language Acquisition*, **18**, 91–126.

Ellis, R. (1990). *Instructed Second Language Acquisition*. Oxford: Blackwell.

Ellis, R. (1994). *The Study of Second Language Acquisition*. Oxford: Oxford University Press.

Ellis, R. (1997). *SLA Research and Language Teaching*. Oxford: Oxford University Press.

Ellis, R., Loewen, S., & Basturkmen, S. (1999). *Focussing on Form in the Classroom. Occasional Paper 13*. Auckland, New Zealand: University of Auckland, Institute of Language Teaching and Learning.

Ehrenreich, S. (2009). English as a lingua franca in multinational corporations: exploring business communities of practice. In: A. Mauranen & E. Ranta, eds., *English as a Lingua Franca: Studies and Findings*. Newcastle upon Tyne: Cambridge Scholars Publishing, pp. 126–51.

Ehrenreich, S. (2015). English as a lingua franca (ELF) in international business contexts: key issues and future perspectives. In K. Murata, ed., *Exploring ELF in Japanese Academic and Business Contexts*. London: Routledge, pp. 135–55.

Elder, C. and Davies, A. (2006). Assessing English as a lingua franca. *Annual Review of Applied Linguistics*, 26, 282–304.

ELFA website. (2008). *The Corpus of English as a Lingua Franca in Academic Settings*. Director: Anna Mauranen. Available at http://www.helsinki.fi/elfa/elfacorpus

El Kadri, M.S., Calvo, L.C.S., & Gimenez, T. (2017). English as a lingua franca in an online teacher education program offered by a state university in Brazil. In A. Matsuda, ed., Preparing Teachers to Teach EIL: Curricular Description. Bristol: Multilingual Matters, pp. 181–94.

Evans, L. & Davies, K. (2000). No sissy boys here: a content analysis of the representation of masculinity in elementary school reading textbooks. *Sex Roles*, **42**(3), 255–70.

Faez, F. & Valeo, A. (2012). TESOL teacher education: novice teachers' perceptions of their preparedness and efficacy in the classroom. *TESOL Quarterly*, **46**(3), 450–71.

Farrell, T. S. C. (2012). Novice-service language teacher development: bridging the gap between preservice and in-service education and development. *TESOL Quarterly*, **46** (3), 435–49.

Ferguson, G. (2003). Classroom code-switching in post-colonial contexts: functions, attitudes and policies. In S. Makoni & U. Meinhof, eds., *Africa and Applied Linguistics: AILA Review 16*. Amsterdam: John Benjamins, pp. 38–51.

Ferguson, G. (2009). Issues in researching English as a lingua franca: a conceptual enquiry. *International Journal of Applied Linguistics*, **19**(2), 117–35.

Fetterman, D. M. (2010). *Ethnography: Step-by-Step*. London: Sage.

Firth, A. & Wagner, J. (1997). On discourse, communication, and (some) fundamental concepts in SLA research. *The Modern Language Journal*, **81**(3), 285–300.

Forbes-Mewett, H. & Nyland, C. (2012). Funding international student support services: tension and power in the university. *Higher Education*, **65**(2), 181–92.

Frawley, W. & Lantolf, J. (1984). Speaking as self-order: a critique of orthodox L2 research. *Studies in Second Language Acquisition*, **6**, 143–59.

Frawley, W. & Lantolf, J. (1985). Second language discourse: a Vygotskyan perspective. *Applied Linguistics*, **6**, 19–44.

Freire, P. (1996). *Pedagogy of the Oppressed*. London: Penguin.

Fullan, M. (2007). *The New Meaning of Educational Change*, 4th edn. Abingdon, UK: Routledge.

Galloway, N. (2011). *An Investigation of Japanese Students' Attitudes towards English*. Unpublished Ph.D. dissertation. University of Southampton.

Galloway, N. (2013). Global Englishes and English Language Teaching (ELT)–Bridging the Gap between Theory and Practice in a Japanese Context. *System*, **41** (3), 786–803.

Galloway, N. (2017a). *Global Englishes and Change in English Language Teaching*. Abingdon, UK: Routledge.

Galloway, N. (2017b). *Global Englishes for Language Teaching: preparing MSc TESOL students to teach in a globalized world*. In A. Matsuda, ed., *Preparing Teachers to Teach English as an International Language*. Bristol: Multilingual Matters.

Galloway, N. (2017c). Researching your own students: negotiating the dual teacher-researcher role. In J. McKinley & H. Rose, eds., *Doing Research in Applied Linguistics Realities, Dilemmas, and Solutions*. London: Routledge.

Galloway, N. (2018a). ELF and ELT teaching materials. In J. Jenkins, W. Baker, & M. Dewey, eds., *The Routledge Handbook of English as a Lingua Franca*. New York: Routledge, pp. 468–80.

Galloway, N. (2018b). NESTs (native English speaker teachers). In A. Shehadeh, ed., *The TESOL Encyclopedia of English Language Teaching, Vol. II*. Hoboken, NJ: Wiley-Blackwell.

Galloway, N., Kriukow, J., & Numajiri, T. (2017). *Internationalisation, Higher Education and the Growing Demand for English: An Investigation into the English Medium of Instruction (EMI) Movement in China and Japan. ELT Research Papers 17–02*. London: British Council.

Galloway, N. & Rose, H. (2013). "They envision going to New York, not Jakarta": the differing attitudes toward ELF of students, teaching assistants, and instructors in an

English-medium business program in Japan. *Journal of English as a Lingua Franca*, **2**(2), 229–53.

Galloway, N. & Rose, H. (2014). Using listening journals to raise awareness of global Englishes in ELT. *ELT Journal*, **68**(4), 386–96.

Galloway, N. & Rose, H. (2015). *Introducing Global Englishes*. Abingdon: Routledge.

Galloway, N. & Rose, H. (2018). Incorporating Global Englishes into the ELT classroom. *ELT Journal*, **72**(1), 3–14.

Garcia, E. (2009). *Bilingual Education in the 21st Century: A Global Perspective*. Malden, MA: Wiley-Blackwell.

García, O. & Flores, N. (2014). Multilingualism and common core state standards in the United States. In S. May, ed., *The Multilingual Turn: Implications for SLA, TESOL and Bilingual Education*. New York: Routledge, pp. 147–66.

García, O. & Wei, L. (2014). *Translanguaging: Language, Bilingualism and Education*. New York and Basingstoke: Palgrave Macmillan.

Gardner, R. (1985). *Social Psychology and Second Language Learning: The Role of Attitudes and Motivation*. London: E. Arnold.

Gass, S. (1997). *Input, Interaction, and the Second Language Learner*. Mahwah, NJ: Lawrence Erlbaum Associates Publishers.

Gass, S. & Selinker, L., eds. (1983). *Language Transfer in Language Learning*. Rowley, MA: Newbury House.

Gass, S. & Varonis, E. M. (1984). The effect of familiarity on the comprehensibility of nonnative speech. *Language Learning*, **34**(1), 65–87.

Gasser, M. (1990). Connectionism and universals of second language acquisition. *Studies in Second Language Acquisition*, **12**, 179–99.

Gattegno, C. (1972). *Teaching Foreign Languages in Schools: The Silent Way*, 2nd edn. Reading, UK: Educational Explorers.

Gimenez, J. C. (2014). Multi-communication and the business English class: research meets pedagogy. *English for Specific Purposes*, **35**, 1–16.

Gimenez, T., Salles El Kadri, M., & Cabrini Simões Calvo, L (2018). ELF in Brazil: recent developments and further directions. In J. Jenkins, W. Baker, & M. Dewey, eds., *The Routledge Handbook of English as a Lingua Franca*. Abingdon & New York: Routledge, pp. 176–85.

Giri, R. A. & Foo, J. M. S. (2014). On teaching EIL in a Japanese context: the power within and power without. In R. Marlina & R. A. Giri, eds., *The Pedagogy of English as an International Language: Perspectives from Scholars, Teachers, and Students*. New York: Springer, pp. 239–56.

Giroux, H. A. (1983). *Theory and Resistance in Education: A Pedagogy for the Opposition*. South Hadley, MA: Bergin & Garvey

Grant, N. (1987). *Making the Most of Your Textbook*. London: Longman.

Graves, K. (1999). *Designing Language Courses: A Guide for Teachers. TeacherSource*. Boston: Heinle & Heinle.

Graves, K. (2016). Language curriculum design. Possibilities and realities. In G. Hall, ed., *The Routledge Handbook of English Language Teaching*. Abingdon and New York: Routledge, pp. 79–94.

Gray, J. (2010). The branding of English and the culture of the new capitalism: representations of the world of work in English language textbooks. *Applied Linguistics*, **31**(5), 714–33.

Gray, J. (2016). ELT materials: claims, critiques and controversies. In G. Hall, ed., *The Routledge Handbook of English Language Teaching*. Abingdon and New York: Routledge, pp. 90–104.

Grazia Guido, M (2008). *English as a Lingua Franca in Cross-Cultural Immigration Domains*. Bern: Peter Lang.

Grazia Guido, M (2018). ELF and translation/interpreting. In J. Jenkins, W. Baker, & M. Dewey, eds., *The Routledge Handbook of English as a Lingua Franca*. Abingdon: Routledge, pp. 369–84.

Guo, S. & Maitra, S. (2017). Revisioning curriculum in the age of transnational mobility: towards a transnational and transcultural framework. *Curriculum Inquiry*, **47**(1), 80–91.

Halkier, B. (2010). Focus groups as social enactments: integrating interaction and content in the analysis of focus group data. *Qualitative Research*, **10**(1), 71–89.

Hall, C. J., Wicaksono, R., Liu, S., Qian, Y., & Xiaoqing, X. (2013). *English Reconceived: Raising Teachers' Awareness of English as a 'Plurilithic' Resource through an Online Course. ELT Research Papers 13–05*. London: British Council.

Hall, G. (2016). Method, methods and methodology: historical trends and current debates. In G. Hall, ed., *The Routledge Handbook of English Language Teaching*. Abingdon: Routledge, pp. 209–23.

Hall, G. (2017). *Exploring ELT: Language in Action*, 2nd edn. London: Routledge.

Hamid, M. O., Nguyen, H. T. M., & Baldauf Jr, R. B. (2013). Medium of instruction in Asia: context, processes and outcomes. *Current Issues in Language Planning*, **14**(1), 1–15.

Handford, M. & Matous, P. (2011). Lexicogrammar in the international construction industry: a corpus-based case study of Japanese–Hong-Kongese on-site interactions in English. *English for Specific Purposes*, **30**(2), 87–100.

Harklau, L. (2005). Ethnography and ethnographic research on second language teaching and learning. In E. Hinkel, ed., *Handbook of Research in Second Language Learning and Teaching*. Mahwah, NJ: Lawrence Erlbaum, pp. 179–94.

Hartley, B. & Viney, P. (1978). *American Streamline*. Oxford: Oxford University Press.

Hellekjaer, G. O. (2010). Lecture comprehension in English-medium higher education. *Hermes*, **45**(45), 11–34.

Henrichsen, L. (1989). *Diffusion of Innovations in English Language Teaching: The ELEC Effort in Japan, 1956–1968*. New York: Greenwood Press.

Hino, N. (2017). Training graduate students in Japan to be EIL teachers. In A. Matsuda, ed., *Preparing Teachers to Teach English as an International Language*. Bristol: Multilingual Matters.

Hobbs, V. (2013). "A basic starter pack": the TESOL certificate as a course in survival. *ELT Journal*, **67**(2), 163–74.

Holliday, A. (1994). *Appropriate Methodology and Social Context*. Cambridge: Cambridge University Press.

Holliday, A. (2001). Achieving cultural continuity in curriculum innovation. In D. R. Hall & A. Hewings, eds., *Innovation in English Language Teaching: A Reader*. Abingdon: Routledge, pp. 169–77.

Holliday, A. (2005). *The Struggle to Teach English as an International Language*. Oxford: Oxford University Press.

Holliday, A. (2015). Native-speakerism: taking the concept forward and achieving cultural belief. In A. Swan, P. Aboshiha, & A. Holliday, eds., *(En)Countering Native-Speakerism: Global Perspectives*. Basingstoke: Palgrave Macmillan UK, pp. 11–25.

Holliday, A. (2006). Native-speakerism. ELT Journal, 60(4), 385–387.

Horner, B., Zhan-Lu, M., & Matsuda, P., eds. (2010). *Cross-Language Relations in Composition*. Carbondale: Southern Illinois Press.

House, J. (2014). English as a global lingua franca: a threat to multilingual communication and translation? *Language Teaching* **47**(3), 363–76.

Hu, G. (2009). The craze for English-medium education in China: driving forces and looming consequences. *English Today*, **25**(4), 47.

Hu, G. & Lei, J. (2014). English-medium instruction in Chinese higher education: a case study. *Higher Education*, **67**(5), 551–67.

Hu, G., Li, L., & Lei, J. (2014). English-medium instruction at a Chinese university: rhetoric and reality. *Language Policy*, **13**(1), 21–40.

Huang, F. (2006). Internationalization of curricula in higher education institutions in comparative perspectives: case studies of China, Japan and the Netherlands. *Higher Education*, **51**(4), 521–39.

Humphries, S. & Burns, A. (2015). 'In reality it's almost impossible': CLT-oriented curriculum change. *ELT Journal*, **69**(3), 239–48.

Hymes, D. H. (1966). Two types of linguistic relativity. In W. Bright, ed., *Sociolinguistics*. The Hague: Mouton, pp. 114–58.

Hymes, D. H. (1972). On communicative competence. In J. Pride & J. Holmes, eds., *Sociolinguistics: Selected Readings*. Harmondsworth: Penguin, pp. 269–93.

Ilieva, R. & Waterstone, B. (2013). Curriculum discourses within a TESOL program for international students: Affording possibilities for academic and professional identities. *TCI (Transnational Curriculum Inquiry)*, **10**(1), 16–37.

Inoue, N. & Stracke, E. (2013). Non-native English speaking postgraduate TESOL students in Australia: why did they come here? *University of Sydney Papers in TESOL*, **8,** 29–56.

Jenkins, J. (1998). Which pronunciation norms and models for English as an International Language? *ELT Journal*, **52**(2), 119–26.

Jenkins, J. (2000). *The Phonology of English as an International Language: New Models, New Norms, New Goals*. Oxford: Oxford University Press.

Jenkins, J. (2003). *World Englishes: A Resource Book for Students*. Abingdon: Routledge.

Jenkins, J. (2006). Points of view and blind spots: ELF and SLA. *International Journal of Applied Linguistics*, **16**(2), 137–62.

Jenkins, J. (2007). *English as a Lingua Franca: Attitude and Identity*. Oxford: Oxford University Press.

Jenkins, J. (2009). *World Englishes: A Resource Book for Students*, 2nd edn. Abingdon: Routledge.

Jenkins, J. (2012). English as a lingua franca from the classroom to the classroom. *ELT Journal*, **66**(4), 486–94.

Jenkins, J. (2014). *English as a Lingua Franca in the International University: The Politics of Academic English Language Policy*. London: Routledge.

Jenkins, J. (2015). *Global Englishes: A Resource Book for Students*, 3rd edn. Abingdon: Routledge.

Jenkins, J., Cogo, A. & Dewey, M. (2011). Review of developments in research into English as a lingua franca. *Language Teaching*, **44**(3), 281–315.

Jenks, C. (2013). "Your pronunciation and your accent is very excellent": orientations of identity during compliment sequences in English as a lingua franca encounters. *Language and Intercultural Communication*, **13**(2), 165–81.

Johnson, K. (2016). Language teacher education. In G. Hall, ed., *The Routledge Handbook of English Language Teaching*. Abingdon: Routledge, pp. 121–34.

Jeyaraj, J. J. & Harland, T. (2016). Teaching with critical pedagogy in ELT: the problems of indoctrination and risk. *Pedagogy, Culture and Society*, **24**(4), 587–98.

Jørgensen, J. N. (2008). Poly-lingual languaging around and among children and adolescents. *International Journal of Multilingualism*, **5**(3), 161–76.

Kachru, B. B. (1992). *The Other Tongue: English Across Cultures*. Urbana: University of Illinois Press.

Kachru, Y. (1986). Nominal complement construction in Hindi. In V. V. Rav, ed., *Bhasa shiksan aur bhasa vijnan*. Agra: Central Institute of Hindi, 119–30.

Kachru, Y. (2005). Learning and teaching of world Englishes. In E. Hinkel, ed., *Research in Second Language Learning and Teaching*). Mahwah, NJ: Lawrence Erlbaum, pp. 155–73.

Kankaanranta, A. & Louhiala-Salminen, L. (2007). Business communication in BELF (Business English as a Foreign Language). *Business Communication Quarterly*, **70** (1), 55–9.

Kankaanranta, A. & Louhiala-Salminen, L. (2010). "English? – Oh, it's just work!" A Study of BELF Users' Perceptions. *English for Specific Purposes*, **29**(3), 204–9. https://doi.org/10.1016/j.esp.2009.06.004

Kankaanranta, A. & Louhiala-Salminen, L. (2018). ELF in the domain of business – BELF: what does the B stand for? In J. Jenkins, W. Baker, & M. Dewey, eds., *The Routledge Handbook of English as a Lingua Franca*. Abingdon: Routledge, pp. 309–20.

Kankaanranta, A. & Planken, B. (2010). Belf competence as business knowledge of internationally operating business professionals. *Journal of Business Communication*, **47**(4), 380–407.

Kelly, L. B. (2018). Preservice teachers' developing conceptions of teaching English learners. *TESOL Quarterly*, **52**(1), 110–36.

Kemmis, S. & McTaggart, R. (1988). *The Action Research Planner*. Geelong: Deakin University.

Kim, E. G. (2017). English medium instruction in Korean higher education: challenges and future directions. In B. Fenton-Smith, P. Humphreys, & I. Walkinshaw, eds., *English Medium Instruction in Higher Education in Asia-Pacific: From Policy to Pedagogy*. Cham: Springer, pp. 53–70.

Kirkpatrick, A. (2007). *World Englishes: Implications for International Communication and English Language Teaching*. Cambridge: Cambridge University Press.

Kirkpatrick, A. (2012). English as an Asian Lingua Franca: the "Lingua Franca Approach" and implications for language education policy. *Journal of English as a Lingua Franca*, **1**(1), 121–39.

Kirkpatrick, A. (2017). The languages of higher education in East and Southeast Asia: will EMI lead to Englishisation? In B. Fenton-Smith, P. Humphreys, & I., eds.,

English Medium Instruction in Higher Education in Asia-Pacific: From Policy to Pedagogy. Cham: Springer, pp. 21–36.

Kirkpatrick, A (2018). The development of English as a lingua franca in ASEAN. In J. Jenkins, W. Baker, & M. Dewey, eds., *The Routledge Handbook of English as a Lingua Franca*. Abingdon, New York: Routledge, pp. 138–50.

Kirkpatrick, A. & Xu, Z. (2002). Chinese pragmatic norms and 'China English.' *World Englishes*, **21**(2), 269–79.

Kirkpatrick, T. (2011). *Internationalization or Englishization: Medium of Instruction in Today's Universities. Working Paper Series No. 2011/003*. Hong Kong: Centre for Governance and Citizenship, Institute of Education. Retrieved from http://repository.lib.eduhk.hk/pubdata/ir/link/pub/AK%20CGC%20occasional%20paper%20final_final_—%20Prof%20%20Kirkpatrick.pdf

Knight, J. (2003). Updated internationalisation definition. *International Higher Education*, **33**, 2–3.

Kormos, J. & Csizér, K. (2008). Age-related differences in the motivation of learning English as a foreign language: attitudes, selves, and motivated learning behavior. *Language Learning*, **58**(2), 327–55.

Kormos, J., Kiddle, T., & Csizer, K. (2011). Systems of goals, attitudes, and self-related beliefs in second-language-learning motivation. *Applied Linguistics*, **32**(5), 495–516.

Kramsch, C. (2012). Authenticity and legitimacy in multilingual SLA. *Critical Multilingualism Studies*, **1**(1), 107–28.

Kramsch, C. (2014). Teaching foreign languages in an era of globalization: introduction. *The Modern Language Journal*, **98**(1), 296–311.

Krashen, S. (1982). *Principles and Practice in Second Language Acquisition*. Oxford: Pergamon Press.

Kroll, J. F., Gullifer, J. W., & Rossi, E. (2013). The multilingual lexicon: the cognitive and neural basis of lexical comprehension and production in two or more languages. *Annual Review of Applied Linguistics*, 33, 102–27.

Krueger, R. A. (1994). *Focus Groups: A Practical Guide for Applied Research*. London: Sage.

Krueger, R. A. (1998). *Developing Questions for Focus Groups: Focus Group Kit 3*. Thousand Oaks, CA: Sage.

Krueger, R. & Casey, M. (2015). *Focus Groups: A Practical Guide for Applied Research*, 5th edn. Los Angeles, CA: Sage.

Kubota, R. (2001). Teaching World Englishes to native speakers of English in the USA. *World Englishes*, **20**(1), 47–64.

Kubota, R. & Lin, A. (2006). Race and TESOL: introduction to concepts and theories. *TESOL Quarterly*, **40**(3), 471–93.

Kuckartz, U. (2014). *Qualitative Text Analysis: A Guide to Methods, Practice and Using Software*. Los Angeles, CA: Sage.

Kumaravadivelu, B. (1994). The postmethod condition: (e)merging strategies for second/foreign language teaching. *TESOL Quarterly*, **28**(1), 27–48.

Kumaravadivelu, B. (2005). *Understanding Language Teaching: From Method to Postmethod*. New York: Lawrence Erlbaum Associates.

Kumaravadivelu, B. (2006). *Understanding Language Teaching: From Method to Postmethod*. Mahwah: Routledge.

Kumaravadivelu, B. (2012). Individual Identity, Cultural Globalization and Teaching English as an International Language: The Case for an Epistemic Break. In L. Alsagoff, S. L. McKay, G. Hu, & W. A. Renandya, eds., *Teaching English as an International Language: Principles and Practices*. New York: Routledge, pp. 9–27.

Kuo, I.-C. (Vicky). (2006). Addressing the issue of teaching English as a lingua franca. *ELT Journal*, **60**(3), 213–21.

Kvale, S. (1996). *Interviews: An Introduction to Qualitative Research Interviewing*. Thousand Oaks, CA: Sage.

Lado, R. (1957). *Linguistic Across Cultures: Applied Linguistic for Language Teachers*. Ann Arbor, MI: University of Michigan Press.

Lamb, M. (2012). A self system perspective on young adolescents' motivation to learn English in urban and rural settings. *Language Learning*, **62**, 997–1023.

Lantolf, J. (2011). The sociocultural approach to second language acquisition. In D. Atkinson, ed., *Alternative Approaches to Second Language Acquisition*. New York: Routledge, pp. 24–47.

Larsen-Freeman, D. (1997). Chaos/complexity and second language acquisition. *Applied Linguistics*, **18**, 141–65.

Larsen-Freeman, D. (2006). On dynamism of grammar in contexualising communicative competence. *Review of Applied Linguistics in China*, **2**, 51-63.

Larsen-Freeman, D. (2009). Teaching and testing grammar. In M. Long & C. Doughty, eds., *The Handbook of Language Teaching*. Oxford: Blackwell Publishing, pp. 518–42.

Larsen-Freeman, D. (2011). A complexity theory approach to second language development/acquisition. In D. Atkinson, ed., *Alternative Approaches to Second Language Acquisition*. Abingdon: Routledge, pp. 48–72.

Larsen-Freeman, D. (2012). The emancipation of the language learner 1. *Studies in Second Language Learning and Teaching*, **2**(3), 297–309.

Larsen-Freeman, D. & Anderson, M. (2011). *Techniques and Principles in Language Teaching*, 3rd edn. Oxford: Oxford University Press.

Larsen-Freeman, D. & Cameron, L. (2008). *Complex Systems and Applied Linguistics*. Oxford: Oxford University Press.

Lasagabaster, D. & Doiz, A. (2017). A longitudinal study on the impact of CLIL on affective factors. *Applied Linguistics*, **38**(5), 688–712.

Lee, H. (2012). World Englishes in a high school English class: a case from Japan. In A. Matsuda, ed., *Principles and Practices of Teaching English as an International Language*. Bristol: Multilingual Matters, pp. 154–68.

Lee, J.-H. & Macaro, E. (2013). Investigating age in the use of L1 or English-only instruction: vocabulary acquisition by Korean ESL learners. *The Modern Language Journal*, **97**(4), 887–901.

Lee, W. Y. (1995). Authenticity revisited. *ELT Journal*, **49**(4), 323–8.

Leung, C. (2014). Communication and participatory involvement in linguistically diverse classrooms. In S. May, ed., *The Multilingual Turn. Implications for SLA, TESOL and Bilingual Education*. New York: Routledge, pp. 123–46.

Li, D. & Edwards, V. (2013). The impact of overseas training on curriculum innovation and change in English language education in western China. *Language Teaching Research*, **17**(4), 390–408.

Lie, J. (1995). From international migration to transnational diaspora. *Contemporary Sociology*, **24**(4), 303–6.

Lim, L., Pakir, A., & Wee, L. (2010). *English in Singapore: Modernity and Management*. Hong Kong: Hong Kong University Press.

Littlejohn, A. (1992). *Why Are ELT Materials the Way They Are?* Unpublished Ph.D. dissertation. Lancaster University.

Littlejohn, A. (2011). The analysis of language teaching materials: inside the Trojan Horse. In B. Tomlinson, ed., *Materials Development in Language Teaching*. Cambridge: Cambridge University Press.

Llurda, E. (2013). English-medium instruction at universities: Global challenges. *ELT Journal*, **67**(4),497–500.

Llurda, E. (2016). *'Native speakers', English and ELT: changing perspectives*. In G. Hall, ed., *The Routledge Handbook of English Language Teaching*. Abingdon, UK: Routledge, pp. 51–63.

Lo, Y. Y. & Macaro, E. (2015). Getting used to content and language integrated learning: what can classroom interaction reveal? *The Language Learning Journal*, **43**(3), 239–55.

Long, M. (1983). Does second language instruction make a difference? A review of the research. *TESOL Quarterly*, **17**, 359–82.

Long, M. (1988). Instructed interlanguage development. In L. Beebe, ed., *Issues in Second Language Acquisition: Multiple Perspectives*. New York: Newbury House, pp. 115–41.

Long, M. (1991). Focus on form: a design feature in language teaching methodology. In K. de Bot, R. Ginsburg, & C. Kramsch, eds., *Foreign Language Research in Cross-Cultural Perspective*. Amsterdam, Netherlands: John Benjamin, pp. 39–52.

Long, M. H. (1983a). Linguistic and conversational adjustments to nonnative speakers. *Studies in Second Language Acquisition*, **5**, 177–94.

Long, M. H. (1983b). Native speaker/non-native speaker conversation and the negotiation of comprehensible input. *Applied Linguistics*, **4**, 126–41.

Long, M. H. (1985). Input and second language acquisition theory. In S. M. Gass & C. Madden, eds., *Input in Second Language Acquisition*. Rowley, MA: Newbury House, pp. 377–93.

Long, M. H. (1996). The role of the linguistic environment in second language acquisition. In W. Ritchie & T. Bhatia, eds., *Handbook of Second Language Acquisition*. New York: Academic Press, pp. 413–68.

Lopriore, L. (2016). ELF in teacher education: a way and ways. In L. Lopriore & E. Grazzi, eds., *Intercultural Communication. New Perspectives from ELF*. Rome: Roma TrE-Press, pp. 167–88.

Louhiala-Salminen, L., Charles, M., & Kankaanranta, A. (2005). English as a lingua franca in Nordic corporate mergers: two case companies. *English for Specific Purposes*, **24**(4), 401–21.

Lowie, W., Plat, R., & de Bot, K. (2014). Pink noise in language production: a nonlinear approach to the multilingual lexicon. *Ecological Psychology*, **26**(3), 216–28.

Lozanov, G. (1978). *Suggestology and Outlines of Suggestopedy*. London: Gordon and Breach Science Publishers.

Macaro, E. (2014). Overview: where should we be going with classroom codeswitching research. In R. Barnard & J. McLellan, eds., *Codeswitching in University English-Medium Classes: Asian Perspectives*. Bristol: Multilingual Matters, pp. 10–23.

Macaro, E., Curle, S., Pun, J., An, J., & Dearden, J. (2018). A systematic review of English medium instruction in higher education. *Language Teaching*, **51**(1), 36–76.

Macaro, E. & Lee, J. H. (2013). Teacher language background, codeswitching, and English-only instruction: does age make a difference to learners' attitudes? *TESOL Quarterly*, **47**(4), 717–42.

MacKenzie, I. (2010). *English for Business Studies*. Cambridge: Cambridge University Press.

MacWhinney, B. (1997). Second language acquisition and the competition model. In A. M. de Groot & J. Kroll, eds., *Tutorials in Bilingualism: Psycholinguistic Perspectives*. Hillsdale, NJ: Lawrence Erlbaum, pp. 113–44.

Mahboob, A. (2004). Native or nonnative: what do students enrolled in an intensive English program think?In L. D. Kamhi-Stein, ed., *Learning and Teaching from Experience: Perspectives on Nonnative English-Speaking Professionals*. Ann Arbor: University of Michigan Press, pp. 121–48.

Mahboob, A. & Golden, R. (2013). Looking for native speakers of English: discrimination in English language teaching job advertisements. *Voices in Asia Journal*, **1**(1), 72–81.

Makoni, S. & Pennycook, A. (2012). Disinventing multilingualism: from monological multilingualisim to multilingua francas. In M. Martin-Jones, A. Blackledge, & A. Creese, eds., *The Routledge Handbook of Multilingualism*. New York: Routledge, pp. 439–53.

Mala, D. (2016). Dept kicks off teacher "boot camp". *Bangkok Post*, 8 March, p. 3. Retrieved 24 January 24 2018, from www.pressreader.com/thailand/bangkok-post/20160308/281522225182612

Manara, C. (2014). 'So what do you want us to do?': A critical reflection of teaching English as an international language in an Australian context. In R. Marlina & R. A. Giri, eds., *The Pedagogy of English as an International Language: Perspectives from Scholars, Teachers, and Students*. New York: Springer, pp. 189–202.

Marlina, R. (2018). *Teaching English as an International Language: Implementing, Reviewing, and Re-Envisioning World Englishes in Language Education*. Abingdon: Routledge.

Masuhara, H. & Tomlinson, B. (2008). Materials used in the UK. In B. Tomlinson & H. Masuhara, eds., *English Language Learning Materials: A Critical Review*. London: Continuum.

Matsuda, A., ed. (2012a). *Principles and Practices of Teaching English as an International Language. New Perspectives on Language and Education*. Bristol: Multilingual Matters.

Matsuda, A. (2012b). Teaching materials in EIL. In L. Alsagoff, S. L. Mckay, G. Hu, & W. A. Renandya, eds., *Principles and Practices for Teaching English as an International Language*. New York: Routledge.

Matsuda, A. (2017). Introduction. In A. Matsuda, ed., *Preparing Teachers to Teach English as an International Language*. Bristol: Multilingual Matters, pp. 3–18.

Matsuda, A. & Duran, C. S. (2012). EIL activities and tasks for traditional EFL classrooms. In A. Matsuda, ed., *Principles and Practices of Teaching English as an International Language*. Bristol: Multilingual Matters, pp. 201–38.

Matsuda, A. & Friedrich, P. (2012). Selecting an instructional variety for an EIL curriculum. In A. Matsuda, ed., *Principles and Practices of Teaching English as an International Language*. Bristol: Multilingual Matters, pp. 17–27.

Mauranen, A. (2003). The corpus of English as lingua franca in academic settings. *TESOL Quarterly*, **37**(3), 513–27.

Mauranen, A. (2012). *Exploring ELF: Academic English Shaped by Non-Native Speakers*. Cambridge: Cambridge University Press.

May, S. (2014a). Disciplinary divides, knowledge construction, and the multilingual turn. In S. May, ed., *The Multilingual Turn. Implications for SLA, TESOL and Bilingual Education*. New York, NJ: Routledge, pp. 7–31.

May, S. (2014b). *Introducing the 'Multilingual Turn'*. In S. May, ed., *The Multilingual Turn. Implications for SLA, TESOL and Bilingual Education*. New York, NJ: Routledge, pp. 1–6.

May, S. (2014c). *The Multilingual Turn: Implications for SLA, TESOL and Bilingual Education*. London: Routledge.

Mayring, P. (2000). Qualitative content analysis. *Forum: Qualitative Social Research*, 1 (2). Retrieved from http://dx.doi.org/10.17169/fqs-1.2.1089

Mazak, C. M. & Carroll, K. S., eds. (2017). *Translanguaging in Higher Education*. Bristol: Mulitlingual Matters.

McCarthy, M., McCarten, J., & Sandiford, H. (2005). *Touchstone*. Cambridge: Cambridge University Press.

McDonough, J., Shaw, C., & Masuhara, H. (2013). *Materials and Methods in ELT: A Teacher's Guide*, 3rd edn. Oxford: Wiley-Blackwell.

McGrath, I. (2013).*Teaching Materials and the Roles of EFL/ESL Teachers: Practice and Theory*. Edinburgh: Edinburgh University Press.

McGrath, I. (2016). *Materials Evaluation and Design for Language Teaching*, 2nd edn. London: Bloomsbury.

McKay, S. L. (2002). *Teaching English as an International Language: Rethinking Goals and Approaches*. Oxford: Oxford University Press.

McKay, S. L. (2003). Toward an appropriate EIL pedagogy: re-examining common ELT assumptions. *International Journal of Applied Linguistics*, **13**(1), 1–22.

McKay, S. L. (2012). Teaching Materials for English as an International Language. In A. Matsuda, ed., *Principles and Practices of Teaching English as an International Language*. Bristol: Multilingual Matters, pp. 70–83.

McKay, S. L. (2013). Globalization, localization and language attitudes: the case of "foreign workers" in Singapore. *Multilingual Education*, **3**(3). https://doi.org/10.1186/2191-5059-3-3

McKay, S. L. & Brown, J. D. (2016). *Teaching and Assessing EIL in Local Contexts Around the World*. New York: Routledge.

McKinley, J. (2018). Making the EFL to ELF transition at a Global Traction University. In A. Bradford & H. Brown, eds., *English-Medium Instruction at Universities in Japan: Policy, Challenges and Outcomes*. Bristol: Multilingual Matters, pp. 238–49.

McNamara, T. (2000). *Language Testing*. Oxford: Oxford University Press.

McNamara, T. (2012). English as a lingua franca: the challenge for language testing. *Journal of English as a Lingua Franca*, *1*(1), 199–202.

Medgyes, P. (1986). Queries from a communicative teacher. *ELT Journal*, **40**(2), 107–12.

Medgyes, P. (1992). Native or non-native: who's worth more? *ELT Journal*, **46**(4), 340–49.

Medgyes, P. (1994). *The Non-Native Teacher*. London: Macmillan.

Meier, G. S. (2014). Multilingualism and social cohesion: two-way immersion education meets diverse needs. In J. Conteh & G. Meier, eds., *The Multilingual Turn in Languages Education: Opportunities and Challenges*Bristol: Multilingual Matters, pp. 179–208.

Meier, G. S. (2017). The multilingual turn as a critical movement in education: assumptions, challenges and a need for reflection. *Applied Linguistics Review*, **8**(1), 131–61.

Mickan, P. (2013). *Language Curriculum Design and Socialisation*. Bristol: Multilingual Matters.

Mitchell, R., Myles, F., & Marsden, E. (2013). *Second Language Learning Theories*, 3rd edn. New York & London: Routledge.

Montgomery, S. L. (2013). *Does Science Need a Global Language? English and the Future of Research*. Chicago: University of Chicago Press.

Mora, R. A. & Golovátina-Mora, P. (2017). A new model for reflexivity and advocacy for master's-level EIL in-service programs in Colombia: the notion of 'learning and teaching processes in second languages'. In A. Matsuda, ed., *Preparing Teachers to Teach English as an International Language*. Bristol: Multilingual Matters.

Morrow, K. (1977). Authentic texts in ESP. In S. Holden, ed., *English for Specific Purposes*. London: Modern English Publications.

Moussu, L. & Llurda, E. (2008). Non-native English-speaking English language teachers: history and research. *Language Teaching*, **41**(3), 315–48.

Munby, J. (1978). *Communicative syllabus design*. Cambridge: Cambridge University Press.

Murata, K. & Iino, M. (2018). EMI in higher education: an ELF perspective. In J. Jenkins, W. Baker, & M. Dewey, eds., *The Routledge Handbook of English as a Lingua Franca*. Abingdon: Routledge, pp. 400–12.

Murray, H. (2003). Swiss English teachers and Euro-English: attitudes to a non-native variety. *Bulletin Suisse de Linguistique Appliqué*, **77**, 147–65.

Naji Meidani, E. & Pishghadam, R. (2013). Analysis of English language textbooks in the light of English as an International Language (EIL): a comparative study. *International Journal of Research Studies in Language Learning*, **2**(2). https://doi.org/10.5861/ijrsll.2012.163

Nation, I. S. P. & Macalister, J. (2010). *Language Curriculum Design*. New York & London: Routledge.

Nero, S. (2012). Languages without borders: TESOL in a transient world. *TESL Canada Journal*, **29**(2), 143–54.

Nickerson, C. (2005). English as a lingua franca in international business contexts. *English for Specific Purposes*, **24**(4), 367–80.

Nickerson, C. (2013). English for specific purposes and English as a lingua franca. In B. Paltridge & S. Starfield, eds., *The Handbook of English for Specific Purposes*. Walden, MA: Wiley-Blackwell, pp. 445–60.

Norris, J. & Ortega, L. (2000). Effectiveness of L2 instruction: a research synthesis and quantitative meta-analysis. *Language Learning*, **50**, 417–528.

Norton, B. (1995). Social identity, investment, and language learning. *TESOL Quarterly*, **31**, 409–29.

Norton, B. (2013). *Identity, literacy and the multilingual classroom*. In S. May, ed., *The Multilingual Turn. Implications for SLA, TESOL and Bilingual Education*. New York: Routledge.

Norton, B. (2014). Identity and poststructuralist theory in SLA. In S. Mercer & M. Williams, eds., *Multiple Perspectives on the Self in SLA*. Bristol: Multilingual Matters, pp. 59–74.

O'Grady, W. (1996). Language acquisition without universal grammar: a general nativist proposal for L2 learning. *Second Language Research*, **12**, 374–97.

Ortega, L. (2009). *Understanding Second Language Acquisition*. London: Hodder Education.

Ortega, L. (2013). SLA for the 21st century: disciplinary progress, transdisciplinary relevance, and the bi/multilingual turn. *Language Learning*, **63**(suppl. 1), 1–24.

Ortega, L. (2014). Ways forward for a bi/multilingual turn in SLA. In S. May, ed., *The Multilingual Turn. Implications for SLA, TESOL and Bilingual Education*. New York, NJ: Routledge, pp. 32–53.

Överlien, C., Aronsson, K., & Hydén, M. (2005). The focus group interview as an in-depth method? Young women talking about sexuality. *International Journal of Social Research Methodology*, **8**(4), 331–44.

Owston, R. (2007). Contextual factors that sustain innovative pedagogical practice using technology: an international study. *Journal of Educational Change*, **8**(1), 61–77.

Paikeday, T. M. (1985). *The Native Speaker is Dead! An Informal Discussion of a Linguistic Myth with Noam Chomsky and Other Linguists, Philosophers, Psychologists, and Lexicographers*. Toronto and New York: Paikeday Publishing.

Paulsrud, B. Y. (2016). English-medium instruction in Sweden: perspectives and practices in two upper secondary schools. *Journal of Immersion and Content-Based Language Education*, **4**(1), 108–28.

Pavlenko, A. & Lantolf, J. (2000). Second language learning as participation and the (re) construction of selves. In J. Lantolf, ed., *Sociocultural Theory and Second Language Learning*. Oxford & New York: Oxford University Press, pp. 155–77.

Pennycook, A. (1989). The concept of method, interested knowledge, and the politics of language teaching. *TESOL Quarterly*, **23**(4), 589-618.

Pennycook, A. (1998). *English and the Discourses of Colonialism*. London: Routledge.

Pennycook, A. (2003). Global Englishes, rip slyme, and performativity. *Journal of Sociolinguistics*, **7**(4), 513-33.

Pennycook, A. (2007). *Global Englishes and Transcultural Flows*. Abingdon and New York: Routledge.

Pennycook, A. (2010). *Language as Local Practice*. London: Routledge.

Pfenninger, S. E. & Singleton, D. (2017). *Beyond Age Effects in Instructional L2 Learning: Revisiting the Age Factor*. Bristol: Multilingual Matters.

Phan, L. H. (2007). Questioning the validity and appropriacy of presenting communicative language teaching as 'the best' teaching method in TESOL teacher training courses. In J. Mukundan, S. Menon, & A. Hussin, eds., *ELT Matters 3: Developments in English Language Learning and Teaching*. Selangor, Malaysia: Universiti Putra Malaysia Press, pp. 232–40.

Phillipson, R. (1992a). ELT: the native speaker's burden? *ELT Journal*, **46**(1), 12–18.

Phillipson, R. (1992b). *Linguistic Imperialism*. Oxford: Oxford University Press.

Pietikäinen, K. (2014). ELF couples and automatic code-switching. *Journal of English as a Lingua Franca*, **3**(1), 1–26.

Pietikäinen, K. S. (2018). ELF in social contexts. In J. Jenkins, W. Baker, & M. Dewey, eds., *The Routledge Handbook of English as a Lingua Franca*. Abingdon: Routledge, pp. 321–32.

Prodromou, L. (1992). What culture? Which culture? Cross-cultural factors in language learning. *ELT Journal*, **46**(1), 39–50.

Quirk, R. (1990). Language varieties and standard language. *English Today*, **6**(1), 3–10.

Rajagopalan, K. (2018). Divide between NESTs and NNESTs: dichotomy and continuum perspectives. In A. Shehadeh, ed., *The TESOL Encyclopedia of English Language Teaching, Vol. II*. Hoboken, NJ: Wiley-Blackwell, pp. 1–7.

Ramanthan, V. & Morgan, B. (2007). TESOL and policy enactments: perspectives from practice. *TESOL Quarterly*, **41**(3), 447–63.

Rampton, B. (2011). From 'multi-ethnic adolescent heteroglossia' to 'contemporary urban vernaculars'. *Language and Communication*, **31**(4), 276–94.

Rampton, M. B. H. (1990). Displacing the 'native speaker': expertise, affiliation, and inheritance. *ELT Journal*, **44**(2), 97–101.

Richards, J. C. (2001). *Curriculum Development in Language Teaching*. Cambridge: Cambridge University Press.

Richards, J. C. (2017). *Curriculum Development in Language Teaching*, 3rd edn. Cambridge: Cambridge University Press.

Richards, J., Hull, J., & Proctor, S. (2005). *Interchange 3*, 3rd edn. Cambridge: Cambridge University Press.

Richards, J. & Rodgers, T. (2014). *Approaches and Methods in Language Teaching*, 3rd edn. New York: Cambridge University Press.

Richterich, R. & Chancerel, J.L. (1977). *Identifying the Needs of Adults Learning a Foreign Language*. Oxford & New York: Pergamon Press.

Rizvi, F. & Beech, J. (2017). Global mobilities and the possibilities of a cosmopolitan curriculum. *Curriculum Inquiry*, **47**(1), 125–34.

Robinson, B. & Latchem, C. (2003). *Teacher Education through Open and Distance Learning*. London: Routledge.

Rogers, E. (2003). *Diffusions of Innovations*, 5th edn. New York: Free Press.

Rogier, D. (2012). *The Effects of English-Medium Instruction on Language Proficiency of Students Enrolled in Higher Education in the UAE*. Unpublished Ph.D. dissertation. University of Essex.

Rose, H. (2017). A global approach to English language teaching: integrating an international perspective into a teaching methods course. In A. Matsuda, ed., *Preparing Teachers to Teach English as an International Language*. Bristol: Multilingual Matters.

Rose, H. (2018). Popular approaches to EAL instruction. In S. Abrar-ul-Hassan, ed., *The TESOL Encyclopedia of English Language Teaching, Vol. I*. Hoboken, NJ: Wiley-Blackwell, pp. 1–12.

Rose, H. & Galloway, N. (2017). Debating standard language ideology in the classroom: using the 'Speak Good English Movement' to raise awareness of Global Englishes. *RELC Journal*, **48**(3), 294–301.

Rose, H. & Galloway, N. (2019). *Global Englishes for Language Teaching*. Cambridge: Cambridge University Press.

Rose, H. & McKinley, J. (2017). The prevalence of pedagogy-related research in applied linguistics: extending the debate. *Applied Linguistics*, **38**(4), 599-604.

Rose, H. & McKinley, J. (2018). Japan's English-medium instruction initiatives and the globalization of higher education. *Higher Education*, **75**(1), 111–29.

Rose, H. & Montakantiwong, A. (2018). A tale of two teachers: a duoethnography of the realistic and idealistic successes and failures of teaching English as an international language. *RELC Journal*, **49**(1), 88–101.

Rose, H. & Syrbe, M. (2018). Assessment practices in teaching English as an international language. In S. Abrar-ul-Hassan, ed., *The TESOL Encyclopedia of English Language Teaching, Vol. I*. Hoboken, NJ: Wiley-Blackwell, pp. 1–12.

Rossman, G. & Rallis, S. (2016). *Learning in the Field: An Introduction to Qualitative Research*, 4th edn. London: SAGE Publications.

Rubdy, R. (2001). Creative destruction: Singapore's Speak Good English Movement. *World Englishes*, **20**(3), 341–55.

Rubin, D. L. (1992). Nonlanguage factors affecting undergraduates' judgments of nonnative English-speaking teaching assistants. *Research in Higher Education*, **33**(4), 511–31.

Ruecker, T. (2011). Challenging the native and nonnative English speaker hierarchy in ELT: new directions from race theory. *Critical Inquiry in Language Studies*, **8**(4), 400–22.

Ruecker, T. & Ives, L. (2015). White native English speakers needed: the rhetorical construction of privilege in online teacher recruitment spaces. *TESOL Quarterly*, **49**(4), 733–56. https://doi.org/10.1002/tesq.195

Sampasivam, S. & Clement, R. (2014). The dynamics of second language confidence: contact and interaction. In S. Mercer & M. Williams, eds., *Multiple Perspectives on the Self in SLA*. Bristol: Multilingual Matters, pp. 23–40.

Samuda, V. & Bygate, M. (2008). *Tasks in Second Language Learning*. Basingstoke: Palgrave Macmillan.

Sangiamchit, C. (2018). ELF in electronically mediated intercultural communication. In J. Jenkins, W. Baker, & M. Dewey, eds., *The Routledge Handbook of English as a Lingua Franca*. Abingdon: Routledge, pp. 345–56.

Saraceni, M. (2015). *World Englishes: A Critical Analysis*. London: Bloomsbury Publishing Company.

Saussure, D. (1966). *Course in General Linguistics*. New York: McGraw-Hill.

Saussure, F. (1959). The object of linguistics – nature of the linguistic sign, a course in general linguistics. In R. Innis, ed., *Semiotics: An Introductory Anthology*. London: Hutchinson, pp. 28–40.

Savignon, S. (1972). *Communicative Competence: An Experiment in Foreign Language Teaching*. Philadelphia: The Centre for Curriculum Development, Inc.

Savignon, S. J. (1983). *Communicative Competence: Theory and Classroom Practice. Texts and Contexts in Second Language Learning*. Reading, MA: Addison-Wesley Publishing Company.

Schmidt, R. (1990). The role of consciousness in second language learning. *Applied Linguistics*, **11**, 129–58.

Schreier, M. (2014). Qualitative content analysis. In U. Flick, ed., *The SAGE Handbook of Qualitative Data Analysis*. London: SAGE Publications, pp. 170–83.

Seargeant, P. (2009). *The Idea of English in Japan*. Bristol: Multilingual Matters.

Seidlhofer, B. (2001). Closing a conceptual gap: the case for a description of English as a lingua franca. *International Journal of Applied Linguistics*, **11**(2), 133–58.

Seidlhofer, B. (2004). Research perspectives on teaching English as a Lingua Franca. *Annual Review of Applied Linguistics*, **24**, 209–39.

Seidlhofer, B. (2008). Of norms and mindsets. *Australian Review of Applied Linguistics*, **31**(3), 1–7.

Seidlhofer, B. (2011). *Understanding English as a Lingua Franca*. Oxford: Oxford University Press.

Seidlhofer, B. & Widdowson, H. (2003). House work and student work: a study in cross-cultural understanding. *Zeitschrift Für Interkulturellen Fremdsprachenunterricht*, **8** (2/3), 115–27. Retrieved from http://tujournals.ulb.tu-darmstadt.de/index.php/zif/article/view/539/515

Selinker, L. (1972). Interlanguage. *International Review of Applied Linguistics in Language Teaching*, **10**, 209–32.

Selvi, A. F. (2010). All teachers are equal, but some teachers are more equal than others: trend analysis of job advertisements in English language teaching. *WATESOL NNEST Caucus Annual Review*, **1**, 156–81.

Selvi, A. F. (2011). The non-native speaker teacher. *ELT Journal*, **65**(2), 187–9.

Selvi, A. F. (2017). Preparing teachers to teach English as an international language: reflections from Northern Cyprus. In A. Matsuda, ed., *Preparing Teachers to Teach English as an International Language*. Bristol: Multilingual Matters.

Sembiante, S. (2016). Translanguaging and the multilingual turn: epistemological reconceptualization in the fields of language and implications for reframing language in curriculum studies. *Curriculum Inquiry*, **46**(1), 45–61.

Sharifian, F. ed. (2009). *English as an International Language: Perspectives and Pedagogical Issues*. Bristol: Multilingual Matters.

Sharwood Smith, M. (1981). Consciousness-raising and the second language learner. *Applied Linguistics*, **2**, 159–68.

Sherman, T. (2018) ELF and the EU/wider Europe. In: J. Jenkins, W. Baker, & M. Dewey, eds., *The Routledge Handbook of English as a Lingua Franca*. Abingdon, New York: Routledge, pp. 115–25.

Shim, R. J. (2002). Changing attitudes toward TEWOL in Korea. *Journal of Asian Pacific Communication*, **12**(1), 143–58.

Shohamy, E. (2006). *Language Policy: Hidden Agendas and New Approaches*. London: Routledge.

Shohamy, E. (2012). A critical perspective on the use of English as a medium of instruction at universities. In A. Doiz, D. Lasagabaster, & J. M. Sierra, eds., *English-Medium Instruction at Universities: Global Challenges*. London: Longman, 196–213.

Sifakis, N. & Bayyurt, Y. (2016). ELF-aware teacher education and transformative learning. Comments on Éva Illés. *Journal of English as a Lingua Franca*, **5**(1), 147–53.

Sifakis, N. C. (2014). ELF awareness as an opportunity for change: a transformative perspective for ESOL teacher education. *Journal of English as a Lingua Franca*, **3** (2), 317–35.

Sifakis, N. C. (2017). ELF awareness in English language teaching: principles and processes. *Applied Linguistics*. Advance Article, https://doi.org/10.1093/applin/amx034

Sifakis, N. C. & Bayyurt, Y. (2015). Insights from ELF and WE in teacher training in Greece and Turkey. *World Englishes*, **34**, 471–84.

Sifakis, N. C. & Bayyurt, Y. (2018). ELF-aware teacher education and development. In J. Jenkins, W. Baker, & M. Dewey, eds., *The Routledge Handbook of English as a Lingua Franca*. Abingdon: Routledge, pp. 456–67.

Sifakis, N. C. & Sougari, A.-M. (2005). Pronunciation issues and EIL pedagogy in the periphery: a survey of Greek state school teachers' beliefs. *TESOL Quarterly*, **39**(3), 467–88.

Siqueira, D. S. P. (2015). English as a lingua franca and ELT materials: is the "plastic world" really melting? In Y. Bayyurt & A. Sumru, eds., *Current Perspectives on Pedagogy for English as a Lingua Franca*. Berlin: De Gruyter.

Skehan, P. (1996). Second language acquisition research and task-based instruction. In J. Willis & D. Willis, eds., *Challenge and Change in Language Teaching*. London: Heinemann.

Smit, U. (2018). Beyond monolingualism in higher education: a language policy account. In J. Jenkins, W. Baker, & M. Dewey, eds., *The Routledge Handbook of English as a Lingua Franca*. Abingdon: Routledge, pp. 387–99.

Smithson, J. (2000). Using and analysing focus groups: limitations and possibilities. *International Journal of Social Research Methodology*, **3**(2), 103–19.

Soars, J. & Soars, L. (2008). *New Headway: Upper-Intermediate. The New Edition*. Oxford: Oxford University Press.

Söderlundh, H. (2012). Global policies and local norms: sociolinguistic awareness and language choice at an international university. *International Journal of the Sociology of Language* (216), 87–109.

Song, M.-M. & Tai, H.-H. (2007). Taiwan's responses to globalisation: internationalisation and questing for world class universities. *Asia Pacific Journal of Education*, *27* (3), 323–40.

Sridhar, K. & Sridhar, S. (1986). Bridging the paradigm gap; second language acquisition theory and indigenised varieties of English. *World Englishes*, **5**(1), 3–14.

Starfield, S. (2013). Historical development of language for specific purposes. In C. Chappelle, ed., *The Encyclopedia of Applied Linguistics*. Malden, MA: Wiley-Blackwell, pp. 2485–91.

Starfield, S. (2016). English for specific purposes. In G. Hall, ed., *The Routledge Handbook of English Language Teaching*. Abingdon, UK: Routledge, 150–63.

Sung, C. C. M. (2014a). English as a lingua franca and global identities: perspectives from four second language learners of English in Hong Kong. *Linguistics and Education*, **26**(1), 31–9.

Sung, C. C. M. (2014b). Global, local or glocal? Identities of L2 learners in English as a lingua franca communication. *Language, Culture and Curriculum*, **27**(1), 43–57.

Sung, C. C. M. (2014c). Exposing learners to Global Englishes in ELT: some suggestions. *ELT Journal*, 69(2), 198–201.

Sung, C. C. M. (2015). Implementing a Global Englishes component in a university English course in Hong Kong. *English Today*, **31**(4), 42–9.

Sung, C. C. M. (2018). Out-of-class communication and awareness of English as a lingua franca. *ELT Journal*, **72**(1), 15–25.

Suzuki, A. (2011). Introducing diversity of English into ELT: student teachers' responses. *ELT Journal*, **65**(2), 145–53.

Swain, M. (1985). Communicative competence: some roles of comprehensible input and comprehensible output in its development. In S. Gass & C. Madden, eds., *Input in Second Language Acquisition*. New York: Newbury House, pp. 235–56.

Swain, M. (1995). Three functions of output in second language learning. In G. Cook & B. Seidlhofer, eds., *For H.G. Widdowson: Principles and Practice in the Study of Language*. Oxford: Oxford University Press.

Swain, M. (2000). The output hypothesis and beyond: mediating acquisition through collaborative dialogue. In J. P. Lantolf, ed., *Sociocultural Theory and Second Language Learning*. Oxford: Oxford University Press, pp. 97–114.

Swain, M. (2005). The output hypothesis: theory and research. In E. Hinkel, ed., *Handbook of Research in Second Language Teaching and Learning*. Mahwah, NJ: Lawrence Erlbaum, pp. 471–83.

Swales, J. M. (1985). *Episodes in ESP: A Source and Reference Book on the Development of English for Science and Technology*. Oxford: Pergamon Institute of English.

Swan, A. (2015). Redefining English language teacher identity. In A. Swan, P. Aboshiha, & A. Holliday, eds., *(En)Countering Native-Speakerism*. London: Springer, pp. 59–74.

Swan, M. (2006). Teachers' beliefs and practices. In P. Garrett & J. Cots, eds., *Collaborative Learning in Mathematics*. London: Routledge, pp. 75–91.

Syrbe, M. (2017). *The Representation of Global Englishes in English Teaching and Testing Materials. An Investigation of International Textbooks and Proficiency Tests*. Unpublished Ph.D. dissertation. Trinity College Dublin.

Syrbe, M. & Rose, H. (2018). An evaluation of the global orientation of English textbooks in Germany. *Innovation in Language Learning and Teaching*, 12(2):152–163. https://doi.org/10.1080/17501229.2015.1120736

Tajeddin, Z. & Teimournezhad, S. (2015). Exploring the hidden agenda in the representation of culture in international and localised ELT textbooks. *The Language Learning Journal*, **43**(2), 180–93.

Takahashi, R. (2016). The attitudes of learners and teachers towards ELF-oriented materials, with related implications. In N. Tsantila, J. Mandalios, & M. Ilkos, eds., *ELF: Pedagogical and Interdisciplinary Perspectives*. Athens: Deree-The American College of Greece.

Tang, E. L., Lee, J. C. & Chun, C. K. (2012). Development of teaching beliefs and the focus of change in the process of pre-service ESL teacher education. *Australian Journal of Teacher Education*, *37*(5), 90–107.

Tarnopolsky, O. B., & Goodman, B. A. (2014). The ecology of language in classrooms at a university in eastern Ukraine. *Language and Education*, **28**(4), 383–96.

Tarone, E. (1983). On the variability of interlanguage systems. *Applied Linguistics*, **4**, 142–63.

Tarone, E. (2015). Second language acquisition in applied linguistics: 1925–2015 and beyond. *Applied Linguistics*, **36**(4), 444–53.

Tarone, E. & Allwright, D. (2005). Second language teacher learning and student second language learning: shaping the knowledge base. In D. Tedick, ed., *Second Language Teacher Education* Mahwah, NJ: Lawrence Erlbaum, pp. 5–23.

Taylor, S. K. & Snoddon, K. (2013). Plurilingualism in TESOL: promising controversies. *TESOL Quarterly*, **47**(3), 439–45.

Teachers of English to Speakers of Other Languages (TESOL). (1991). *A TESOL Statement on Non-Native Speakers of English and Hiring Practices*. Retrieved 29 December 2016, from http://nnest.moussu.net/docs/TESOL_PositionStatement(1991).pdf

Teachers of English to Speakers of Other Languages (TESOL). (2006). *Position Statement against Discrimination of Nonnative Speakers of English in the Field of TESOL*. Retrieved 29 December 2016, from http://nnest.moussu.net/docs/TESOL_PositionStatement(2006).pdf

Thiel, M. & Friedman, R. (2016). Introduction: culture and narratives of transnational belonging. In R. Friedman & M. Thiel, eds., *European Identity and Culture: Narratives of Transnational Belonging*. Abingdon: Routledge, pp. 1–16.

Thornbury, S. (2016). Communicative language teaching in theory and practice. In G. Hall, ed., *The Routledge Handbook of English Language Teaching*. Abingdon: Routledge, pp. 224–37.

Tian, L. & Macaro, E. (2012). Comparing the effect of teacher codeswitching with English-only explanations on the vocabulary acquisition of Chinese university students: a Lexical Focus-on-Form study. *Language Teaching Research*, **16**(3), 367–91.

Tilbury, A. (2011). *English Unlimited. B2 Upper Intermediate*. Cambridge: Cambridge University Press.

Timmis, I. (2002). Native-speaker norms and international English: a classroom view. *ELT Journal*, **56**(3), 240–9.

Tollefson, J. W. (2007). Ideology, language varieties, and ELT. In J. Cummins & C. Davison, eds., *International Handbook of English Language Teaching. Part 1*. New York: Springer, pp. 25–36.

Tomlinson, B. (2010). Principles of effective materials development. In N. Harwood, ed., *English Language Teaching Materials: Theory and Practice*. Cambridge: Cambridge University Press, pp. 81–108.

Tomlinson, B. (2016). Current issues in the development of materials for learners of English as an International Language (EIL). In W. Renandya & H. Widodo, eds., *English Language Teaching Today. English Language Education Vol. 5*. Cham: Springer, pp. 53–66.

Tudor, I. (2001). *The Dynamics of the Language Classroom*. Cambridge: Cambridge University Press.

Ullucci, K. (2007). The myths that blind: the role of beliefs in school change. *Journal of Educational Controversy*, **2**(1), Article 4. Retrieved from https://cedar.wwu.edu/jec/vol2/iss1/4

Ur, P. (2012). *A Course in English Language Teaching*. Cambridge: Cambridge University Press.

van der Walt, C & Evans, R (2018). Is English the lingua franca of South Africa? In J. Jenkins, W. Baker, & M. Dewey, eds., *The Routledge Handbook of English as a Lingua Franca*. Abingdon, New York: Routledge, pp. 186–98.

Van Lier, L. (1996). *Interaction in the Language Curriculum. Awareness, Autonomy & Authenticity*. London: Longman.

Van Lier, L. (2009). Action-based teaching, autonomy and identity. *Innovation in Language Teaching and Learning*, **1**(1), 1–19.

Vertovec, S. (2007). Super-diversity and its implications. *Ethnic and Racial Studies*, **30** (6), 1024–54.

Vettorel, P. (2013). ELF in international school exchanges: stepping into the role of ELF users. *Journal of English as a Lingua Franca*, **2**(1), 147–73.

Vettorel, P. (2016). WE-and ELF-informed classroom practices: proposals from a pre-service teacher education programme in Italy. *Journal of English as a Lingua Franca*, **5**(1), 107–33.

Vettorel, P. (2018). ELF and communication strategies: are they taken into account in ELT materials? *RELC Journal*, **49**(1), 58–73.

Vettorel, P. & Lopriore, L. (2013). Is there ELF in ELT coursebooks? *Studies in Second Language Learning and Teaching*, **3**(4), 483–504.

Vettorel, P. & Lopriore, L. (2017). WE, EIL, ELF and awareness of their pedagogical implications in teacher education programs in Italy. In A. Matsuda, ed., *Preparing Teachers to Teach English as an International Language*. Bristol: Multilingual Matters.

Viney, P., Hartley, B., Frankel, I, & Falla, T. (1994). *New American Streamline: Departures*. Oxford: Oxford University Press.

Virkkula, T. & Nikula, T. (2010). Identity construction in ELF contexts: a case study of Finnish engineering students working in Germany. *International Journal of Applied Linguistics*, **20**(2), 251–73.

VOICE website. (2013). *The Vienna-Oxford International Corpus of English (version 2.0)*. Director: Barbara Seidlhofer; Researchers: Angelika Breiteneder, Theresa Klimpfinger, Stefan Majewski, Ruth Osimk-Teasdale, Marie-Luise Pitzl, Michael Radeka. Available at www.univie.ac.at/voice

Vygotsky, L. S. (1978). *Mind in Society: The Development of Higher Psychological Processes*. Cambridge, MA: Harvard University Press.

Wächter, B. & Maiworm, F. (2014). *English-Taught Programmes in European Higher Education: The State of Play in 2014. ACA Papers on International Cooperation in Education*. Brussels: Academic Cooperation Association.

Walkinshaw, I., Fenton-Smith, B., & Humphreys, P. (2017). Introduction. In B. Fenton-Smith, P. Humphreys, & I. Walkinshaw, eds., *English Medium Instruction in Higher Education in Asia-Pacific: From Policy to Pedagogy*. Cham: Springer International Publishing.

Wallwork, A. & Sheard, N. (2001). *International Express: Upper Intermediate*. Oxford: Oxford University Press.

Wang, Y. (2013). Non-conformity to ENL norms: a perspective from Chinese English users. *Journal of English as a Lingua Franca*, **2**(2), 255–82.

Wang, Y. (2015). Chinese university students' ELF awareness: impacts of language education in China. *Englishes in Practice*, **2**(4), 86–106.

Wang, Y (2018). Chinese English as a lingua franca: an ideological inquiry. In J. Jenkins, W. Baker, & M. Dewey, eds., *The Routledge Handbook of English as a Lingua Franca*. Abingdon, New York: Routledge, pp. 151–64.

Wang, Y. & Jenkins, J. (2016). 'Nativeness' and intelligibility: impacts of intercultural experience through English as a lingua franca on Chinese speakers' language attitudes. *Chinese Journal of Applied Linguistics*, **39**(1), 38–58.

Waters, A. (2014). Managing innovation in English language education: a research agenda. *Language Teaching*, **47**(1), 92–110.

Wedell, M. (2003). Giving TESOL change a chance: Supporting key players in the curriculum change process. *System*, **31**(4), 439–56.

Wedell, M. (2009). Innovation in ELT. *ELT Journal*, **63**, 397–9.

Wei, L. & Martin, P. (2009). Conflicts and tensions in classroom codeswitching: an introduction. *International Journal of Bilingual Education and Bilingualism*, **12**(2), 117–22.

Wenger, E. (1998). *Communities of Practice: Learning, Meaning, and Identity*. New York: Cambridge University Press.

White, R., Martin, M., Stimson, M., & Hodge, R. (1991). *Management in English Language Teaching*. Cambridge: Cambridge University Press.

Widdowson, H. G. (1983). *Learning Purpose and Language Use*. Oxford: Oxford University Press.

Widdowson, H. G. (1998). EIL: squaring the circles. A reply. *World Englishes*, **17**(3), 397–401.

Widdowson, H. G. (2004). A perspective on recent trends. In A. P. R. Howatt & H. G. Widdowson, eds., *A History of English Language Teaching*. Oxford: Oxford University Press, pp. 353–72.

Widdowson, H. G. (2012). ELF and the inconvenience of established concepts. *Journal of English as a Lingua Franca*, **1**(1), 5–26.

Wilkins, D. (1976). *Notional Syllabuses*. Oxford: Oxford University Press.

Wilkinson, R. (2013). English-medium instruction at a Dutch university: challenges and pitfalls. In A. Doiz, D. Lasagabaster, & J. M. Sierra, eds., *English-Medium Instruction at Universities World-wide: Global Challenges*. Bristol: Multilingual Matters, pp. 3–24.

Williams, C. (1996). Secondary education: teaching in the bilingual situation. In C. Williams, G. Lewis, & C. Baker, eds., *The Language Policy: Taking Stock*. Llangefni: CAI, 193–211.

Willis, D. & Willis, J. (2001). Task-based language learning. In R. Carter & D. Nunan, eds., *The Cambridge Guide to Teaching English to Speakers of Other Languages*. Cambridge: Cambridge University Press, pp. 173–9.

Willis, J. (1996). *A Framework for Task Based Learning*. Harlow: Longman.

Wolcott, H. F. (2008). *Ethnography: A Way of Seeing*. Plymouth: Altamira Press.

Xu, Z. (2013). Globalization, culture and ELT materials: a focus on China. *Multilingual Education*, **3**(6). https://doi.org/10.1186/2191-5059-3-6

Yashima, T. (2002). Willingness to communicate in a second language: the Japanese EFL context. *Modern Language Journal*, **86**(1), 199–210.

Young, A. (2014). Looking through the language lens: monolingual taint or plurilingual tint? In J. Conteh & G. Meier, eds., *The Multilingual Turn in Languages Education: Opportunities and Challenges*. Bristol: Mulitlingual Matters, pp. 89–110.

Young, R. (1988). Variation and the interlanguage hypothesis. *Studies in Second Language Acquisition*, **10**, 281–302.

Yu, M. H. (2015). Developing critical classroom practice for ELF communication: a Taiwanese case study of ELT materials evaluation. In H. Bowles & A. Cogo, eds., *International Perspectives on English Language Teaching*. New York: Palgrave Macmillan.

Zacharias, N. T. (2005). Teachers' beliefs about internationally-published materials: a survey of tertiary English teachers in Indonesia. *RELC Journal*, **36**(1), 23–37.

Index